BORROWED LAND

ALSO BY KAPKA KASSABOVA

Street without a Name
Twelve Minutes of Love: A Tango Story
Border: A Journey to the Edge of Europe
To the Lake: A Journey of War and Peace
Elixir: In the Valley at the End of Time
Anima: A Wild Pastoral

BORROWED LAND

A HIGHLAND STORY

KAPKA KASSABOVA

JONATHAN CAPE
LONDON

1 3 5 7 9 10 8 6 4 2

Jonathan Cape, an imprint of Vintage, is part of the Penguin Random House group of companies

Vintage, Penguin Random House UK, One Embassy Gardens,
8 Viaduct Gardens, London SW11 7BW

penguin.co.uk/vintage
global.penguinrandomhouse.com

First published by Jonathan Cape in 2026

Copyright © Kapka Kassabova 2026

Epigraph p. vii: 'A Man in Assynt' by Norman MacCaig, from *The Poems of Norman MacCaig* (Polygon, 2005), Birlinn Limited. Reproduced with permission of the Licensor through PLSclear. Extracts on pages 206 and 209 from *Children of the Dead End* by Patrick MacGill (Birlinn, 1999) reproduced with permission from Birlinn Ltd.

The moral right of the author has been asserted

Penguin Random House values and supports copyright.
Copyright fuels creativity, encourages diverse voices, promotes freedom
of expression and supports a vibrant culture. Thank you for purchasing
an authorised edition of this book and for respecting intellectual property
laws by not reproducing, scanning or distributing any part of it by any
means without permission. You are supporting authors and enabling
Penguin Random House to continue to publish books for everyone.
No part of this book may be used or reproduced in any manner for the purpose
of training artificial intelligence technologies or systems. In accordance
with Article 4(3) of the DSM Directive 2019/790, Penguin Random House
expressly reserves this work from the text and data mining exception.

Typeset in 13.4/16pt Bembo Book MT Pro by Six Red Marbles UK, Thetford, Norfolk
Printed and bound in Great Britain by Clays Ltd, Elcograf S.p.A.

The authorised representative in the EEA is Penguin Random House
Ireland, Morrison Chambers, 32 Nassau Street, Dublin D02 YH68

A CIP catalogue record for this book is available from the British Library

ISBN 9781787335349

Penguin Random House is committed to a sustainable future
for our business, our readers and our planet. This book is made
from Forest Stewardship Council® certified paper.

Mo ghleann

To my glen

Who owns this landscape?
Has owning anything to do with love?

> Norman MacCaig, 'A Man in Assynt'

Leig ise sgal aiste le tùrsa
A chluinnt' thar sheachd beannan.
She gave a shriek with wailing
That was heard over seven hills.

> 'Glaistig Lianachain' (The Spirit Keeper
> of Lianachan), Gaelic folk poem

These plunderers of the world, after exhausting the land by their devastations, are rifling the ocean . . . And where they make a wasteland, they call it peace.

> Calgacus, leader of the Caledonian Confederacy against
> the Romans, from the *Agricola* by Tacitus

Contents

Maps	xi
Preface	xv
A note on terms	xvii
The Glen	1
Chì mi	11
The Crossing Place, home	12
Chì mi	30
Under Fairie Hill	33
The Cougies	42
Chì mi	58
The Crossing Place, roaming	60
Chì mi	75
Silver Falls	76
Chì mi	95
The Crossing Place, transmission	97
Chì mi	104
Strathfarrar	105
River People	129
The Keepers	146
Chì mi	179
The Crossing Place, gravel	182

Chì mi	189
The Dam Builders	190
The Crossing Place, loss	219
Chì mi	223
Back to the Land	227
Chì mi	245
The Crossing Place, endurance	246
Chì mi	255
The Good Woodsman	256
Chì mi	272
Deer People	273
The Glen	316
Acknowledgements and Sources	329

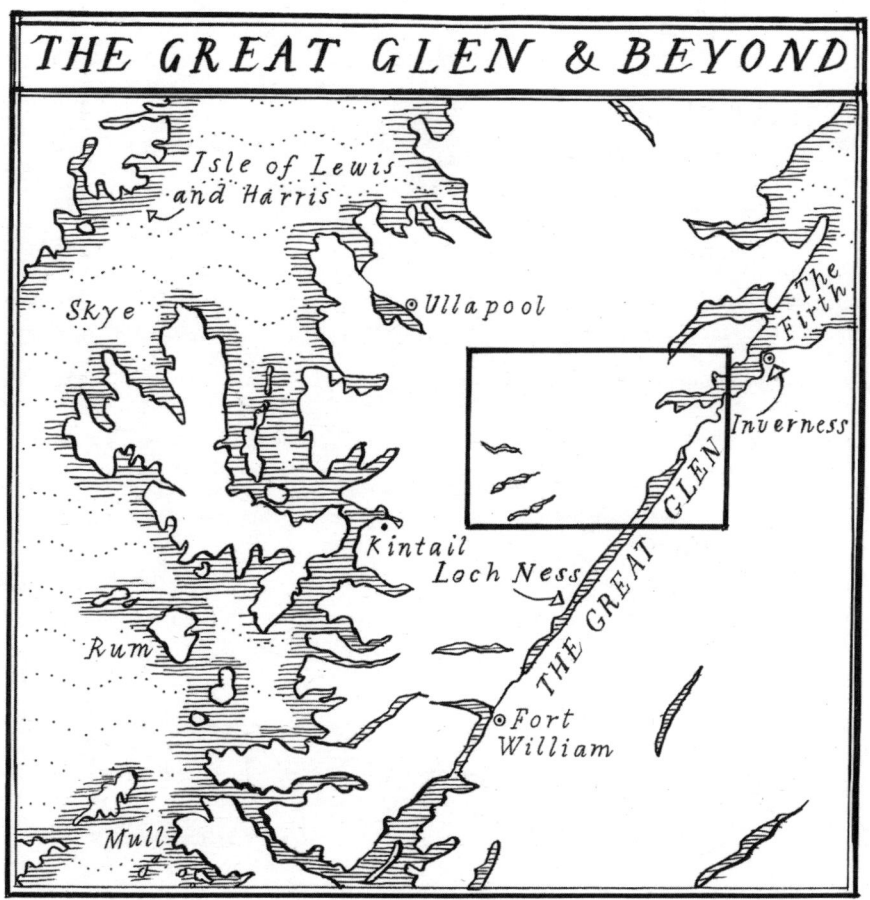

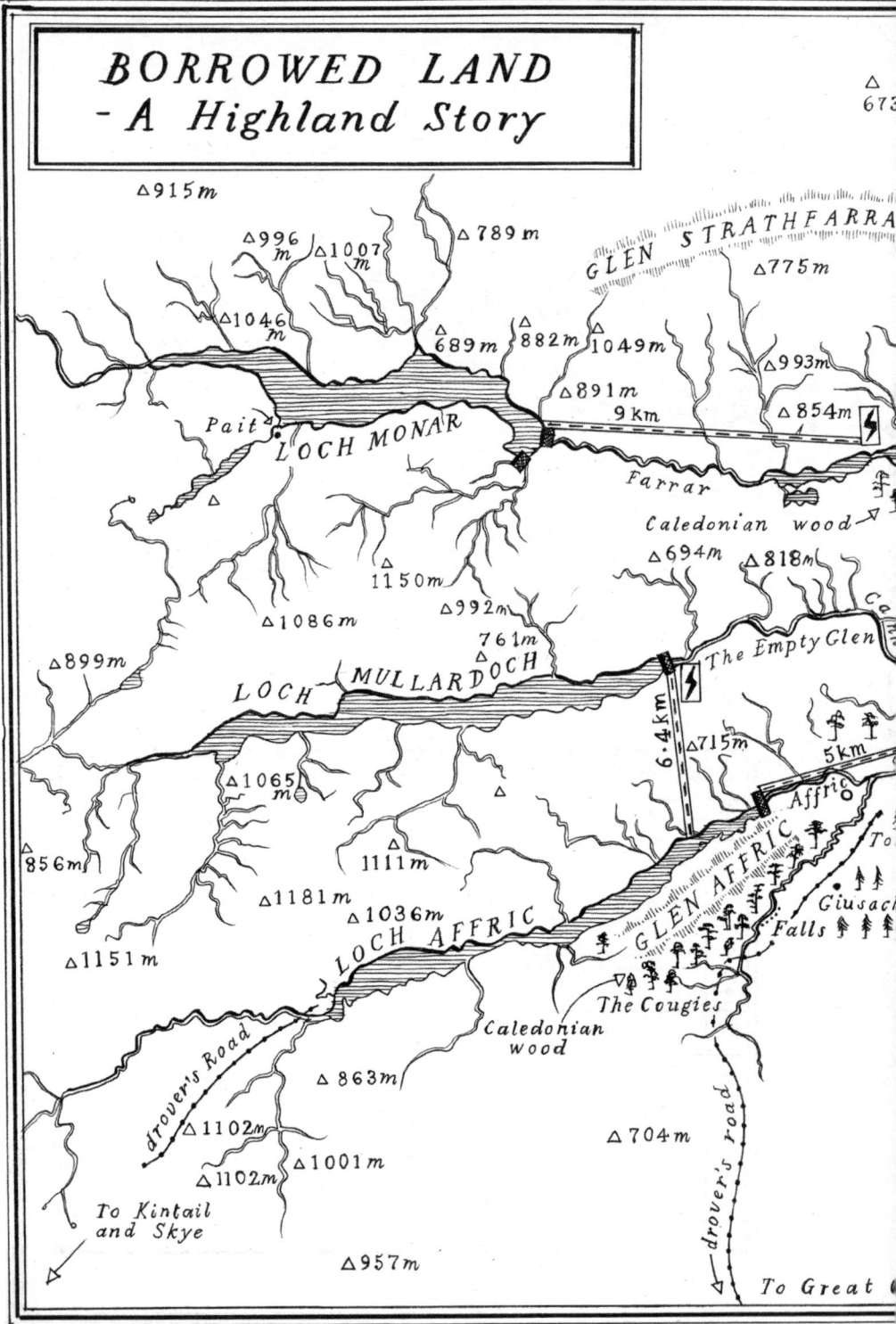

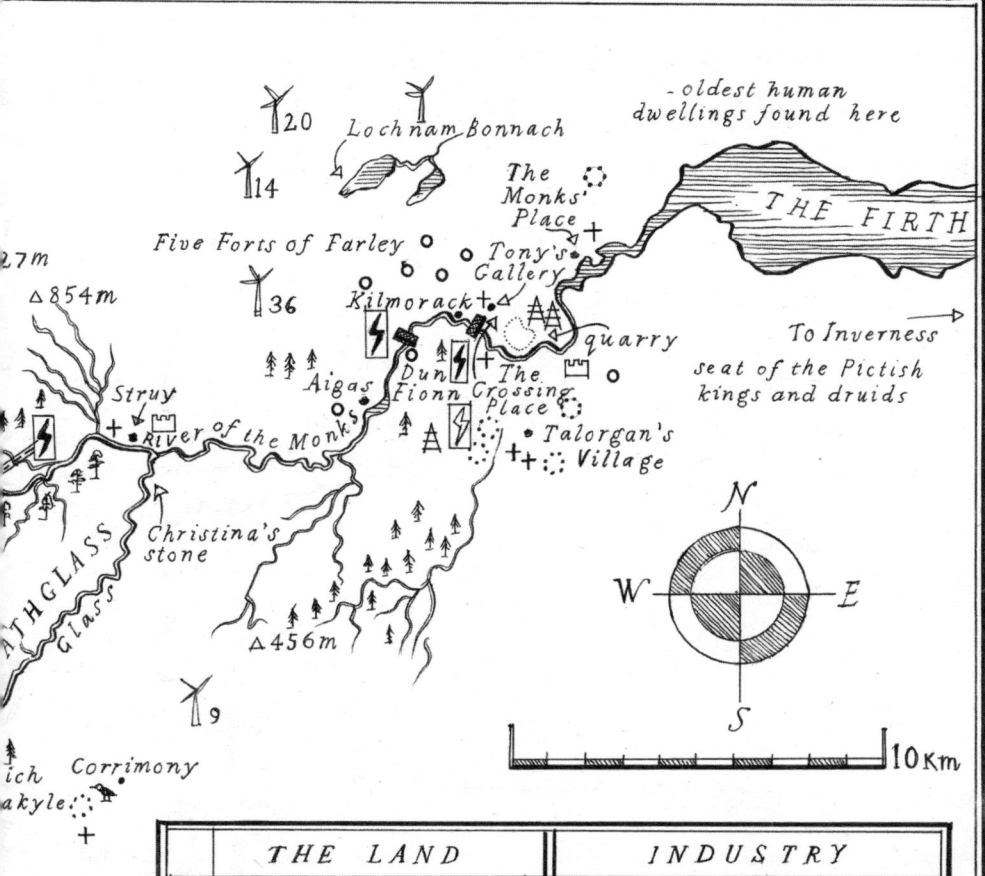

Preface

This is the story of a Scottish glen and its inhabitants, and of how I came to call it my glen. *Mo ghleann*. In the Gaelic worldview, *mo* expresses affection more than possession. My glen runs 80 kilometres west to east and is second to none in beauty and story, not even to its neighbour the Great Glen of Loch Ness.

A glen is a long river valley. A long and wide valley is a strath. Lake is loch (pronounced with a hard h) and streams are called burns. Straths and glens, burns and lochs define the character of the Scottish Highlands. The balance of water, land, air and sentient beings has shaped this northern land.

But the balance is on the brink. I came to this place at a time when industry is rapidly changing the face of the land and the sea. Energy companies are building industrial hubs across the Highlands and Islands on a scale not seen before. Their appetite is insatiable and their footprint expands horizontally and vertically. Their industrial networks are everywhere – underground, overhead, on hills, inside lochs, rivers and the ocean.

Sixteen power stations, including the country's two largest switching stations. Over 1,000 wind turbines up to 230 metres high. Forty battery energy storage systems (BESS). Five or maybe eight national transmission lines with pylons 59 to 100 metres high, converging over the same river. Three or maybe six major pumped storage Hydro schemes on Loch Ness. This is the projected footprint by energy companies in the Great Glen area, not counting the old Hydro schemes. The north of Scotland has become a target for big developers to build industrial hubs and extract wind, water and solar energy and export it hundreds of miles from where it is produced – which is why the transmission grid expands in all directions. This deployment of industry in a delicate ecology is driven by net-zero targets in the race to stop climate change. But what is happening on the ground increasingly feels like a war on nature and communities.

What to do? I went into my glen. To discover it with fresh eyes. To capture how it feels to live in a microcosm where everything alive is in relationship. To record what may be lost.

A note on terms

I use the terms industrial and industrialisation in an existential sense, to describe both practice and mindset. It covers the mechanical and technological extraction of resources on a large scale for profit, which is often presented by the extractors and their political enablers as necessary for progress, security and growth. This includes the large-scale extraction of animals, minerals, forests, sealife, oil, coal, gravel, water, air, space, data, intellectual and creative property, and human health and peace.

In this book's geography, the north is the Highlands. The south is often used for south of the Highlands, whether it's the rest of Scotland or the rest of Britain. This is a geographical locator in instances where more detail isn't needed. South and north are charged notions, but the charge depends on the context. In the context of this book, I have used the north to signal the dignity and sovereignty of the Highlands, beloved of so many around the world.

The Glen

The weather doesn't change inside the cave. Water seeps through the rock and when you sink your hand in the moss, the pulse of the mountain comes through. Something is germinating. It unfolds and spreads. Then folds back and retreats. A blueprint dwells here like a presence. You look for it but can't find it because it's everywhere. This is the inner ear of the glen.

In autumn when the bracken wilts and flops down and covers the land like rust, there are no signposts to go by. You have to find it on faith – like an abandoned childhood home – and when you find it you see with surprise that something cares for it.

The inner chambers are reached through a long crack in the rockface, and I squeeze through. Is that a waterfall? I know there isn't a waterfall but squeeze further in to reach it. The faultline narrows like a lens and continues to the interior of the mountain where you can't follow. Bella barks and the chamber reverberates with a chorus as if all the dogs that ever lived in these hills have woken up. Sheep dogs, cattle-droving dogs, hunting dogs, companion dogs of the dam builders, dogs who left with their people when the dams flooded their homes by appointment. Bella's voice is sent to the interior of the Earth like a message. Then the chorus fades.

When we emerge, the breeze has risen and plays eerie tunes through the birches that haven't shed their golden leaves yet. Far west into the glen, the hills of Monar are white-capped.

It's darkening. This happens every time in the Painted

Glen. It takes longer to get out than to go in. Time warps. I emerge from the cave and things have happened in my absence. Quickly. And very slowly. Aeons run parallel to minutes. I must reach the car at the gate before night hides the world and brings me too close to the unseen. I walk fast on the tarmac. Bella finds a deer leg with hoof on. I worry about her getting trampled by a herd of them, she is quite small. A stag bellows from across the river and another answers him. It's bear-like, thick and guttural. Oooo. Your instinct is to run. It's October, the rut. Seized with fever, the stags fight with each other and mate with up to sixty hinds a day to exhaustion and even death.

At the gate, Heather with her pixie face opens the padlock. But she is retiring. Has it really been twenty years?

'I know,' she smirks. 'I was young and naïve when I started and now I'm not.'

The Painted Glen is inside Glen Strathfarrar. And Glen Strathfarrar is one of four interior glens that converge into the trunk of the main glen, and all of that makes up mo ghleann. All tarmac roads end at the dams out west, and the only way to carry on to the west coast is by foot, mountain bike, horse and second sight. The glens are the children of the rivers. The rivers mate in pairs and give rise to a third one, then again, until there is a single river and then – the sea. Affric and Cannich become Glass. Glass and Farrar become the River of the Monks whose fresh estuary opens into the salty waters of the Firth in a widening funnel. When you see the Firth, coming in from the east, you see how the melting glaciers slipped down the mountains and shaped these coastal terraced plains. Behind the terraced plains hills rise into a shimmering infinity of mountains to the west and the north. When you stand in this gateway of the sea and look inland, you are drawn in irresistibly. On the south shore of the Firth is Inverness, gate city to the Highlands.

THE GLEN

To the north is a fertile peninsula called the Black Isle. And here is a low-lying plain where the first people of this land set up camp, as they drifted in their canoes through marshy estuaries. Strange to think, but the Firth was not always like this – because the British Isles were once connected to the continent. The first people glided into this wild silent land untrodden by two-leggeds, built huts not unlike the huts of pastoral nomads in the twentieth century, and lived in small groups, hunting and gathering in this mild and wooded land of birdsong and beasts for several thousand years. Until the herding-farming folk of the Neolithic arrived with cattle, sheep, and barley and wheat seeds. Land became more contested and people drifted further inland.

And so to Strathglass.

Our main glen is called Strathglass because it's wide enough to be a strath. But you always say I'm going up the glen, not I'm going up the strath, I don't know why. A dead-end, that's what some call our glen of Strathglass. But if it's a dead-end, then poor politics made it so, not poor geology, nor geography. In fact it leads upstream to the source of life – the multiple springs in the interior glens. Without all this water, none of us would be here.

Strathglass – the valley of the grey-green water. *Glas* can be green, grey, shadowy, grassy, mossy, and not completely there. Glas an latha is shadow of the day and it embraces me forgivingly. Twilight is like that. Then the night will erase all the *glasan*. That's what Highlanders called all shadowy creatures. The Highlanders are gone and only their words remain. Like ghosts.

In the night I stop and get out to feel the cold of the air and the passion of the river, and all the glen inhabitants feel this with me. An old woman from the Islands once said: I like listening to the radio because everyone listens together.

I like being cold together.

Behind me are twenty Munros – that's a hill 3,000 feet high or more. The glen opens and closes ahead of the car. How quickly the elemental embraces you, like a lover, once the chatty electric lights vanish. How quickly you turn to the stars and the river for company. The old Scots pines are serrated against the moonlit sky like art.

I turn off the headlights. Only in its natural night can I hear the glen. It's a self-dare too: do I know each turn in the road? Or will the car end up in the boggy alder whose sap runs a red for which there is no word.

Or halt in the beeches, elephant-footed, where an old iron gate stands without a fence. If you open the gate and climb the forest path, you'll find the gravestones of an old clan. Boar heads and Celtic swords are carved in red stone 3 metres high. The clan folk are gone from the glen, the castle lies empty but tenants still live in the grounds. One of them is Laughing Lachlan, a handyman who fixes broken things but you must catch him in the morning because there are just too many broken things in this world.

Behind me the glen folds back like a sleeping fern. Its beinns and lochs are silent.

This river runs parallel to the Great Glen that splits Scotland sideways like a lightning bolt. Ours is the first major waterway north of that faultline. There are others to the north of us. The glens are like constellations that expand and contract parallel to each other, but all of them in the same galactic neighbourhood of the Great Glen. From time to time, they send news to each other. Lately the news has been bad. The news is large energy companies moving in and drilling into the land tonnages of steel and concrete.

I'm driving west to east. That's how the rivers run in these glens – west to east. Drovers drove their cattle west to east.

Two men who embody the Highlands travelled west to east: the Christian missionary Columba and the Brahan Seer. The mystic Columba was born in Ireland. Before his birth, his mother had a visitation from an angel who gave her a robe in all the colours of the rainbow, a presage of divine grace, but then took it away and she saw the robe rise above the mountains and woods, illuminating the world with beauty. When Columba was a grown man, the holy spirit came to him in the form of a *columba*, dove. From his base in Iona to our Firth, where the Pictish King Brudei welcomed him. And as he made his way along the Great Glen, Columba became the first in recorded history to see the monster of Loch Ness. The episode was called by his biographer 'Of the driving away of a water beast'. The Pictish 'heathen barbarians' were so awed by the holy man's ability to repel the creature with nothing but the spell 'You shall not advance further' that they converted on the spot.

A millennium later, a man of humbler origins but equal spiritual power retraced this trail. His name was Coinneach Odhar, Sallow Kenneth, who went down in history as the Brahan Seer. It is said that, like Columba, he saw the shape of things past, present and future. He had a small stone with a hole in it and such stones are found on the islands and the west coast, the perfect creations of magma and waves. This is a country of stone, soil and water. But his stone was not what gave him second sight, for that's an inner gift. Some say his stone might lie at the bottom of a dam in this glen, whose flooding he foresaw:

'A loch above the Monks' Place will burst its banks and destroy in its rush a village.'

I've reached the River of the Monks. Its keystone village is the Monks' Place because a Benedictine monastery has been here for eight centuries but empty and roofless since the Reformation.

When archaeologists excavated the estuary plains near the Monks' Place, the fragments that came up showed that people have lived here since the Mesolithic. Chunks of bloodstone were brought by travellers from the western isles just like Columba, the Brahan Seer and the drovers. The bloodstone made the trip first – around 7,000 years ago – and was used to make tools.

West to east was the way of gifts and also the way of theft.

Goods were harvested deep in the glens and sent downstream to the Firth, then south by boat and lorry. Timber, fish, animal flesh. And human too – for the imperial army, for the emigrant ships. And more recently, Hydro power and wind power.

Industry arrived in the glens lured by their generous waters. And once it had a foothold, it grew. The first large-scale Hydro scheme was built at the turn of the twentieth century in the Highlands to power British Aluminium. By the 1930s, all the wild rivers were well mapped out. And between the 1940s and 1960s, the entire network of northern rivers was industrialised. Rivers were dammed, tunnels blasted into hills, Hydro power stations built. Power from the glens, it was called. Electricity was to be brought to all corners of Scotland. Highlanders and Islanders were promised free energy in exchange for the reshaping of their country. This did not happen, and most of the electricity generated in the north was sent to the south, whose industrial needs were growing.

Our glen hosts seven dams and each, bar one, is connected to a power station – either through a tunnel or next to the dam. That's three overground and three underground Hydro power stations. Monar, Mullardoch, Culligran, Fasnakyle,

Aigas, Kilmorack — for years I thought these were the names of dams and power stations. But inside the dams are lochs with the submerged skeletons of animals, houses and forests. And inside the hills are tunnels and turbine halls.

Yes, the lifeblood of the glen struggles, but it's still flowing. And I haven't crashed yet. All above me, the braes light up with spirits like twinkling stars in the Milky Way. I pass Aigas gorge overlooked by Dun Fionn. I glimpse things with the corner of my eye, shadowy creatures that are sometimes grey and pale, sometimes animal and sometimes human like children, but also dart across your field of awareness like spotted fish. They are the glasan, the creatures of the Glass river. The veil is thin, when you get close.

Do I digress? I think not. I'm still on the road, driving home.

I pull over at Aigas dam where the water churns darkly. Tony and I used to paddle in the gorge in a canoe built by him. Everything looks different from the water. To discover something is easy — you just turn up. But to know it takes time. We saw remains of the wooden platforms from which loggers and ferrymen floated the trees felled deeper in, and were sometimes maimed. The river was a trade artery between glen and sea and it took away the green gold of the Highlands: its forests. Eventually the glens ran out of native trees and native people, or almost. But the land still sings in Gaelic. It's just there's hardly anyone to make sense of it. I want to tune in, but the broadcast is fuzzy.

It is said that Columba received revelations through holy light, but that the Brahan Seer was triggered by anger and sorrow. A curtain fell and the Seer was seized with jolts and catapulted down the timeline where the future waited. As in the famous utterance:

'Oppressors will appear in the land, and the people change their own land for a strange one.'

I once fell asleep above Aigas gorge. The underwater turbine purred like a bass undertone to the main melody of birdsong. It was the last summer of something. Time was compressing. Ten years in the glen, and something was shifting under my feet and over my head. I felt a great loss coming.

When I woke up, I saw where I really was – in a place alive to itself, not just to me. Metamorphic rocks rose from the river and I saw what it was like for the children who swam here before the dams. They called these rocks the Frogs, and after the dams the shape was lost. But Aigas gorge is so noble it makes even the dam look good. In the glen, every living thing is multiplied. *A thousand welcomes*, goes the Gaelic greeting. *A thousand somethings or other*, goes the glen whose vocal cords are cut but it still wants to welcome you because that's the way of the living land. I got up from among the snake-patterned fritillaries and ran towards the opening light of the Firth and the rest of my life. To meet the ghost behind the face. The country behind the country. My life has become inextricably tied to this land. It was like going to meet myself before it's too late.

I drive past the stone church of Kilmorack and next to it the hermit who hasn't left her house for years. She lives with a parrot under a big chestnut tree next to the old spring. The spring supplies the church with water. The church is now a fine-art gallery. The windows glimmer like treasure chests full of paintings and sculptures of birds, animals, humans and planets. The stained-glass window features a rosette of perfect proportions. The spring has a resident frog that has been there for decades and sometimes it blocks the flow, and then Tony who owns the gallery puts on his waders and plunges into the spring and coaxes the frog out.

THE GLEN

Across from the church and the spring is the last dam. By the dam are two houses, and in the small one I spent ten years with Tony and our dogs. This patch of land is the Crossing Place. It's dark under the brilliant galaxies. I remember my first months here – no streetlamps, just stars and the outlines of the forest. I dreaded the darkness in the mouth of the glen. How I've changed. Everything has changed. The forest is gone. In its place is an open-pit quarry. A highway of steel pylons rides the hills, unnatural in size and intent. Cows with eyes like torches huddle around the base of a pylon. Their field is shrinking. Tony will be dozing with the radio on, the dog asleep under the stairs. I drive past like a stranger but I am not a stranger.

The odd streetlight appears now. Past the security gates of the country's largest switching substation, like a forest of steel.

Before I reach the Monks' Place I see the shack of the dam builder's son with his rusty pick-up truck and then – electric lights everywhere! Streetlights flood the empty road. Shop fronts and hairdressers are lit up, lots of hairdressers in this tiny village because sometimes it's all that's left – to get your hair done. The stars disappear and the glasan too. The night smells of estuary at low tide, and of whisky you can't taste because the distillery makes it for export.

These days I live with Bella in the Monks' Place where the river becomes tidal. In the morning the tide is in and the river so high, its silver light enters my windows. The willows are half-submerged like mangroves. A canoe glides in the morning mist – my neighbour the ex-soldier. He now walks barefoot like a penitent, and we talk about trees a lot because he is a tree surgeon. An otter lives in the first river bend, the sleek head pops up to check if things are still here and is gone. The swans honk-quarrel about which direction to take, there is a schism but they make up and move downstream as one. Hundreds of geese take off and you are almost lifted up by the flap of their wings.

I face the Firth full of reeds but keep turning around to scan the far hills of the glen. As if waiting for news. Or just to make sure they are still there.

And I hear it, especially at night when the thunder of industry stops and the land is left alone.

Something folds and unfolds in the hinterland. A vibration. If you tune in, you hear the glen hum its ancient nasal chant any way it can – through the animal skins of long-ago bagpipes, through fish bones, dead mouths, corries named by girls and women who walked with animals through blooming heather, peaty cascades, stones with a hole in them, dam sluices, high-voltage electricity lines, power stations ticking underground, and tunnels blasted in the hills by men whose song and screams are forgotten, except by the wind.

Chì mi

Chì mi (hee mee), I see. This is how a type of Gaelic poem begins.

And you name the places you see with your eyes. When you run out, you continue with places and things you see with your inner eye. There are chì mi prophecies and chì mi songs, like 'Chì mi na mòrbheanna'. It was written in 1856 by an exiled islander who sailed to Canada but returned to the Highlands and their misty mountains.

> *O chì, chì mi na mòrbheanna*
> *O chì, chì mi na còrrbheanna*
> *O chì, chì mi na coireachan*
> *Chì mi na sgoran fo cheò*

> Oh I see them, I see the great mountains
> I see the great hills
> I see the great corries
> I see the peaks of mist

It goes on – I see the place where I was born, where I am greeted in a tongue I understand, where love welcomes me, and I wouldn't trade that for a ton of gold.

When you listen to this song, you feel what it's like to lose your land. It is the same as losing people you love, your health, your peace. So you visit it in your mind's eye. You develop second sight.

The Crossing Place, home

When you are new to a place you love, your senses are reborn. You hear sounds you've never heard before, or not like this.

The panicked flaps of grouse in the bushes. The river rushing in its bed. The scratch of mice in the walls. The darting of bats at twilight. They live under the roof and like to come out at night to feed and circle above the dam, then they come home and cover the ledge of the small bath window with droppings. The cosmic silence of the glen at night.

On summer nights when it didn't get dark we stayed out on the patio, ate foraged greens we called the thirty-leaf salad, made plans for home improvements, and sneezed from the flowering elder. The elders were bone-white in winter but burst into leaf in spring. They lived in the neighbour's field where you could see the contours of grassed-up furniture and ruined dwellings. The metal frame of a bedstead poked out and sometimes the grass inside it assumed the shape of a body sleeping on its side. Through the garden ran the ghost of the old road that led to the river's Crossing Place.

Three generations of a family had lived together in this cottage in the 1970s. Their bath and latrine was outside. The next tenants brought the bath inside and the steam made the wallpaper fall off, but they liked the mugginess because it helped grow their cannabis. When Tony moved in, he gutted the upstairs and put in a modern floor. Even the doors and their latches were crafted by him with salvaged materials, learning trades as he went along: plumbing, carpentry, electrics, painting-decorating, gardening, architecture and general heavy lifting.

There had been a midden in the garden and the soil kept churning up fragments. The first years when it was just Tony, it was coils of wire. Even now, the earth threw up shards of thick glass, hand-painted cream jugs and horseshoes crafted by the famed cobblers of the glen. We lived inside an archaeological pit. You dig a vegetable bed and the earth sends up a message.

And stones. Moving them made me feel like a convict. But Tony enjoyed it, like a desert hermit building an oasis. Already as a child, he'd dragged stones around for fun. Sometimes I looked at him and saw him in a long hemp robe like a Benedictine monk. Same long hair, same look in the eyes that could go from hyperfocused to tripped out. Old and young at once, knowing that all shall come to pass but you must cultivate your garden.

Sometimes I wondered if both of us had returned in this lifetime to complete some unfinished business in the Highlands. There was something fated about it.

When I first met Tony, I felt a blast of freshness, a purity of heart like quartz. Every time I drove north to visit him and the glen, something lifted me up and made me fly as if released from a cage. That cage was the city. I liked the city or maybe I was just used to it. But going north set me free. The silent stoic glens, that low-key kindness of the north, it embraced me at once. Everything here was real.

But the stones! So many types of stones. That's why Tony had studied Geography and Geology, to understand what made this country the way it is. Lewisian, Moinian, Torridonian, Dalradian. And all that before the Cambrian Age, long before the dinosaurs. This dragon land was so old, the fire had gone out of it and left it stone cold. Or that's how it felt on a chilly damp day. The thaw of the most recent ice had left behind a sandy ground. Hunter-gatherers in animal skins had drifted in their canoes from the east in the wake of the thaw, when the British Isles were still a part of the European continent. And here we were, 10,000 years later, next to the quarry.

'On the other hand, sandy soil is why we don't have midges!' Tony looked at the positive.

Midges like soggy ground. One summer, we built our very own stone circle under the geans (cherry trees) and sat inside it on upturned postal boxes with the birds and the blossoms full of buzzing bees, surveying the Crossing Place. How effulgent it was.

I liked roaming the forest above the dam, and Tony liked projects. One winter he built a garden study, another a potting shed, with salvaged materials – doors, windows, corrugated tin. It's amazing what you can find in the tips of industrial estates. All this lifting will give me a hernia and you a third one! I complained, and I also complained about the rough driveway with its potholes that we filled with gravel once a year, which we got in trailer loads from the quarry. The woman at the gate kiosk weighed your gravel by the ton on a weighbridge. For twenty years she sat behind the small window, chain-smoking and weighing gravel with a poker face.

It had started in the 1950s as a gravel pit for the construction of our dam. Then it was sold to a bigger company, then a bigger one worth a billion pounds. It kept expanding and went from a small pit to an industrial zone the size of an airport. The dust from the quarry aggravated our hay fever and our neighbour's asthma but at least we were shielded by a woodland and the crashing sounds were distant.

In spring, our family of geans burst into white blossom and doubled in size. The cherries were small and destoning them for smoothies produced blood-like jets that stained the skin. Our neighbour rented her croft for a peppercorn rent from the largest local estate. She kept sheep as pets, because when you live on a croft, by law you have to keep animals or plant a crop. In the Highlands and Islands, the croft stands for two things: self-sufficiency and hard-earned rights to have a working relationship with the land. But in practice there are hardly any crofters left.

The head sheep Baa would come to the wire fence to look at you and chew thoughtfully. When Baa died, the others followed one by one, and ten years on it was two sheep on six acres. If crops, orchards and animals were raised here, they would feed a township full of milk, cheese, vegetables, grains and occasionally meat. Just as they used to, when the Crossing Place had been productive.

'It is still productive!' the neighbour pointed out. 'Because of Tony's gardening.'

Tony kept a full vegetable garden. In the potting shed he planted up seeds for courgettes, beans and all sorts of salad leaf and transferred the shoots to bigger pots after a few weeks. I didn't have that kind of patience. The week I moved in, rats chomped through the potatoes in the kitchen. The neighbour's husband used to shoot them from his wheelchair with an old army shotgun, but he died and the rats moved into our compost and then kitchen. 'Don't worry, my love!' Tony said, and put out blue poison cakes. A baby rat dragged itself into the kitchen and died. We gave up on the poison cakes and flatted with the rats for a couple of weeks till the fields filled up with grain and the rats moved out. Then the field mice moved back in and started squirrelling nuts and seeds under the mattresses.

We were friendly with our neighbour but did not breach each other's doors. We exchanged chutneys, raspberries, eggs and books. Ten years after moving in, I will knock on her door to say that I'm moving out and burst into tears, and she will usher me in:

'For God's sake, you can't have a meltdown! Pull yourself together and think about your readers!'

Stoic and sensible: the tonic for those who wash up in the North on a sea of uncontrollable emotions.

This was the mouth of the glen, fertile despite the stones, with sloping fields. The braes (heights) were Kilmorack and our small patch on the river side was the Crossing Place. Before the bridge, you were ferried across by a boatman with a crooked smile. I see him: callused hands from rowing, unwashed hair, biting a coin to check it's genuine. He drinks creamy sheep's milk brought down from the braes by his daughter. They speak Pictish, then Gaelic, then nothing.

Across the road, the farmer moved his cows around to vary their grazing. Another sound I'd never heard before was the mothers when their male calves are taken away. Two days a year, the mouth of the glen was filled with a holler of grief that haunted my sleep.

Our house and the neighbour's were the only two houses left in the Crossing Place. There was one other guy in a caravan upstream. We lived by Kilmorack dam and he lived by Aigas dam. The Crossing Place had once supplied nearby communities with grain milled on the river. The mill had been powered by the Kilmorack cascades that flowed over stunning terraces of red stone and were renowned as one of the natural wonders of the Highlands, before they were replaced with the dam.

A cold jet of water the size of a man's thumb used to spring from the river banks, a priest had written in his parish notes. It never changed in size or temperature, the priest wrote, and we kept looking for it.

In winter, when darkness came at four in the afternoon, we lounged by the fire with whisky macs (green ginger wine and whisky). On clear nights we stood by the fast-growing willow and looked for the seven sisters of the Pleiades like glow-worms in the cosmic cave. And millions of other stars folded into galaxies with heads and tails and presumably bodies.

'Each star is a sun like ours. Some are already dead by the time we see this,' Tony would say. 'It blows your mind.'

But the mind gets it for a second, the time for a bat to dart past the edge of your awareness.

Winters, and other seasons, had that uniquely Scottish, bone-rotting dampy cold. Tony had happily survived with a log-burning stove and a cooking-gas stove. The ground floor was small and cosy but retained a medieval dinge. The cottage had thick stone walls but the floor was concrete and the thin entrance door that opened up straight into the living space – no vestibule – brought in draughts. I've always liked old houses, old people and old things in general, and here was – old. Not to worry, my love, I'll put in radiators, Tony said, and did. He also gave me a pair of wellies and soon enough I assumed the ways of the glen – thick jumpers, sleeves stained with soot from the fireplace and leaves in my hair. We piled up thick rugs on the floor to stop the stone-cold of the centuries. It took some getting used to. But it's how country living is. The inside and the outside fuse. You are close to a myriad living things that are not human and it fills you with delight. You become the child you forgot. It releases you from the paralysis of self-consciousness and makes room for self-reliance.

Tony had learned all his practical skills through doing things. Restoring on a shoestring budget the church and the miller's cottage had been his school. I learned to stack logs in the shed, which became my favourite activity; tell a red kite from a buzzard; recognise basic trees like beech, rowan and alder, and smell the change in weather. Crouching in the vegetable beds to weed, I remembered the last time I had done this – when I was a child in my great-aunt's garden in the fertile pre-Danubian plains of northern Bulgaria. She and my grandmother were green-fingered and all the green stuff we ate came from their gardens. I started drying herbs like thyme, mint and nettle, the way my grandmother had done – on newspapers spread out on spare beds. It had taken me decades to return to the land, but here I was at last.

I liked living next to the dam. It was big, but one of the smaller ones. It existed in its mechanical reality, reliable and dull. It had done its job of powering fridges, washing machines and factories for seventy years. It was a veteran. On misty mornings when we walked down to the dam and the dog collected pinecones in her mouth, we saw deer swimming across the river. They came to the small island that was partially submerged when the dam released excess water. In summer, the odd angler was rowed out to the island and left there for the day. Come May, we watched the silver trout flip and later the salmon. Some years there were lots, others not, but the overall trend was down.

Willie the gillie patrolled in his car for poachers. I don't know if he saw any, but I did. I always thought fishing should be democratic. And it was, once. The country known as the Highlands and Islands makes up one third of Scotland and it was once the home of one third of its people. Kinship safeguarded ecology. The folk of the glens lived just like in the Gaelic saying: everyone can take a deer from the hill, a tree from the forest and a salmon from the river – and no more. Then came the Highland Clearances. Once they were completed, just 8 per cent of Scotland's people were left in the Highlands and Islands. The people were gone, the kinship was gone, and the ecology was gone.

Fishing became a commercial 'sport'. Our stretch of the river is more expensive than upstream because there are more salmon here. Then the obstacle course of the dams begins and they struggle. The fishing tourists came from the south. A week in August on this river is a highlight of their year. Willie, who came from a dynasty of fishing gillies, handled them with a gentle hand and plenty of whisky. He had a drooping moustache and spaniels, and he'd sit in his car on the riverbank, enveloped in cigarette smoke, in his tatty waxed jacket, play 1980s rock music, his eyes flowing with memories like the river. Raise of hand, curt sideways shake of the head the Highland male way like a horse, the rare word. 'Aye, it's nippy' on a freezing day. The river was a part of him, the best part. Every day I took the dog past the first fishing hut and the old cemetery with the ruined church of Talorgan – and if I didn't see him, I'd wonder. Once he saw me picking nettles and his eyes watered. He remembered his mother's nettle soup. But a fresh-faced gillie from the south replaced him and soon after, Willie fell while cutting sticks (logs) and never got up again.

After heavy rain, the sluice gate of the dam is opened to stop it overflowing, and we hear the blast and go down to watch it. A massive jet shoots through the sluice gate and makes waves in the river.

And that natural spring the size of a man's thumb that

gushed from the rock – we can't find it because the sluice gate replaced it, just as the dam replaced the waterfall. The spring was smashed and its water diverted into cement extracted from the gravel pit next door.

We're above the banks but when the sluice disgorges a damful at our feet in fast-travelling fury – then it all feels very close. It's fine, Tony says, even if the reservoir overflows, they'll let the water through the dam and the water will burst through the glass front of the power station. Now that's a thought! But it gives me dreams of flooding. And a fascination with dams. Each dam has a power station next to it or near it. Why are there so many of them and so close together?

The post-war era brought mass industrialisation to the most pristine places.

If the Highlands and Islands were to be electrified like the rest of the modern world, the Hydro-Electric schemes had to go ahead. So went the argument. The builders of the Hydro schemes were hailed as pioneers of renewable energy, and they were. But the schemes were built at the cost of a drastic modification of the land. But that's what nature was here for, wasn't it? To be pummelled into a more useful shape, extracted, monetised and put to work. Soon the true purpose of the mass Hydro schemes became clear: to supply the production of other large industries. Within a few years of being built, 80 per cent of Hydro energy generated in the Highlands went south of the Highlands. Highlanders got a raw deal out of it. They lost some of their natural wonders like the Kilmorack Falls, they lost a way of life, and instead of getting free electricity, they picked up a double bill. Their nature was impoverished and their electricity expensive.

Tony and I made special trips to the innermost dams of the glen – Monar and Mullardoch. Monar is big and Mullardoch is gigantic. They prop up the great Highland waters like Atlases. These key dams had their own clocks and their own law, like Roman garrisons inside Hadrian's Wall. They have held out very well, but now hairline cracks run through them.

Is it a matter of time? we wondered.

There were old mutterings in the glen: Mullardoch was built the wrong way around, Monar is cracked. Or maybe: Monar was built the wrong way around, Mullardoch is cracked. Were the Brahan Seer's prediction of a flood to come true, it'll be one of these two. The old timers know it, because a Highlander knows that the Brahan Seer has the last word, even if it takes four centuries.

When you approach our dam, you can hear the turbines. It's an overground station that is part of the dam. We peer through the glass front of the turbine hall with its shuddering machines and alarm buttons. The maintenance engineer used to come every week and chat to us but these days the workers on the dams are rare, and they are not local anymore. Valves and switches are now remote-controlled from the headquarters 200 miles south. Our neighbouring dam upstream used to have a viewing room where you could see the fish ladders but this has been shut. New barriers and gates have appeared, cameras too. The engineers, workers and surveyors of the energy company that owns the dams, the power stations and the electricity grid itself would drive around in large vehicles, wearing safety helmets and orange jackets, avoiding eye contact while prospecting for something they called *preferred routes* for the new transmission line. Then they started building the new steel towers. Woods were felled to make way for them – the preferred route seemed to rip through the most beautiful places, like an army of vandals. I passed the contractors on my walks and chatted to them. They worked hard, didn't really know where they were, and left when the job was done. The new pylons were twice the height of the existing power lines. The materials were surprisingly outdated: steel and concrete – and the production of steel is completely dependent on coal. The ripping up of so much nature was hard to witness.

An army of gleaming new pylons marched across the Highlands now. They were built too close to houses, schools, farms, sometimes almost on top of them. We acquired one in the Crossing Place, just across the neighbour's field, maybe a hundred metres from our house. They dwarfed everything and made the dams look small. But surely, there was a good reason, we need renewable energy. There have to be sacrifices . . .

I'd got to know the dams and the power stations, but I hadn't a clue about the world of energy generation, transmission, speculation, storage and global trading. I wanted to trust that all was being taken care of, for the benefit of our planet. We had a progressive government, didn't we? We were going to decarbonise not just ourselves, but the whole of Europe. That had to be good.

But I knew in my bones that something had gone wrong – how can you destroy so much nature to replace it with steel and concrete?

I sought comfort in graveyards, I've always liked them. They were quiet and green. Above our dam was the old graveyard of Kilmorack. The graveyard keeper's bothy was still here because once, graveyards had watchmen against body snatchers. In the bothy were discarded clothes and bottles, from whoever had last squatted in it. From this vantage point, you could see the drop of the dam and appreciate its height of 26 metres. You saw how the river was split, like an atom. Once this split is made, power is released. Life becomes more efficient, and more dangerous.

Across the road was the gallery-inside-a-church, with its

healing spring. Until the early twentieth century, people walked to attend service. In summer it was held outside, and the minister stood at the top of the rumbling cascades and delivered a sermon in Gaelic to a thousand people wearing their Sunday best. Worshippers walked barefoot and only put on their shoes for the service. Then walked home barefoot again.

In the 1960s, the church fell out of use for a generation, until a young guy in an old sweater bought it from a mysterious man called Black Alan who collected valuable old things but lived in a damp room with his mother. The young guy was Tony. Black Alan turned up a few times to see how the restoration was going, glowed with approval at Tony's progress, and vanished without a trace.

The new graveyard, which is quite old, was still in use, and when a procession of sombre cars parked along the road, we started guessing who had died. There were three grave diggers that Tony was friendly with. One wrote short stories, another painted, and the boss was Mr Fridge – not a nickname. Mr Fridge was always in a good mood and even worked on weekends when he turned up in a little MG car just to hang out in the lushness of the glen. I heard that he used to shoot aggressive seagulls that attacked funeral processions and especially people's heads, but maybe this is a true story that never happened.

A clan of settled Travellers lived in Talorgan's Village on the other side of the river from us. Once or twice, a sight rarely seen, like an apparition: two men in singlets with pomaded hair and a woman in a long skirt on a painted cart drawn by two horses. They galloped past our house with a clatter of hooves and vanished. Once, a guy turned up at the cottage with a gleaming smile. We hadn't heard him arrive.

'I won't ask for yir old junk, pal.'

That's exactly what he was asking for. The slang of Travellers. You invert the meaning. It's a protection, like a spell. The roots of this slang are in medieval bardic cant. And with their unmatched genius, the Travellers also created a back-to-front pidgin-Gaelic called Beurla Reagaird. It's like nothing else. To disguise the meaning from both English and Gaelic speakers, they introduced random elements into a word. I wanted to invite him in and take his life story, but Tony didn't. Last time he'd been pally, all his tools went missing. A fairish swap for a life story, I thought, but the man never returned.

Some nights the stars were so bright, the sky looked painted above the birch which grew before my eyes, and one day, Tony said, even this birch will come down, and everything will go south, but I will still love you when all your teeth fall out.

Tony had come to the Highlands in his twenties, driven by an instinct to leave the central belt and keep going north until something changed. He too had felt that euphoria when the Great Glen comes into view like the edge of another continent. Highlanders were welcoming and he felt at home even as he moved between damp flats and held odd jobs, like grubbing in spring, when you hike all day scattering grass seeds on bare hills – a great job, but you can't do it forever. Then he stumbled across the abandoned church. He had exactly the right amount of money which wasn't much – nobody wanted an eighteenth-century church. Tony had an eye for beauty. He restored it – on his own, with a shaky scaffold – and started showing Highland artists and sculptors. Beauty and nature: his two great loves since childhood. He slept upstairs in a small alcove, washed with cold water that froze in winter, cooked noodles on a camping stove, and lived like a monk – him and the bats in the roof, moonlight streaming through the perfect rosette of stained glass.

It's about what you have to give up, Tony liked to say, and that was it.

It was the same for the artists. Those who were possessed by the creative daimon had given something up. When the old miller's cottage in the Crossing Place came up for rent, he moved in and set about renovating it. Unexpectedly, the gallery became a success and his stable of artists grew until he was working with the country's best artists and sculptors. He never took holidays until I came along.

In his notebook, Tony drew architectural plans for an improved cottage.

'What about a porch here. And a small extension here?'

'But I like the gable end! A shame to take it out. And that would wipe out the vegetable beds.'

I wanted a more comfortable house but the cottage was perfectly proportioned. Ten years on, we still couldn't afford to improve it, and maybe we were meant to keep it as it was – for people with simple needs. And try to be more like them. Our ancestors of the Crossing Place.

In winter when the gallery closed for a few weeks, we'd go on holiday to some island colder than here. We'd drive across a land pouring with water – down hills, across roads, waterfalls swelling with glee, and rivers flowing where there weren't any before, a symphony of water all around us – then onto a ferry and across choppy seas. The standing stones of Orkney were alive and hummed when you hugged them. Orkney was flat and had winds that lifted you off and chucked you somewhere else. The Isle of Mull had the misty mountains described in 'Chì mi na mòrbheanna'. Once, 8,000 people lived in Mull, in a self-reliant economy. But forced emigration banished three quarters of them to the ends of the world. Down a jetty, in a bay enjoyed by glistening seals that trumpet like elephants, the saddest scenes took place some generations ago: the destitute people of Mull boarded ships and sailed to Canada. Some died en route. Made destitute by their own clan chiefs, they could no longer survive in the island. Or anywhere in Scotland. The small tenancies that the clansfolk held in the land were not lucrative for the clan chiefs who became indebted to the Crown. To commodify the land, they evicted their own people and populated the north with a single imported crop: Cheviot sheep.

This evisceration of the land of its natives happened with sickening regularity in almost every corner of the Scottish Highlands and Islands over a century. It became known as the Highland Clearances. The people were extracted and left to their own devices to transplant themselves wherever they could. By the time this operation without anaesthetic was completed, it left the body of the land nearly bloodless. This is how the Highlands became known for being *empty*. The Clearances took place in the long aftermath of the Battle of Culloden (1746) when Jacobite rebels were defeated by the British Army. This battle was the culmination of half a century of schismatic conflict, and its aftermath sounded the death knell of Highland culture which was synonymous with Gaeldom. So much so that the earlier name for the Highlands and Islands is Gàidhealtachd – the realm of the Gaels.

In the north of Scotland, people still speak of Culloden with sadness. And in the south, with detachment. The south benefited from the tragedy of the north – and to this day. The south does not know the north – to this day. When I lived in the south, I thought the Highlands and Islands were a place for holidays and second houses for the rich. They were *empty*, weren't they? The cliché was *majestically empty*. And it puzzled me how something so long ago as Culloden could be evoked with such sorrow by the Gaels. Then I came to live in Gaeldom. Among the ruined cottages, abandoned villages, immigrant jetties, haunted glens, extinct families and place names in a forgotten language. A catastrophe is not a single event. It ticks on in some infernal mechanism out of view. It casts a shadow over the land like the hand of a broken clock. One day, 280 years later, you walk across a strath and realise that there's no one to tell you the name of that hill. That everything good in this land has been, or is targeted to be, harvested for export. And you start hearing the raven's caw in a different way. The silent scream of a swept country, once you hear it you can't unhear it.

One winter we sailed to Shetland mainland to visit artists. It's called that because there are other islands off the main island. Shetland is not close to anything. It is its own country. The ferry crossing is ten to twelve hours and on the way back there was a storm. Mountains of water rising and falling. You lay on your bed if you had one, standing was impossible. Twenty-four hours later we docked in granite-grey Aberdeen. On deck, we could tell the Shetlanders – woollen-hatted, waterproofed and smiling like sailors on duty, never mind that they had missed hospital appointments and flights. My notion of the north shifted. Seen from Shetland, the Great Glen is the far south. I grasped the quintessential thing about Highlanders and Islanders. It was the ability to not merely endure the elements but relish them.

Our life at the Crossing Place revolved around the gallery and the seasons. Every month there was a preview of a show, people would come from all corners of Scotland, and on occasion Tony put on his great-grandfather's kilt, heavy and moth-eaten, and holding in it the memory of the trenches from 1917 when its wearer would fall asleep in the mud, a piece of cheese stuck on his bayonet to keep it from rats. In the days of busy gallery previews, kilts were still a thing. I looked at these kilted men with their bare knees and high woollen socks, and behind them lined up I saw all the men of the millennia who wore patterned tunics, from my native Thrace and Macedonia to Caledonia, via the Romans. A man in a tunic can't be pompous. The day after the Brexit referendum, I went for the usual walk with the dog. Two young guys in kilts were carrying the Saltire on a pole, as if to some battle of independence or maybe reunion, and they were in tears.

After previews, artists and hangers-on would come back to the bohemian gloom of the cottage with the spare bottles of wine. We'd have a pot of stew waiting. Tony used to make the stew, in between hanging the latest show, fixing the roof, turning the vegetable beds and attending to artists' nervous breakdowns. But I took over the stew-making. Previews were on a Saturday, which meant that Sundays were for putting wine glasses through the dishwasher at home and recovering from it all. When things didn't sell, I was distraught for Tony. When they did, we were elated.

Otherwise, I spent my days in a studio above the garage also built by Tony. From that high room I ventured out to fantastical places. I was here and elsewhere. I belonged to some moving landscape of the mind and followed its siren call. That was my destiny, and the guardianship of Kilmorack was his. The creative daimon drove us both. That's how it was, in the Crossing Place.

Tony had a habit of popping back to get lunch. He'd materialise and grab a pack of oatcakes and a tub of hummus, and touch base as if to make sure I was still there. The lunch-time interruptions were brief.

'It's me! Goodbye!' Tony would call up to the studio.

And I'd watch him run up the driveway back to the gallery wearing his jumper back to front. He would turn to see me perched at my high window, and I would wave.

Chì mi

Every time Tony and I go into the inner glens for a day's trip, we fall in with the land and a music rises like mist off the river and makes us sing. It's more sounds than words and it's never the same, though we pass the same places.

We see the Five Forts of Farley above, purple with blooming heather. The hermit and her horse chestnut by the gallery. The bridge of wild garlic. The blue landscape artist I suspect to be a selkie who shed her sealskin to have a life on land, but is often sad in her human guise, and one day she'll return to sea, Tony says. The people in their houses with lives stranger than fiction and quieter than a pond. Aigas gorge, Dun Fionn. The nature park. The golf course. 'I see the golf course overgrown in some future time, taken over by the nature park, and are you glad?' asks Tony. I am glad.

I see the church of Struy 'the confluence', and the inn where shepherds and foresters, stalkers and dam builders had a dram then stumbled in the dark to their digs. I see the turn-off that nobody takes but if you do, you'll go past the Meadow of the Heads where two clans clashed and heads rolled, and you'll reach a thin stone by the road where this is carved:

W C & C F
1746
Mo rùn geal òg

A coded message that tells you how the Highlands became a tragic cliché of *majestic emptiness*. I see William Chisholm the way his wife saw him – sensitive, handsome, broad of shoulder, because Christina Fergusson painted him in her poem of lament 'My fair young love'. *Mo rùn geal òg*. He was a smith and standard-bearer of his clan and when the battle at Culloden Field was lost, he took his clansmen to a barn on a hilltop and fought the government army to the end. Christina's poem starts by addressing Bonnie Prince Charlie, the pretender to the throne who led the Highlanders to their doom.

> Oh little Charlie Stuart,
> It's your cause that has grieved me,
> you took everything from me in this selfish war

And ends addressing her beloved:

> Time has gone by
> and there is nobody like you.
> Till I am buried beneath the ground
> your love will not leave me –
> my fair young love.

I see them parting in the spot where the stone stands today. He goes downstream with the white linen flag of his clan and all the other men who will be killed. I see Christina wrapped in her black wool shawl by the river, gathering nettles in a willow basket. And all the other war widows of the next 200 years, young and already old.

We see glasan in the fields, in the alder grove, people and animals that are gone.

We see the piles of stones that were houses, entire villages.

They were emptied of their people in the Clearances. Today, quite a lot of this land belongs to the energy giant.

We see the high drove roads to the west where only the wind gallops because people were forced off the high road to the low. Everyone is a lowlander now.

We see Sgùrr na Lapaich, Peak of the Bogland. The Forest of Fasnakyle. And Fasnakyle power station, built in the 1950s from red stone quarried locally. We see the stone reliefs reminiscent of Pictish carvings and emblematic of now-eclipsed clans: the boar, a dragon, the stag – and if you look again, the stag has an erection, to show the thrust of industry through the glens. The Fasnakyle church reminds us that Fasnakyle was not always owned by industry. The name means hazel wood. A great hazel wood grew here once and many people lived in it. Now the church is for sale. Everything is for sale.

But we don't despond because we see the icy waterfalls of the future crash down the brown hills like a hundred fiddlers jamming together, and it makes us glad to arrive one summer morning at a fork in the glen. Right to Affric where nobody lives. And left to green Giusachan which means pine wood and where we like to visit because it's the last inhabited place in the glen.

Under Fairie Hill

We are 27 kilometres into the main glen. The village here is Tomich. Its gingerbread lattice-roofed houses line the road which continues uphill to farmhouses, the waterfalls — and higher up, a place called Cougie where a family lives off-grid, and they are the last inhabitants. Then the land turns wild all the way to the west coast.

Something's off here, I said the first time we came. I knew little about the glen in my first years. Maybe it's the closed doors, the silence of the houses. A cold shadow falls over the tranquil river road. Maybe it's the topography — this is a frost bowl in winter. And in the warm months, the woods of Giusachan are chlorophyl-green and silent like a midsummer night's dream, or nightmare.

It's the history, Tony said. Tomich is a *model village* that did not arise spontaneously. It was built along this lower road from the ashes of displaced communities from the higher road. Their ruined houses, mills, animal pens and whisky stills were engulfed by a pine plantation. This happened a hundred years after the Clearances started. A latter-day clearance. People were taken from their hillside dwellings and brought down to the low road — so that the owner of Giusachan could have a model village with model peasants and a model farm to show off to his guests when they came to shoot everything that moved and have meetings behind closed doors, in which the fate of individuals and nations was informally decided on the back of a napkin.

The village has a hotel-restaurant and a post-office shop that closed when the ninety-year-old postmistress died. The houses are occupied by recent settlers and second-home owners. Of the old timers, there's Ali the gillie, the family with the big farm, the Cougies way up at the top, and at the foot of Fairie Hill, Iain the Wood.

He used to stop in the gallery with his girlfriend but Tony hadn't seen him lately and we came to see if he was still alive.

Iain lives in the woods in a self-built house so fairie-like it has become a tourist attraction. Iain too is an attraction, with his hobbit looks, kilt with sporran and feathered beret. In summer, visitors drop in on their way to the falls, to see the woodsman and his creations. In winter, neighbours come to check up on him.

Radio music blasts from the shed. We admire his sun-struck garden that backs onto the dark forest: his arched bridges over the pond, the lilac trees. Iain comes out and smiles a practised smile. He is in wellies.

'This is a catenary bridge. From Latin *catena*. How did the Romans make bridges? Inverted catenary. And the meaning of catenary?' He tests us.

'Padlock,' I say.

'Very good. Chain. Havenae seen you in a wee while,' to Tony. 'You look like Jesus these days.'

'And you still look about eighty years old.'

Iain is pleased. He is ninety. Iain is known in the glen for giving his income to a family in Vietnam, his pension and any money that tourists leave in the post-box at the bottom of the driveway.

There's no small talk because when I ask about Vietnam, he starts from the beginning. But soon we lose the thread of his story.

'I was in a regiment. Then you join a battalion. I hated the army. The Korean War had just finished. Actually it never finished. It just stopped.'

The cuckoo clock goes off twelve times. He made it out of cherry wood. He made everything. Every door handle is a work of art. A table from red wood that shines like autumn.

'Also called sequoia. Introduced from the United States by large estates. Hard wood is everything with leaves. Soft wood has needles. The best tree for building shelters is larch. That's introduced too.'

His house is made from larch. Lots of things are traditionally made from larch. Wheelbarrows, horse carts, fishing boats, field posts, gates and cabins in the wood. Next to oak it's number one for standing up to the weather. A set of rounded stools is made from yew and elm, with little drawers from sequoia. The stairs are oak. An ornate table from Caledonian pine.

'I like beauty. I'm visual, like.'

He shows us the diamond stool, from sycamore, with diamond-shaped hollows inside the legs. It was made from cast-offs.

'Ach, everything is made out of rubbish. I'm not clever, or strong, or lucky. Just curious.'

Something scurries in the roof: pine martens. They have moved in to keep him company while his girlfriend is away. The window frames are exquisite.

'I knew these windows when they were a tree.' All his lines

are well rehearsed, but behind the hosting manner, there is pain and loss.

After Korea, Iain came back and set up a sawmill. A one-man organisation. He made good money. But he couldn't stay put. In those days, you could buy a sailing ticket to Australia for £10. He told us that he spent a decade in Australia, had a child with a First Nations woman, then married another woman and had two more children with her. He worked as a builder and they moved from house to house, following his jobs. In his spare time he built their dream house. Later, it transpires that he fabricated two women out of one. His biography shifts all the time. The couple came back to the glen, back to the sawmill, and lived in a cabin. His wife went on walkabouts deep in the glen, but he didn't tell us that, he only talked about himself. She'd walk out the door of the cabin with nothing but the clothes on her back and would be gone for two or three days. The odd person would see her and think she was lost, but she was getting to know the glen.

In his spare time he did up this place, which was then a roofless byre.

'It was all temporary but I got carried away.'

The Australian house he'd built was on the edge of an Aboriginal reserve and they couldn't sell it. They returned to Australia but became estranged, she sickened and died young, and once again he came back to the glen, and the children drop out of the story altogether.

'You're leaving already!'

Next time we visit, he has dressed for the occasion in full kilt regalia. He tells us about the time he and his friend the priest were walking along this road. It was around Samhain, the silent month of November.

'The priest's wife ran away with another priest. But that's not the point.'

The point is, Iain and the priest were consoling themselves in the hotel bar and walking back along the road at twilight when a tall man appeared out of nowhere on the edge of the road. He looked at them. He was not of this reality, they could see through him – literally. Staggered, they watched him wade into the bracken and vanish.

'Was he trying to tell us something?'

Or maybe he had popped into this reality to retrieve something. Like the truth. Since then, Iain always walks in the middle of the road and avoids the edges of things. Because the spirit world has its own ways.

'Aye, very much so. See, I don't feel that I did this garden at all. Somebody else did it. Look at that door! I couldn't have done that. I was just the labourer.'

Behind his hobbit house, the forest whispers. Lilac hyacinths drop on the grass and fill the air with sweet decadence.

This land is old and full of spirits. Fairies and spirits are known as the little people. This is why names like Fairie Hill, Fairy Glen, Fairy Mound and Fairy Gate are common in the Highlands. The biggest fairie hill is above Inverness. It's called Tomnahurich and was known as the gathering place of 'fiddlers and fairies'. A source as sober as the New Statistical Account of the mid-1800s states that Tomnahurich was 'the great gathering hill of fairies in the north, its broad and level summit and smooth green sides waving with harebell, broom and bracken, afforded them ample space and seclusion for their elvish orgies.'

But fairies can also be very large and it's no coincidence that the great warrior giants are known to be buried there – not dead but merely sleeping, the saying goes, and when they awaken, the Gaels will be a nation once again. In popular memory, two people are associated with Tomnahurich. Thomas the Rhymer, a medieval seer who received his second sight from the Queen of the Fairies herself after living in the Otherworld for seven fairie years. Seven fairie years could be an hour or a century, in human time. You come out and the world has changed beyond recognition. The second person is the Brahan Seer who foresaw many changes in the Highlands.

'The day will come when English mares with hempen bridles shall be led round the back of Tomnahurich,' he predicted, and it sounds like poetry in Gaelic. It means: The day will come when full-rigged ships will be seen sailing from the top of Tomnahurich Hill.

This was fulfilled with Telford's Caledonian Canal in the early nineteenth century. Twenty years later, the hill became a burial ground and the largest cemetery of the Great Glen, complete with fence and a gate – an alien sight for the people of the Highlands. Fences and gates arrived after the Clearances. The Brahan Seer had foreseen this too:

'The day will come when Tomnahurich will be under lock and key, with spirits secured within.'

A fairie hill is very likely to contain a mound from Neolithic times and the original fairies were the spirits of the dead. Over time, they became indistinguishable from the spirits of the place. Our land ancestors.

Iain lives at the foot of a fairie hill too. The day will come when a big German developer will build a wind farm on it, with an access road, a locked gate and a battery storage plant filled with lithium batteries the size of trucks. The red lights of masts will flash in the deep night of the glen. Fairie Hill Wind Farm sounds so good that tourists may come to look for fairies among the mechanical hum of turbines. Will Iain's house be levelled by a developer and something more useful put in its place, like industrial offices?

'Take the Nessie,' Iain is off on another narrative. 'Nessie is still around.'

What, the Loch Ness Monster?

'It's a plesiosaurus. I know three people who seen it.'

So do I, scoffs Tony who is a Nessie sceptic. Everyone knows three people who have seen it. Recorded mass sightings of unknown creatures in Loch Ness – including on land – started in the 1930s. That's when the modern road was built. Perhaps it was all the drilling that brought the creatures to the surface! But sightings have faded. Only the potency of the symbol remains, like a totem.

The kelpie of Celtic folklore is a seahorse. And the kelpie is the heir to the Pictish beast carved on Pictish stones. They are the same thing. The kelpie, the Nessie, it's an animal that should be extinct and we fully expect extinction. And don't trust resurrection. But there is much we don't know – about Loch Ness and about life itself. In the Gaelic indigenous view, the approach to the uncanny is the opposite to the scientific approach. You don't talk with confidence about things that you don't understand. You just hold the knowledge of their existence the way you hold ancestral memories in your body. The uncanny is not an attraction but an aspect of life. We need the uncertainty of Nessie, if nothing else as a backup against the certainty of extinction. Iain is a believer in nature and therefore possibility. Crafting a world from living wood has saved him from his own hell.

'But that's not my point.'

What is your point?

'The Korean war. I still remember things. You remember the things you want to forget.'

The money he gives to that family in Vietnam is atonement. Iain sees us off to the bottom of the garden and we pass a lump of resin with a paw print.

'The big cat of Giusachan,' he explains, 'I took this from the woods just behind the house before they caught her.'

The big cat of Giusachan, the puma of Cannich, the ghost cat of Affric, the beast of the Highlands – an odd tale and a true one. For decades, large wild cats have been sighted across the Highlands. Sheep found by farmers with their throats ripped, calves with torn-off tails and ponies with wounds. The puma of Cannich roamed over large distances. Was it a creature between realms? The Gaels had a name for the fairie cat – *cat-sìthe* (shee). There is fairie dog, King of the Fairies, Queen of the Fairies, big fairies, places that abound in fairie mounds like here and pretty much everywhere in the Highlands, and all manner of fairie plants that belong to the banshee because they are shaped like fairie distaffs. And the banshee is fairie woman, *ban-sìthe*. Lus na ban-sìthe: foxglove. Cuigeal na ban-sìthe: bulrush. The banshee rides on these plants, unseen, and lets out a scream of warning.

But it was a real cat. In the 1970s, a law was changed about exotic animals in captivity. Some private estates that held exotic animals released them in the wild. There was an old woman who lived in a cottage on the quiet side of the river where it flows more slowly. At night, she heard a lion's roar. Nobody believed her, except the farmer next door whose sheep were mauled. After spending a night in her house, he heard the roar and set up a trap. A puma was caught. She was taken to a wildlife park, given a name, and died famous. But many still see glimpses of strange animals. Aye, it roams. You don't talk about it, but you belong to the Highlands when you know that *it roams*.

Iain waves from his catenary bridge. The hyacinth blossoms cast a lilac eyeshadow over his old womanly face. The story of his life is another of his creations. In his round house, he is like the dweller of a broch. Brochs are round drystone towers built by the Picts and the Norse, and you see hundreds of them in the coastal Highlands, sometimes very well preserved. For the Gaels, a broch could be one of two things: a human dwelling or a fairie dwelling. You just never know who squats in it. Careful when you go in, lured by little voices, or the world will be changed beyond recognition by the time you come out.

And what is the uncanny but truth unseen? The more you press it down, the more it pops up from the submerged contents of the psyche like a family of plesiosauruses in the faultline of the Great Glen, or a fairie cat that sometimes rips out the throats of lambs as a reminder that everything, even the unseen, leaves a footprint.

The Cougies

Cougie does not come down. You go up to it. It is six miles above Giusachan and the highest inhabited place in the glen. There is just one family, some call them the Cougies.

You get a bird's-eye view from the high road. Brown-purple hills unfold to the west like a story, pages damp and illegible. A highway of steel rides the backs of the hills as far as the eye can see: the new transmission line. It's big. And it's why wind farms have started mushrooming on the hills, to hook onto it. Many trees were felled to make way for the pylon line, and more for the wind farms, but there is still the odd pine plantation darkening a hillside, and even from a distance you can tell that no light gets in because they were planted to be harvested by appointment. Corduroy forests, Tony calls them, because they are in tight straight rows.

White yarrow flashes on the verges of the gravel road like the whites of eyes that are watching you. I've come up here once before with Tony, but I am struck anew by how remoteness has a majesty. How far and free the Highlanders used to live. And how this freedom amounts to a wealth, a generosity of the land that is still here, like an invitation. Do you dare to be a Highlander?

I've been wanting to go riding with the Cougies for years. Seven miles up, and you leave behind the darkness of Giusachan and the sky rushes in. You arrive in a good mood. Geese scatter. Mossy ponds. Horses grazing. A few sheep and cows. Wooden cabins. A weather-board bungalow built around a static caravan. A whitewashed cottage. Sheds. Piles of scrap for recycling. Saddles, belts and other wild-west apparel. It's like a frontier outpost.

Roddy shouts from the open stable:

'There's a fine for late arrivals!'

The two of them are saddling the horses. Eilidh has a brooding intensity, and Roddy a buccaneer-like charm. They are local heroes but the only other time I've met them was at a party down the glen some years ago. She wore a dress with animal prints, he wore farming boots, and Tony freakishly guessed their star signs although he doesn't practise astrology. Eilidh is a riding champion and when I saw her horse-riding at a show, she looked like a Pictish queen.

Living in Cougie is not for everyone. You need a sense of humour for those unromantic winter days when the generator fails and you run out of logs for the Rayburn stove. The couple have four children and several grandchildren, and they're still in their prime. It is the horses – the horses are their passion and horse trekking their living. Today there's a family with kids, helmeted and in the saddle, and Eilidh sets off with them.

Roddy introduces me to Angus who appraises me from the corner of his eye, he is used to all sorts. The two house dogs come along – a small Pitbull with a red hanky round her neck like a biker, and a Jack Russell who rolls in smelly things and is having the best time. An outing with any kind of animal has the euphoria of a pastoral exodus every time. You don't know what's going to happen. It's a controlled chaos of hooves, wet fur, open road, munching, barking and excrement. I discover that on horseback, you are at the mercy of the horse and the ground.

'When was the last time you rode?' Roddy asks.

'Last summer,' I lie, but he can see that I can't hold the reins and shows me till I get it.

'Angus is very very chilled. He'll not let you down.'

Angus is a Highland purebred pony, I like him very much. We take a track Roddy has trodden since he was first on horseback, aged three.

In 1962, a young family arrived in a van. They were Welsh Travellers in search of somewhere better to set up camp than the docks of Cardiff. They came here, entered the labyrinth of the glens and drove until they reached the end of the road. That was Cougie.

Before the Clearances, it was normal to live in a place like Cougie. But by the time the family arrived, Cougie was a dot on the map that could have been easily rubbed out. A game keeper's family lived up here and that was it. A ruined cottage, an old sheep pen, abandoned fields and a grove of old Scots pine that somehow escaped the axe. A realm of golden eagles, deer, wild goats and freezing winds, a perfect place to settle. Especially if you never want to be found, and glen rumour had it that the father had a 'leather hand' and was running from trouble. But who isn't running from trouble? Roddy's parents set about building their compound from the ground up. Roddy was one of seven. The Cougies were all on the wild side. One became a general, another got into all sorts of dealings and died in a road accident, yet another became a master carpenter.

'Anyway, how's Tony the Gallery?' Roddy stands in his stirrups like an acrobat and turns around. 'You know we used to get taken for each other?'

People would stop Roddy in town and ask to buy a painting. And other people would burst into the gallery:

I'll break your kneecaps, you Cougie bastard, where's my money!

'Not so much anymore,' Roddy says breezily. 'The similarity was more pronounced in youth.'

The stories tumble out and the bleak hills come to life. There are old-growth pine groves with birches growing through, filled with light and little beasties. An echo of the old forest.

'When my parents arrived, the only trees here were these old Scots pines. They're between a hundred and two hundred years old. You can see which ones they are. The other pine groves were planted by us.'

When he was a kid, these hills were white with sheep, for a while.

'Then they reduced the subsidies and the sheep dwindled. In came the subsidies for tree planting.'

His father was employed to plant trees by the estate owner, a Dutchman who comes to stalk deer. Roddy and his brothers helped their dad.

'We planted one and a half million native trees.'

Then Eilidh got pregnant. They had no money so they came to live with his parents. Eilidh liked it at once and they raised their kids on the farm, free like Roddy had been. It was a wrench when their daughter went to university, but then she returned.

To this day, they kill their own sheep for food, from time to time – with a shotgun – and skin and process the carcass themselves. Roddy shoots the odd deer too. After gralloching it, he hangs it in the shed. You hang it head down, and start eating the meat from the neck and work your way up to the haunches. It doesn't spoil that way.

'That's the only honest way to eat meat,' says Roddy.

We pass the twenty horses who are off duty. There are

different breeds. More than half of them are rescued. They look wild to me – it's their lean, shiny bodies, the way they're not shoed.

'Horses are wild animals. It's their nature. But they *agree* to the riding for my sake. They do it out of generosity. See, horses are smarter than humans. And nicer.'

Some people who come on the rides have rigid ideas about horses.

'Who breaks your horses? Where's the whip? Nobody *breaks* my horses. We have a relationship.'

Roddy grew up with animals. He'd milk a cow or a goat first thing in the morning, before zooming down the road to school. The Cougie animals always free-grazed. And the horses have a roaming territory of about seventeen by eighteen miles. How do you go looking for them? He knows where they're likely to go. Sometimes they decide to go west for fresh pasture, always moving as a herd. Except when a mare gives birth, then she splits off. Mares prefer to give birth in the same spot where they were born, they remember it, Roddy tells me. They always give birth in the early morning. Two, three, four o'clock. So that by daybreak, the foal is on its legs and able to get away from predators. An old evolutionary habit.

'But even when they go roaming, they return for the morning's ride! They're honest animals. What you see is what you get. And also, you reap what you sow.'

Horses like routine. There's no surprises, they know what happens every day. And Roddy hopes that in the same way, they won't surprise him. He laughs. His high spirits are contagious. We pass through the birdful grove of Scots pine, different ages, birch, and alder and rowan. Mosses everywhere. It's a sunny August day, but in the mossy forest it's muggy like on the west coast. And if we ride on, we'll reach the west coast in a few hours. Angus keeps stopping and munching broom. It's a protest.

'He knows very well that we're walking, and not eating,' Roddy says. 'But they suss you out from the start, horses do. Whether you're tough or gentle. He knows you're gentle and he's taking the piss.'

His horse is a black stallion called Danny.

'I love you, Danny,' Roddy leans on his neck.

The trail we're on is cobbled with stones showing faintly through the grass.

'Aye, this road is very very old.'

The drover's roads connected people and places. They were the pastoral ways.

In contrast, General Wade's military roads, built with great effort through difficult terrain over many decades from the early eighteenth century on, aimed at controlling the Highlands. It brought the industrial ways. To suppress the Jacobite rebels, to flush out rogues and reivers, to centralise trade and transport. Along the road were military posts. The Romans didn't build anything this far north, so Wade's roads were the first colonial highway in the Highlands. Until then, it was all drover's trails from glen to glen. Under the road along the south side of Loch Ness, built in the 1930s when the mass sightings of the strange creatures started, there is a Wade road. The Highlanders of the eighteenth century treated 'the new road' with suspicion and avoided it, preferring their own well-trodden pastoral ways across the hills. While soldiers built it, in the vicinity of Wade's road were always shadowy figures wrapped in tartan, propped on a stick and observing the progress of industry with a hooded eye, then melting into the fog. They spoke no English.

We tackle a steep hill to get the lay of the land from above.

The ground is peaty, water burns zig-zagging it. Angus and Danny struggle uphill and we are a dead weight.

'This is called *Struggle* Hill!' *Stri* in Gaelic. You strive to the top.

The hills of Scotland are not very high but they are harsh. It's the exposure. We haven't reached the top yet and the weather has changed. A cold wind lives up here like a ubiquitous despot in an open-air palace. We are perched on the southern lip of the Affric basin. We can see two peaks – the Rough one and the Bleak one. They all looked the same to me from below but now, face to face, each hill has a distinct shape. The world looks different here. The land becomes country when there is someone to tell you its story. We also see the big new pylons that carry the new transmission line, the lines sagging like unclean linen. When it was strung up through this wild country a few years ago, Eilidh and Roddy thought: at least we'll finally get the electric! A compensation for having their country despoiled and their business threatened. Riders come to this last frontier to get away from industry, and now industry was here. The new pylons were so close to their house, surely they'd hook them up to the grid!

'So, what happened?'

The Cougies became the talk of the glen because of their battle with the energy giant, then it all went quiet. It took many trips to the council. Finally a representative of the energy giant and a councillor paid them a visit, in suits, with safety helmets on. Eilidh put on her best dress. They explained that it was very difficult. Too remote. Unless the family could personally pay £250,000 to be connected to the grid, there was nothing the company could do, sorry.

They didn't get the electric, but the council continued to bill them with rates for – streetlights.

'We're not going to the top. Coz the wind'll blow us off the hill.'

We sit on rocks and munch oatcakes. The horses look at space and see something in it. Roddy has just the lumberjack shirt on his back and an empty canvas bag slung across the chest. On the way up, he pointed out the bleached roots of trees. Scots pines.

'Seventy per cent of Scotland was pine. Twenty per cent birch, and the rest mixed. Oak, rowan, beech, alder, hazel.'

They burned forests during the Clearances, just to be mean. And to clear the land for grazing and shooting.

'They banned the kilt. They banned the skean dhu – that's the knife all Highlanders carried. They banned the language. The food. The songs. What colour are Highland cows?'

'Red.'

'Black. Highland cattle is black. They banned that too coz it was emblematic. And they introduced the red cow from the lowlands.'

Some farmers are reintroducing black cattle. They are ancient-looking and remind me of the buffalo of the Balkans, who suffered near-extinction in the twentieth century for similar reasons: industrial farming killed the pastoral ways.

Bog cotton and heather – that's what's left. The August purple of blooming heather makes me melancholy. Purple heather hills, cold metal sea, no people. Where heather grows, the soil is poor after decades of grouse-shooting – that's why the trees were cut and burned by large estates, to clear the land for bird and deer hunting. When I first came here, I sensed it before I could name it: there is something Balkan about the Highlands. It's an atmosphere. A howl in the perfect land, as if a force has blasted through it and swept it of its creatures, and exiled them to the four corners of the Earth. Empty villages in a land of song and soul.

In my native Bulgaria and its neighbours, such totalising

clearances took place two centuries later than here – when Communism arrived with its industrial doctrine and grabbed land, animals, entire populations, cleared highland villages of their people and forced them down into new industrial towns to work in factories and dams, like slaves. Almost 80 per cent of people had lived well from the land until then.

Here the environmental aftershocks are far worse because the separation of people from the land started longer ago.

'Aye. Over Kintail way were the MacKenzies. That way the Grants. The Chisholms and the Frasers down that way.' Roddy points in all directions. Every glen once linked to a clan.

At the time of Culloden, fourteen of the clans were Jacobites or had mixed loyalties and blew with the changeable political winds. After the defeat in 1746, the lands of wealthy Jacobite supporters were seized, their estates forfeited by an act of parliament, and eventually their clansmen and women were harassed, dispossessed and forced to leave. All this work was done by tacksmen working under instructions from the chiefs-turned-lairds, and the chiefs were increasingly absent and spineless – away in their other properties in Edinburgh and London. Tacksmen, or factors, were the managers of estates and not all of them were cruel and expedient, but many were. By the time their work was done, the wedge driven between people and place was permanent. No longer country, the land became commodity to be rented out to the highest bidder. Tenancies for sheep were taken out over vast territories, and the most aggressive speculators made the most money. The 'Age of Improvement' had arrived in the Highlands.

A Gaelic bard foresaw this:

Mo thruaighe ort a thir, tha'n caoraich mhor a'teachd!
My poor land, I cry for you, the Great Sheep is coming!

'Now that's Shepherd's Hill. It gets snowy here. You know what we used to call snow, back when there were lots of sheep? The white shepherd.'

Because it naturally rustles the sheep down.

'Over there, the Women's Loch. And further down in the open where everyone could see their balls, the Men's Loch!'

It was common to have a men's pool and a women's pool.

'But I can't say it in Gaelic, coz I've got no Gaelic. And over the hill is the Birds' Loch.'

People came down to the lochs to bathe, meet and court.

'Och aye, of course they did. This was the drover's way! People come and say: wow, this is remote. But it was a highway.'

Remoteness is relative to where the centre of power is. Back then, they were self-sufficient micro-economies. It's Edinburgh that was remote – as one of the glen's last speakers of Gaelic and no English discovered. That man was a green keeper all his life. Green keeper was the keeper of an estate, now they are called game keepers or just keepers. I guess there isn't so much green anymore to keep. When that green keeper retired in 1920, his employer, the local lord, asked him what he wanted as a retirement gift. To see London, the man said. He was given a train ticket, but arriving in Edinburgh was a shock: people didn't speak Gaelic. Not a word. He was in a foreign country and London would be the same. Stricken, he took the train back to his glen.

Every twelve miles along the drover's roads were drover's inns. Roddy pointed to a ruined inn by a pine plantation. If we were to head to the Great Glen, we'd pass it. We'd see the ghosts of long-haired, kilted drovers, faded plaids across their chests, knees red with cold, eating barley broth with spoons chained to the tables. Their cattle and horses overnighted in the yard. Villagers from Cougie would sell them cheese, but the drovers moved in their own guarded bubble – an animal nation. And they were armed. Even after Culloden, when firearms were banned by the British government, the drovers were allowed to keep them.

'Aye, the drovers were very very tough.'

When Roddy's mum was pregnant with him, she had a friend: the old woman who lived in a house where the roar of the big cat was heard. And she kept asking: When will you have that bairn?

She herself was born in Cougie. When she married, she moved one glen south, but when that glen was flooded for the Hydro schemes, their house was submerged and she returned to her childhood glen. She didn't think she'd see a child born here again, until the new family arrived from Wales. She held the baby Roddy and died a week later.

One day, Roddy found a cassette tape. It was a recording his father had made with that woman in which she talked about places and people now forgotten.

'I couldn't sleep one night and put the tape on.'

The following day, an American couple turned up at Cougie. Not for the horses, but to look for the old shepherd's cottage. Roddy was stunned by the timing of it.

'I said to them: till last night I couldn't have told you, but now I can.'

On the tape, she described life in Cougie two generations back. Roddy took the couple to the ruined cottage.

'Most Americans who come here have ancestry from the glens.'

That couple's ancestors had been evicted from Cougie.

'There's more Gaelic spoken in Canada than in Scotland. It's sad, is what it is,' Roddy concluded, and not letting the mood drop, he pointed out some clear lines that ran in the elephant-skinned hills.

Parallel lines, from glaciation, when the last great ice melted here between 10,000 and 13,000 years ago. I love the parallel lines of Highland glens! They are like bridges to eternity.

'The ice retreated at a rate of seventeen miles per every hundred years.'

These days, it's by the hundred days that glaciers melt.

'Aye. Did you know that three hundred years ago, there was still a glacier in the Cairngorm Mountains?'

I did not! That was the time of the mini Ice Age. Strange, how much disappeared from this land around the same time – the glaciers, the wolves, the Highlanders.

'That over there is Dove Hill, where the eagle used to nest.'

When the economic tide turned and the estate shepherd turned game keeper, he burned the eagle's nest, to clear the hill for partridge shooting. The eagles moved to the next hill.

'He knows I'm keeping an eye and doesn't dare do that again! But it's traditional to train game keepers to persecute the wildlife. Hopefully that's changing now.'

Roddy's eldest son is studying to be a game keeper. And having grown up here, the boy has a respect for all animals.

'Imagine all the wildlife that used to be here! Have you seen a Roman map of Scotland? It's written across it: great dense forest with barbarians living in it.'

It can't have been so bad, being a barbarian in a great forest.

'It was *one hundred* per cent better than now!' Roddy says.

Was it better, to be one of the peoples of this great Caledonian country? They did not have an army and a state. Their tribes were scattered across large distances. They had no written language. They were not centralised and had no common identity yet they were a nation, because they had a shared country. The first centralised power they encountered were the Roman invaders. And the first recorded large battle on Scottish soil was the battle of Mons Graupius in 83 AD between the Caledonian Confederacy of highland tribes (united for the first time, to resist the common enemy) and the Roman legions who won the battle but lost Caledonia. The only written record of these events comes from Tacitus, who in *The Agricola* gave a voice to a man called Calgacus. That was the leader of the Caledonian Confederacy and he is the first inhabitant of the Highlands recorded in history. Thirty thousand natives of disparate tribes gathered under one banner against the world's largest empire. His soliloquy is quite the immortal tour-de-force. It coins the term 'the last of the free' – that's the people of Caledonia – and it ends with a pithy summary of that oxymoron, the Pax Romana:

'They make a wasteland of a place and call it peace.'

'The Romans made many mistakes,' Roddy asserts. 'One of them was to shoe horses.'

It had not been done until then. The Romans also built roads, and the two are related. But it's also true that during their incursions this far north, they exchanged things with the Picts: skills, clothes, horse saddles, crafts, jewellery and probably bodily fluids too. Roman galleys rowed by slaves came to the Firth and brought cast-off sheets of gold and silver to local craftsmen who made jewellery from them.

'But horseshoes are not good for them. The hoof is naturally adapted. When they tap their hooves, that stimulates a growth hormone in the coronet band of the hoof. That's like the nail.'

He shows me on Danny. When we return to base, he files Danny's hoofs with a big rasp.

'Horses have been evolving for millions of years. And we think we nail a piece of iron to their feet and we're gonna improve them! How can you improve the fact that Angus has zebra stripes that are designed to be insect repellents?'

Angus looks at him in a low-key way. On the way down, Angus and I will fall into a bog. His legs will buckle and I'll manage to unstrap my feet and jump off in time. It's quite something, jumping from a large animal. Angus struggles to unmuck himself and climbs out with peaty legs, and I think of all the war horses who were forced into our human projects of self-extermination. Angus and Danny look back at us, their manes flapping in the wind like banners. The wind blows away my tears but also causes them. We get back in the saddle.

'It hurts like hell to do it but sometimes you have to put them down when their quality of life gets poor. There was this Arabian stallion, he went blind and got stressed by the slightest thing coz he couldn't see. He was spooked by shadows. We had to put him to sleep.'

There is a horse cemetery by their house that they've planted with oaklings. That way, the horses will come back as oaks and host up to a thousand species.

I see the two drove roads – west and south. The drovers covered distances that nobody covers on foot anymore. They travelled with herds of cattle and Border collie dogs. Drovers would pass through these glens en route to the big trysts 200 miles south. At their peak in the mid nineteenth century, 150,000 cattle sold at these trysts. Afterwards, the drovers rode back or sometimes sailed back to avoid brigands. But what to do with the dogs? The dogs were sent back. They knew the way.

'At every drover's inn along the route were bowls of water and food left for them. For the dogs' big trek home.'

Men, horses and dogs would find each other again in the glens a couple of weeks later. The last drover of this glen died in 1960. He had a long beard in the manner of the times and was known as Aly Dhu, Black Sandy, because the beard was black before it turned white. He was the last to walk with cattle along the drover's road from Inverness to the glen. To the end, he was seen surrounded by his collies, in a flat lumberjack's hat and a buttoned-up worker's jacket.

'These drover's roads, could you still find them if you had to?'

'One year, the kids were still wee, I got into a spot of trouble,' Roddy twisted on his saddle. We were returning. 'I was working in a sawmill in Perthshire. For money. Eilidh was here with the kids and my folks.'

He got into a pickle with his employer. One day, he jumped on his horse and rode all the way to Cougie without touching tarmac. He simply followed the drove roads. The 'conman' employer came looking for him here. Roddy made sure to disappear in the hills, leaving Eilidh to explain how they'd broken up and he'd gone to America.

Cougie brings home a simple fact. There are very few people left who really live with the land – with whatever the place throws up, with animals and rain and your own company. Most of us just live on top of the land, creatures of the topsoil who don't know how to get nutrients for ourselves. We rely on a long chain of supply whose origin is out of view. In Cougie, everything is in view. What you see is what you get. What you reap is what you sow.

We stop in the woods and dismount to pick some mushrooms. A large cep – dinner, Roddy grins! And some magic mushrooms which he picks for those winter days when they see no one for weeks.

'I eat a few of these and my sadness goes. They make you happy in a way that lasts for days!'

When there are no happy mushrooms around and he is sad, he goes looking for the horses and lies among them for a few hours. That's how the winters pass. His happiness returns when the daffodils bloom yellow and the yarrow goes white.

Bye, Angus, I'll miss you. I leave Cougie with regret. On the way down the yarrow dazzles under the high orbit of the sun and says something to me with the whites of its eyes. The Gaels call it *lus na fola*, blood herb. I cut some with a knife. This bitter herb aids women, soldiers and anyone who is bleeding in the hills. I cut it and say an old Highland spell for yarrow. I dedicate it to Cougie. May off-grid Cougie be like the blood herb.

> May I be an isle in the sea,
> May I be a hill on the shore,
> May I be a star in waning of the moon,
> May I be a staff to the weak,
> Wound can I every man,
> Wound can no man me.

Chì mi

I see the standing stone in among the trees, but only because Aria told me about it. It's on the edge of Talorgan's Village. The standing stone was once part of a circle. How many times have I driven past it and not seen it?

Aria laughs — I don't know, but there's two stone circles and two Pictish hut circles around my village. She has made it hers. Aria grew up on an orchard in Australia and studied anthropology but didn't enjoy academia and ended up emigrating to these isles where her ancestors had emigrated from.

We are in a mature woodland I hadn't seen either, till she brought me here. I learn to spot mushrooms and lichens. Polypore for immune-boosting tea, you slice it off the birch and dry it. It can also start a fire, stop bleeding wounds, and is a natural antibiotic. Ceps, and these little fairie champignons, Aria says, are nice. She is quick-fingered. She is always giving little jars of pickles, pestos, jams or facial balm out to friends and I'll eat anything she makes.

In the bush it's your feet that do the talking. Aria comes here in all seasons, and her forest trails make a one-woman *ngurra*. Two women now. Ngurra is what the Pintupi people of western Australia call homebase in the wilderness. And also just country. But it has to be named to be country.

Country is another word for self. Ngurra is to make your home across country as you walk, hunt-and-gather, remember, name and story-tell. These are simultaneous activities. Two levels of space–time occur: the Dreaming and the here-and-now. One can't exist without the other. The Dreaming holds everything together, like a law. 'It's a big law. We have to sit down alongside of that law like all the dead people who went before us,' an elder explained to Aria. A cosmology too great for the western mind with its industrial bias. The Pintupi discovered that myth travels like mycelium – underground. 'We thought that story ended, went into the ground at Pinari. But we found that it goes underground all the way to Balgo.' For First Nations Australians, and for First Nation Gaels, country is a continuous entity, like God.

I see that for me and for Aria, this place has become our countryself. Bulldoze the ancestor graves and it sends shockwaves to the unborn. Aria was at one of the endless public 'consultations' given to local communities by one of the many energy developers closing in on the Great Glen. These ones wanted to start by hacking an access road through a forest and a graveyard. An elderly woman got up and said in a shaky voice: 'I'm worried I won't be able to visit my husband coz your road passes through his grave site – will you be wanting to remove that as well?' Aria walked out of the room in tears and joined the community council. 'I feel it's my duty to fight big bullies and protect what matters,' she says, 'I would've done the same in Australia. Or anywhere.'

The Crossing Place, roaming

From the Crossing Place there were three ways to roam.

One was the river walk that started from a ruined early church named after one Talorgan. You went downstream past the fishing huts and old beech trees that carpeted the ground red gold in autumn. The gloomy turreted castle on the other side was hugged by a mature forest. On a cold day, mist lifted from the frosted fields like a ghost. I'd pad among the mossed-up slabs in the old graveyard of Talorgan and become lost in time.

This was my favourite graveyard of the three in our perimeter. It had the best nettles. I'd come with the dog, wave to Willie the gillie by the fishing hut, and stand under the old yew when it rained. Who was Talorgan? Maybe a missionary monk who, like Columba, travelled west to east. Maybe they travelled together on their quest to convert the pagans of Pictland. But the Picts were not completely pagan, already their Druidic cult of nature was becoming illuminated with Christ's teachings on forgiveness. Or was he Talorgan the Druidic priest brother of the Pictish King Brudei who received Columba? Or perhaps Talorgan the Pictish king of the mid seventh century.

I'd like to travel back to that time, Tony said, the most interesting time in the Highlands. A time of great change but gradual. And nature was untouched! It made you dream. Imagine travellers walking in the Great Glen, in all this beauty and wildness, in a state of ecstasy, with birds and animals long extinct. These monks didn't stay in one place but moved on in the way of bards and dervishes. But we know that Talorgan stayed because his tomb is up the road, an unmarked stone forgotten by people but not by the land. He built a small chapel, maybe a single hermit's cell. On top of that was built the thirteenth-century church whose ruin we contemplate now. It's all rounded lintels and arches. These small churches from the early days are in tune with the land. It's to do with scale, location and closeness to the old gods of place.

'The Celtic church gave love, the Roman church gave law,' goes the saying.

The ruin has its resident spirits. Spirits don't need a roof. They are benevolent and live around the ancient yew whose cones turn red and poisonous in autumn. Tony calls them death berries. From the graveyard you could see the weeping wall of our dam – and downstream, the turrets of the castle wrapped in vapours. There was a very old gean here and when our dog died and we were inconsolable, the gean consoled us. We lay under it and looked at the sky through its white blossoms. One year, the gean fell and it was like the fall of a city.

To continue the river walk, you skirted the edge of a lush gully. On the other side of the path was the quarry. There were separate mounds of big rocks, small rocks, gravel and sand, processed and moved around by thundering gravel-crunchers. The quarry chomped its way through the forest, extracted the earth until reaching ground water, then abandoned it and invasive plants took over. We hoped that one day soon, the site would be closed and replanted with a mixed forest or turned into a park. On this walk, I had my patches of mint, nettle, raspberries, blaeberries and bramble which I dried or froze for the winter. The forest was still bigger than the quarry, in those early years.

But with its history of expansion, I could see the quarry eating into the whole forest, an unbearable thought and surely that wouldn't be allowed to happen with a mature woodland. Red ribbons appeared on trees and we reassured each other that this was forestry work, protecting trees and birds.

'You have to show another way, not just criticise,' Tony insisted. If you quarry the land, build a loch for wildlife in its place.

We live in a sympathetic universe. Everything spreads. Everything affects us. We affect each other. Living with Tony in this place of peace affected me like a balm. I learned to relax for the first time in my life.

But things were changing fast in the Crossing Place, in the glen, and across the Highlands. Someone else was envisioning the future, and it looked increasingly like an industrial estate.

The new transmission line to the south was completed. I lay in the chipped enamel bath, listened to the bats chirp like mice at sunset, and contemplated the electricity line that had been strung up the week before. It was a shock to see these double-lane sheets of steel hanging three layers deep from each pylon to the next. Like strange washing lines, they were draped all over the land and filled the sky. This is how the Enclosure Movement must have looked to people on the ground. What was common land became cut up into private parcels and fenced off. Now it was happening in the sky too. And under the oceans.

The line started here and went south because Scotland's largest switching station was here at the mouth of the glen. Actually, it went into the glen too. It was everywhere. But surely, it was needed! The world needs renewable energy. Whatever that actually means. Steel, cement and lithium are not renewable and this is what these structures are built from. The switching station was first built for the Hydro dams. It was small. But like the quarry, it has spread over the clean mouth of the glen like a cancer. The industrial footprint is growing all the time. The pylons, the wind turbines, the roads. Gigantism instead of innovation.

But it must be the final onslaught! Done. Beautiful wild places have been sacrificed, many people will have to live in the shadow of the grid – we already do – but there will be no more. We just have to get on with things.

For a long time, perhaps months, I don't recall now, the new line did not go live. Then it went live but only transmitted low outputs of energy. It was baffling: all that heavy infrastructure, all that destruction and upset – and now there wasn't enough energy generated to transmit. But even with this low transmission, in the first weeks the line went live, we heard a vibration. It was most active at night; an all-pervasive hum, like a presence, like an electrified hologram of something that roamed and entered through the windows. I woke up and closed the windows. That week, workers in the industrial estate on the other side of the Monks' Place developed sudden symptoms and had to be let off work – migraines, panic, nausea, a malaise.

The hum remained. It came through the pillows. It was there like permanent tinnitus. In damp weather, the volume was turned up. Tony paced in the house, went out in the garden. You could not escape it. It was in the atmosphere. Things began to lose their coherence.

I lay in the bath, the steel pylon permanently framed by the little window, and remembered the day I decided to move here from the city. I'd had a lucid dream. They were still building the pylons then, and we couldn't yet imagine the triple electricity lines going live. We were still overwhelmed by the new towers and the way steel was replacing wood. Instead of the other way around.

In my dream, I saw the new highway being electrified, and the whole field flooded by light as by a giant projector, like a lake of fire. A solar storm, or an accident. I saw Tony with his long hair running through the field looking for something, maybe me. It was a call from the future. I made up my mind then: I would move north. And one day, I may write about it all.

Living under a transmission highway forced me to take an interest in energy generation and transmission. How ignorant I'd been! The new transmission line was not built for the reasons I had thought. It was not built for any existing energy generation — for example, it wasn't for the Hydro, which worked perfectly well with the old transmission lines. It was built to *open up a marketplace*. It was built on a speculative hope that other large-scale infrastructure could hook onto it — more Hydro, more wind, more battery storage, more everything. Existing big wind farms, already rapidly proliferating over the hills, and coming ones. This new transmission line that had destroyed forests, peatland, habitats, waterways and health was not the end of large-scale industrialisation, it was the beginning.

The government had an ambition: to turn the Highlands into *the Saudi Arabia of renewables*, to have a *green industrial revolution* that would bring thousands of jobs to the north, while reaching net-zero targets by 2030. And 2050. And beyond. Targets without end. Scotland was going to decarbonise Europe by *decarbonising the grid*. But it looked like this would involve an expansion of the grid so vast that the entire Highlands and Islands of Scotland would end up an industrial park.

Scotland's oil was drying up. The high wages of oil workers were shrinking. In the Firth, I watched three oil rigs, once Dubai-owned, now decommissioned and with nowhere to go. Nobody wants a bunch of giant oil rigs that don't make money. They were caught quietly slinking off to dump themselves illegally on an Indian shipbreaking beach. Now they're waiting to be legally decommissioned in Turkey but years pass and they are still here. Scotland has only two shipbreaking yards and can't cope. Or maybe it doesn't want the waste on its land so it's in the sea instead. Rich countries are used to outsourcing their garbage to poor countries. On the other side of the Firth is the expanding industrial hub. Yesterday it was giant oil rigs. Now it's giant turbine blades and lithium batteries.

But where was all this energy to be transmitted? Who was it for?

The more I learned, the more I wanted to go back to being asleep. But the destruction kept me awake. When the new line was built, nature organisations had asked for *mitigation* from the energy giant, but none of it materialised. The new line was already seen by most as environmental vandalism. There was no evidence of need, yet the energy giant was permitted by the government to go ahead with it. The wishes of Highlanders were overruled by the central government. Not only that, but the company was allowed to take its *preferred route*, which means the cheapest and most convenient for them. The line trampled through one of Scotland's richest montane biospheres – Drumochter Pass. In the same decade, the state allowed the felling of 17 million trees on publicly owned land – to clear the way for wind farms (that's generation). Some of those wind farms didn't have a transmission line to hook onto or a confirmed destination for their energy. They were speculatively proposed, speculatively approved and speculatively built. And so was the actual transmission line. The speculation was this: we are building it to open up a marketplace.

Transmission and generation were building their own piecemeal empires in the hope of joining up, one day.

But back to the trees: that's 1,700 trees cut every day to be replaced with large wind farms. The wind farms are not publicly owned. The peatland destroyed by access roads and concrete bases for the wind turbines took 5,000 years to form. Only 18.5 per cent of Scotland is woodland, and only a tiny fraction of that is primary forest. Primary forest means native and therefore biodiverse. That's half the average for the rest of Europe, and a third of the average for Scandinavia.

Meanwhile, the energy giant was funding housing developments at the tailends of towns and villages, with roundabouts. And introducing their agenda into the educational system from primary to university. Politicians were referring to the energy giant as *our friends*, and energy developers were funding election campaigns, rural fairs, sport events, ugly new infrastructure, widening of pavements, and – rewilding projects for extra kudos. Politicians enthused that *global green investment* had arrived in Scotland. And that it was the future. The future they wanted didn't favour new ideas about education, health, arts, nature and ways to keep young people from emigrating. Just – extraction.

I learned that Scotland already produces eight times the renewable energy that it will need for the next twenty years. Scotland also powers England with renewable energy. This is why the transmission lines are so long and destructive in their path.

And even after that, the excess generation is so great that the grid is overloaded and the energy has nowhere to go. Billions are then paid out to these companies for *not* generating. Until their energy is needed. This is called *constraint payments*. This set up keeps large energy companies in profit, pushes wildlife out of habitats and puts taxpayers out of pocket. When woodlands are felled to make way for steel and concrete cities, diversity is destroyed and replaced with lifeless monoculture. The Earth's climate is the breath of a living organism. If her lungs are industrially removed and replaced with something more profitable, we can't expect her to keep breathing for us.

Tony planted trees and shrubs with an urgency to match the quarry and the energy giant (transmission), both of which were taking down forests, drilling good land and making large pits. He could not bear the void.

That's how eco violence feels on the ground: like a void inside you. It hollows you out.

In the new hedge he planted, two roe deer started sheltering. We left out bowls with water, but they were so shy, we never saw them leave the hedge. Their mothers came to visit them when the road was quiet. Then the mothers would dart back to safety above the dam and disappear in the woods of Aigas gorge.

Up there was the last refuge. This was the second way to roam from the Crossing Place and the least visited by two-leggeds. The woods contained ancient remains. Here, glen people had sought shelter from invading tribes and government soldiers.

The path started from our dam and climbed for an hour through mixed woodland, the gorge plunging to the right. I never met another person, except a group of lost canoers dragging their canoes through the woods, looking for access to the gorge but there's only a sheer drop. Tony and I would wander the woods, pick chanterelles, pull sorrel from the spongy floor and chew it, and spot the ospreys that nested in the gorge. Deer ran through the forest, and the ground shook. And we'd peer through the trees for a glimpse of the guy in the caravan, the only dweller of the gorge. He was elusive.

Even the dam didn't wreck the majesty of the gorge, where in the many millennia preceding the dam, the river had run free and children had jumped, shouting with fear and joy.

Every blue moon, someone died at the dams. An otter photographer fell and drowned. A man took his dog for a walk and was never seen again. When we heard helicopters, we knew they were looking for someone. Either that, or it was the plutocracy arriving in their Highland estates. It's how they travelled — as little contact as possible.

The other occasional air traffic sounded different. It was the fast and furious roar of military planes: the nearest air-force base conducting exercises, perhaps using the dams as mock-targets.

At the top of the woodland was a lochan (little loch) that was the first to warm up for summer swims and the first to form an ice sheet in December. Then — a remote river island with a small bridge. There were two dwellings on it: an old one and a new one, and they symbolised land ownership in the Highlands. The old one was an Edwardian mansion quietly falling into rot. An old chief had lived here. Then a Canadian tech-tycoon bought them out and, finding the mansion too small, built a palace. But the palace lay empty much of the time and the only residents were the keepers, a reclusive couple who mowed the lawns for twenty years. When the new transmission line ripped through the grounds, heralding an industrial future with a wind farm on every hill, the owners gave up on the Highlands and sold the estate. It went to a royal family from a Gulf state. And that was the latest deal in this passing-down of the land: from local aristocracy to business meritocracy to global technocracy to stratospheric plutocracy. When the new owners finally visited with their retinue, one summer, their arrival was announced by the sound of helicopters.

The third way to roam from the Crossing Place was the Five Forts of Farley. You climbed up the braes above the gallery. A loose neighbourhood of houses and grazing fields with the odd cow, sheep and horse. Our dream house was up here, with its own cascading burn and steep-running croftland all the way down to the road. It was one of the last entire crofts not cut up into smaller parcels and sold to developers. But the couple with the croft grew old, and the people who bought it were developers. They immediately hacked a road through the hillside and started their own gravel quarry. No doubt inspired by the big one. Their quarry ate into the hill and only stopped when it almost reached their house. The once peaceful place became an industrial site, the noise and dust filled the glen for years, until the hillside was fully extracted. The land was eaten to a stump and the landslides began. When it rained a lot, the excavated bank slid and blocked the road into the glen, causing a bottleneck. Then more diggers had to be brought in.

It was an illustrated lesson in how like attracts like. Extractive industry brings with it an extractive mindset that spreads like a disease. When an industrial hub moves in next to you, your mind can go two ways – it starts to think like a quarry and joins in with the big diggers, or it continues to think like nature and sickens. It isn't that different from when war comes to a place and predators become profiteers.

To escape the thunder of the two quarries and the shadow of the pylons, we would come up to the Five Forts of Farley two miles above the river.

The Five Forts of Farley were fortified settlements from the Iron Age. You could tell from the shape of the five duns. They were spread out over a few miles of open moor. If you kept walking west for a couple of days, you would end up on the Atlantic coast, but we'd turn back after an hour because of the freezing winds. People had lived and worked the land up here until the last crofting families left and their cottages were the latest ruins that dotted the hills like broken teeth.

The only building on the high moor was a cobbled medieval byre converted into a bothy. It belonged to Duncan the ironmonger who sometimes came up to stay.

Inside this byre, child labourers had lived and slept with the animals. Around the turn of the twentieth century, poor Irish youths came 'beyont the water' to earn money. They worked in potato squads and lived in squalid conditions, sleeping in byres like this. The boys would go first across the field, digging up the potatoes, and the girls followed on their knees in the mud, filling heavy baskets. Some of the girls ended up in the city slums of the south and most of the boys became navvies on big industrial projects like the early Hydro schemes. After the First World War, the same work was done by Scottish orphans. Just like Duncan the ironmonger's father, who walked barefoot until the age of twelve when he got his first shoes, the last of the tough rural kids who walked the hills to survive. They were taken in by farming families here, worked hard, alone on top of this lonely world with nowhere to run until they were sixteen.

Only a few houses remain at Farley now, their windows catch the high sun and look down at the multiplying hills and python coils of the river, and the spreading grey void of the quarry next to the gleaming steel city. Farley is a windscape of absent people and animals. Deer patrol the ridge of the hills with antlers like helmets, the only moving things across the land.

I don't know what year it is but it's June and we've come up to the Five Forts of Farley, this time with Duncan the ironmonger. He bought land in Farley with his life savings. He and Tony have known each other for a long time. Tony buys taps, wellies and birdfeed in his shop, and sometimes Duncan comes into the gallery and gazes at a seascape by his favourite Highland artist. I'd like to buy that one, he mutters, but let me think about it, Tony. And so passed twenty-five years. His ironmonger's is the oldest shop in the area. His father the orphan started as an apprentice and inherited the shop from the owner, then Duncan took over. The shop prospered because this was the road you took when you arrived in the Highlands. Then went up the bridge over the Firth and traffic was diverted, and that was followed by the era of the global chain that eclipsed the local shop. Duncan worked without holidays all his life, but at least he had a large family who were taking over the shop so its future was assured. It wasn't going to be bought out by a large developer and turned into something more useful. Duncan liked things with substance, which meant history and continuity. He bought this swathe of land on the Farley moor to stop it being gobbled by developers. Duncan won't convert his bothy into a house because that would bring industry into the pristine hills. His bothy has a million-dollar view. A million dollars is what developers offer. If you make 100,000 a year from wind turbines (or whatever industry is profitable just now), that's a million in ten years. That's why landowners, big and small, are inviting developers onto their land with open wallets.

How to turn land into money. As if the living land is not good enough in itself. It has to be turned into something more useful.

'A form of psychological damage,' Tony sums up.

'Aye, I had many dreams,' Duncan says. 'Now I have just one. To keep this piece of land unspoilt. At least while I'm alive.'

We don't know this yet, but in a few years' time, the multi-millionaire absentee owners of the hills next door to Duncan's will invite a wind-farm company to build thirty-six turbines 230 metres high.

June is the time for cutting the peat. He shows us how you do it. He cuts the peat every year in memory of the last peat-cutter of Farley. The man grew up in Pait (pronounced Patt), the remotest point in the glen on the far side of Loch Monar. He was the last of the shepherding families there, before the Hydro-Electric Board evicted them. To cut the peat, you need a *toirsgean*. It is like a big hoe with a long wooden handle. You lay the peat cakes in a pile and come for them later. Cutting peat is not bucolic. It gives you blisters, a sore back, wet knees, and when you put your peat cake in the fire, it smokes without burning. You have to dry it first, that's why. In a country that cuts down its trees, peat has been precious domestic fuel, one third as calorific as coal. Its antiseptic fumes might have even protected people from infectious diseases in the black houses when they lived under one roof with cattle and sheep all winter. Not so long ago, the peat fire was kept alive at all times by the woman of the house – because kindling was hard to come by, and because without a hearth there is no food.

Scotland is rich in peatland, a supreme carbon storer. Wherever wind farms, pylons and other non-renewable industrial hubs are built, peatland is destroyed, and in this destruction large amounts of carbon dioxide are released. First the peat is churned by the long tarmac roads the energy company builds for its large vehicles to these remote places. Then it is destroyed and poisoned by the turbines drilled into the land. Even a single large wind turbine needs a new tar-sealed road. The size of turbine blades has grown. Eighty metres long for land turbines, and 100 metres long for sea turbines.

We haven't moved to a post-industrial era. We are heavily industrialised, it's just that the industrial rape of the land happens out of view for most people. To rip up the living, oxygen-producing, carbon-storing systems of the Earth and to replace them with concrete, metal, plastic, lithium and other materials made from rare earth-minerals mined *not in our backyards* by underpaid and underaged workers whose premature deaths don't make the news – this happens every day. Lithium is used in the batteries of wind turbines, electric cars and digital technology. You need cobalt to make lithium. Seventy per cent of the world's cobalt is found in the Democratic Republic of the Congo. The mines there use children, who extract toxic cobalt with their bare hands. The renewable-industry boom has caused a spike in rare-ore mining. At the current rate of turbine construction, mining is expected to increase by 500 per cent in the next two decades.

These non-renewable components ripped from the guts of the Earth are shipped across the oceans in diesel-powered containers, built into wind-turbine blades, driven through a glen like ours in oversized lorries and installed in places like the Five Forts of Farley. The whole area becomes wastelanded. For a large turbine there is a large base. To make that base you need 200 tons of steel-reinforced concrete which is poured on top of a steel grid that is drilled into the ground first. The production of cement alone releases 8 per cent of the world's carbon emissions. That's before the destruction of peatland even begins.

Duncan hands me the toirsgean. He has cut a very small row

of peats, but I sense the disturbance. The earth turns, groans, it is exposed, indignant, why have you come here?

Peat should be left alone to store the past and protect the future. Peat cannot be regrown and anyone who promises to *restore peatland* after pummelling it with industrial tonnage is lying. Peat is a buried jungle. Peat has a long memory. Peat is the body of Scotland. I sink the blade into the earth and feel the pain.

Chì mi

Chì mi, says the Cailleach. The Cailleach has hindsight and foresight both. She is custodian of time.

A Cailleach is crone, wise woman, white witch, healer. The Cailleach births children, spins wool and tales, survives calamities, knows which plant to pick, and is the last speaker of a banished language. To me, the Cailleach is the same as the Balkan *baba*. Because every indigenous people has a Cailleach. If a people don't have a Cailleach, they don't have a memory.

I pass the secret hillside where the last true Cailleach of the glen lived, in a stationary caravan, with chickens and goats, like a proper baba. A friend of mine lived near the Cailleach, but they never met. She was powerful and I was afraid to meet her, my friend said, and make eye contact.

'Aye, but the Cailleach didn't make eye contact,' says Ali the gillie. 'She looked to one side of you, but you knew she seen you. When I was a young lad, she held my hand and told me a few things. They all came true.'

Chì mi. When a Cailleach says this, you pay attention. Highland seers are not palm readers. It's through contact. They hold your hand or put their foot on yours, and something of your past and future strikes them like an electric current.

Silver Falls

It's winter. They are still a long way up, but you sense the pounding chill of the waterfalls. The big one that is an attraction has a name, and the smaller one –

'Silver Falls, that's what we call it,' says Ali the gillie. Because when it freezes it's silver.

And Giusachan is an ice palace today. The trees are frosted in large crystals like cobwebs.

I don't know the inner glen except as a day visitor. Ali the gillie is one of the old timers and I hope we can go on some *wee adventures* even if it's just to the waterfalls. I have seen Ali over the years but he hasn't seen me. He keeps to his territory. He is a fixture in the inner glen, with his skinny frame and leathery face, forest-green jumpers with elbow patches and the tweed stalker's hat under which he hides himself.

Along the frozen road comes a car driven by an unhappy-faced man.

'Unhappy Henry,' says Ali. 'A policeman.'

Today Ali has brought his distaff-like stick the Gaels called *cuigeal* (cookel). He has carved on it a water sprite, a fish with scales like on the Pictish stones, and the Saltire. The stick has a rope attached in two places so you can sling it over your shoulder like a shepherdess. The drovers and shepherds are gone, the Travellers are gone, the women who spin yarn and stories are gone. Their crook was passed down to the gillies.

Ali's stick is made of rowan, which gives it magical

properties. In the Highlands you plant a rowan by your house and you never cut one down, because it protects against evil forces. If you cross something with a rowan stick, you stop it in its tracks. You can do that with a roaming spirit trying to get back into its grave before dawn. That's what the mother of the Brahan Seer did when she came across the wandering spirit of a woman. That night she had been roaming. Please let me back in my grave and I'll give you something in return, pleaded the ghost. The gift was a small stone with a hole in it. The seer's stone. Every Highlander had a rowan stick once, for roaming over river and hill. Ali hands me the stick and I become a witch of the woods.

'Where to now?' I ask, suddenly cheered. 'Cup of tea at the hotel?'

But the hotel is closed, indefinitely. A baby is crying. A pensioner from *Englandshire* bought the hotel, Ali quips, and his young Thai wife has given birth. Doors locked, curtains drawn. Is this what happens to settlers in the inner glen, or does the place attract settlers with colonial fantasies? Those who fancy a house at the end of the world and think it's here.

'And now we have no bar and no meeting place in the village,' Ali says.

Ali suffers from the loss of kinship in the glen.

'No more ceilidh.' Ceilidh is pronounced *kaylee*. It's Gaelic for gathering. A ceilidh is whenever people come together in a spirit of kinship, to share news, stories and song. It's the Highland way. You drop in unannounced, tea and scone is offered at once, sometimes a spontaneous ceilidh could happen. *A thousand welcomes*, because people lived and died together, embedded in river and hill. The ceilidh was still in the glen when Ali was young, and curtains were a luxury. Ali still lives as if he has no curtains. Everything is communal. Why buy something when you can borrow it. In his youth, up to fifty people – that's everyone in the village – gathered in a house on a Friday to share stories, pour drams, sing, smoke and gaze at the fire. Chì mi. In the fire, you see past and future. Ali is a solo dad. The mother died of addiction and he raised his girl with the help of the village. He'd go fishing with guests and leave her with neighbours. Now he is caring for his ancient father at home. In summer, when old clients come up for the fishing, Ali wades in the river with them, the banter is on, and the colour returns to his lonely cheeks.

'Maybe it's your fate,' I say. 'To cheer people even when you're sad.'

'Aye, the Cailleach saw it. I see you happy in love, laddie, but it won't last, is what she told me.'

We walk up the frozen road where the young Winston Churchill learned to drive while visiting relatives at Giusachan House. Past locked doors and puffing chimneys. After the last house are the old kennels where the Golden retrievers were first bred.

'It almost didn't happen.'

The first litter was five puppies. A maid went into the kennel and they ran out and straight to the pond. Three of them drowned and two were left. Those two were the first Golden retrievers. That was during the nineteenth century, when Giusachan was a model estate and Tomich a model village.

The road is lined with beautiful old oaks. Under every tree is buried a horse, Ali tells me. In the fifteenth century, the clan chief buried his favourite horse under an oak and the tradition carried on. And here's the ruin of Giusachan House. The great lime trees, the red sequoias and the Scots pines with bark like rope – which is what it was used for, to make rope – frosted like sculptures. The roofless Edwardian ruin is square, with square windows.

'Of its time,' says Ali. 'The age of improvement. They built everything square. The original house was more round-like. Everything was more round-like, before.'

Because nature is more round-like. A Highland settlement was typically round – built organically around a crossroad and a central place for the ceilidh. This was based on the ancient Celtic settlement. The arrival of the paved road changed that. The circular became linear.

In the wake of the Battle of Culloden, when the Red Coats of the British Army came to terrorise the glens, the old clan chief refused to leave the house. He chained himself to a bedstead. The Red Coats camped on the slope above the big waterfall, and every morning fired rounds of musket shots, to frighten the population and make the chief leave. How do you know?

'I found their camp!' With his metal detector. He dug up a box, and inside it were musket balls that the soldiers made from lead on the evening fire, plus quills from pens, cap badges and a metal toothbrush with a few bristles left. The leader of the military assault on the glens was a general who went down in history as Butcher Cumberland and whose pathological hatred for the Highlanders is summed up in the order he gave his soldiers: 'Kill them all.' The King later promoted these men to guards of honour. One eyewitness wrote: 'Betwixt the bridge end of Inverness and Giusachan, there was not left in my countrie a sheep to bleet, or a cock to crow day, not a house unruffled.'

The bleeding of the Highlands had begun. Kill them all: the same order had been given sixteen centuries earlier by the Roman emperor Septimius Severus to his legionnaires, in the last military campaign against the north before that empire gave up on Caledonia and withdrew to the relative comforts of Hadrian's Wall.

'The old chief couldn't take the daily salvoes and fled,' Ali returned to the Red Coats and the Highlanders.

But the clan kept their land here until, in a familiar scenario, a chief went into debt and sold the estate in the mid nineteenth century. He had seen his neighbouring clan chief do things with their land for money and copied him. The clan chiefs betrayed their people by opening up their country to abuse. They were 'bought and sold for English gold' in a phrase that dates back to the Act of Union in 1707 – a gunshot wedding that united the Scottish and English kingdoms. This resulted in a loss of political sovereignty for Scotland. Highland chiefs started receiving loyalty handouts in the form of land.

The union was prompted by the bankruptcy of lowland Scotland, caused by the failed Darien project – a colonial folly in Central America driven by lowland Scots. One fifth of the country's personal wealth went into this buccaneer's venture, and when the project was abandoned in 1700 it led to ruination. Darien was an attempt to emulate colonial ventures like the East India Company. Everyone wanted to hook onto the colonial grid and generate quick money for themselves. Thousands of jobs, capital investment, economic growth, benefits. Had Darien succeeded, it would have relied on the slave trade. A repulsive duke who had heavily invested in it put it like this: import slaves from Africa 'to be worked to death' in gold mines – that was his vision of economic success. The failure of Darien weakened an already struggling country in the throes of climate change (the mini Ice Age), failed crops, famine and social unrest – a period known as the seven ill years. The way was paved for the Act of Union with England, which in turn stirred up the rebellion of the Jacobites and led to Culloden.

In the Clearances that followed Culloden, many chiefs left the Highlands. With the proceeds from their sold estates or lucrative rentals to large-scale sheep breeders, they gambled away their health and wealth in London and Edinburgh, abandoning their people to the whims of whichever raider came trampling through the land after them to harvest its bounty. Sheep breeders, deer hunters, oil extractors, wind-energy traders, and electric-battery storage speculators, all driven by greed. Just like the Darien project.

In the early nineteenth century, the Giusachan estate was tenanted to the son of an American tycoon whose fortune was made from building railways in Russia. By then, Strathglass was severely reduced. Hundreds of families had been pauperised and forced to emigrate to North America. The tycoon's son rented 1,000 square kilometres and even built a great iron fence to keep the deer on his side.

'A Trumpian fence,' Ali sums up.

Fragments of it are still in the land like dead weight. When his hunting parties arrived in autumn, a hundred stalkers were hired to herd hundreds of deer to the edge of cliffs, where the bands gunned them down. He even won an Olympic medal – in shooting. Drovers and travellers were afraid of his brutal regime and were forced off their trails. In a well-known incident in Kintail out west, a poor cottar had a pet lamb. As soon as his lamb went outside the house, it was considered to be trespassing onto the maniac's shooting ground. And the maniac took the poor cottar to court. That cottar had once been a crofter with land, but like everyone in his Kintail community, he'd been stripped of the land and had just the roof over his head. That's what cottar means: someone living in a cottage without land. To be a cottar in pre-industrial society was to be at the mercy of others. Today, most of us are cottars, at the mercy of an industrial chain of supply. That cottar's name was Murdoch Macrae. It was the poorest man and the richest man in the Highlands pitted against each other. Murdoch Macrae lost his lamb but won the case, the maniac who was hated by everyone left the Highlands forever, and this was the beginning of the right-to-roam act in Scotland. Murdoch Macrae and his lamb made history for their country.

In the mid nineteenth century, Giusachan was bought by an aristocrat and businessman-politician from the Borders who transformed it. He pulled down the old house and built a holiday mansion on its site: Giusachan House. This is when the model village came about.

At the time, Giusachan had two large sheep-farmer families (a legacy from the Clearances), many crofters who tenanted the land, and also many cottars. They practised various crafts and trades.

'A wild, irregular, poverty-stricken people,' wrote a parish minister, 'among whom the demoralising practice of illicit distillation prevailed to a very great extent, favoured and encouraged . . . by the inaccessible nature of the surrounding country.'

They kept whisky stills high in the hills, near the now-vanished villages, but the reason why community whisky stills became illegal was that brewing was monopolised by the state. That way, the indigenous no longer had the legal right to produce their own booze. But they went on doing it of course, with great success. A more sympathetic local writer described the old communities of Giusachan as 'warm-hearted people'. What happened to them?

The new owner turned the glen from an independent subsistence community to a shooting estate with a model village attached to it. First, he made the shepherds leave the glen, and the country, and got rid of the sheep. Then he moved the crofters off the land they had toiled for generations, by not renewing their tenancies. His aim was two-fold: to clear as much land as possible for shooting, and to engineer a self-sufficient monopoly where all 300 workers were his dependents. These were the glen's inhabitants, stripped of their land, their agency and their dwellings. Improved. The model village was built on the ashes of their communities. Not one person was left independent of the laird. The age of improvement was like that – it made the Highlanders *industrious not rebellious*. More like Lowlanders. Those who didn't want to become indentured to the model village were forced to leave. Some emigrated abroad. Others suffered early death in hovels in other glens.

The three cleared villages along the high road were erased from the map. You will not find their names anywhere: Achblair, Easter Achnaheglish, Wester Achnaheglish. Ten years later, the census stated: *There are no inhabitants or houses.*

Achnaheglish (*place of the church* in Gaelic) was the site of an ancient chapel, and Ali points at the site with the distaff, but the construction of the model village obliterated it.

'My neighbours went to the site of the church every year. On the date on which it was destroyed.'

And said a prayer in Gaelic. The women in black scarves, the men in their best tweed jackets.

The biggest of the old villages had eighteen houses. The crofters rotated the land among themselves: the runrig system. Runrig from *roinn ruith,* to divvy up the land. Land was communal, like the whisky stills. Traditionally, the smallest crofting unit consisted of four families sharing the land in this way. Those were the crofters who were obliged to live in the model village, work on the model farm, and become model servants to the lord's model shooting estate. By the end of the nineteenth century, everyone here was a servant of the great estate. A list of occupations reads:

Dairymaid, poultry woman, washer woman, agricultural labourer, sick nurse, tailor and sewer, basket weaver, sawyer, laundry-maid, cattleman, cobbler, journeyman blacksmith.

At least the journeyman blacksmith had the freedom to travel.

We climb through the forest and Ali takes me to a ruined house. He detected it under the trees, and chattels were dug up: pieces of blue Delft china, silver coins from 1682 and a child's necklace.

'People lived in basic houses but they did like fine things.'

He was sure the necklace had belonged to the girl who lived here with her parents and brother. They were made to leave and loaded on a Canada-bound ship. The captains of the ships at first recorded the names, but when it grew from hundreds to thousands, they stopped, says Ali. The girl died en route of smallpox. Nobody lived here again. Under every tree – a buried horse, and the ghost of a family.

Travelling through the Highlands in 1780, a writer reported seeing entire communities walking towards the nearest port. These were the destitute sub-tenants and cottars, stripped by the tacksmen of animals and furniture. 'They edged off the road or hurried along as if shy of an interview.' The shame of the raped. One man said to the writer: 'Our fathers were called out to fight our master's battles, and this is our reward.'

During the Napoleonic Wars and later in the Crimean War when the men were off fighting, the dreaded factors moved in on the women and children and evicted them. In one decade between 1847 and 1857, 16,000 people emigrated from the Highlands and Islands. Entire glens emptied. Thirty thousand people were banished from the Isle of Skye alone. By the end of the Clearances in the 1860s, half a million people were gone.

The Gaelic for the Highland Clearances is telling: *Fuadach nan Gàidheal*. The Expulsion of the Gaels.

For the Victorians who came to own the country of the Gaels after the Gaels were flushed out like vermin, it was normal to do what the Giusachan owners did: they built themselves another lodge in Glen Affric over the hills to complement the mansion here. Weeks in Giusachan, weekends in Affric. That's how they started breeding the Golden retriever, intended as a bird-hunting dog that interbred a retriever with a spaniel. The names of the first dogs and their progeny are well recorded and commemorated with big gatherings – unlike the people who were banished from the land.

'The villagers took him to court. He won the case, came back here and kicked out another twenty-eight families,' Ali said.

The ruin gapes with its square holes. The roof was removed in the 1950s to cut tax. These ghost rooms were once stuffed with the owner's collection of Wedgwood Jasperware.

The Victorians collected objects and the Gaels collected dialects – a Highland expression – because with no roof over their heads, the Gaels felt the cold winds of history rushing in. The model village provided better roofs, and no longer were there paupers in the community, but what it took away was land and dignity. Come summer, the owners would arrive in a cavalcade, and the servants and keepers waited, lined up with the dogs and ponies.

'But the children threw stones at them,' Ali says with relish. It's what he would do.

When the guests at Giusachan House ran out of alcohol, the butler would ride the twenty miles to the Monks' Place grocery shop where booze was hidden under the counter.

The lord junior who inherited the place from his father was, like his father, a Liberal politician and campaigned for labour rights, a touch ironic. His daughter learned Gaelic in her later years and became a social advocate. They were progressive for their time, they loved the place and patronised the people. In short, improvers. No one had *improved* this place before, or invested in it. This word – investment – has been used by those who seek a more 'balanced' view of the Highland Clearances. But the Clearances permanently unbalanced this country with their cruelty, stupidity and venality. Yes, the industrialists and politicians who took over the emptied land did *invest* in their own estates and sometimes made improvements to the living conditions of their tenants. But this *investment* arrived in the Highlands only when the Clearances had gutted the country of its folk to exchange it with something more useful. Thus de-peopled, the land became a commodity. Profit replaced kinship. That's why the legacy is alienation. Ali feels this in his bones, and so do I.

The estate changed hands several times but permanent decline had set in, and nobody regretted its collapse.

The following is from a 1935 auction. The geo-pornography is striking. But it's a typical inventory of a Highland estate for sale in London:

Particulars of
the Sporting and Residential Estate of
    GIUSACHAN
  including
Mansion house, deer forest, grouse moor, fishing, the home farm, and Tomich Village
    7,242 Acres

The particulars are the body parts of the glen, and all the tenants in their houses who are listed as chattel. The land was prostituted and the pimps prospered.

4,200 acres of deer forest. This adjoins a sanctuary where deer are fed during the winter and stags are always plentiful and are well known for fine heads . . . Splendid rough shooting can also be had over this area – Grouse and Woodcock being plentiful, while the shooting also affords Roe, Blackgame and Ptarmigan.

The obsession with shooting is another legacy of these estates. Birds were shot in the hundreds in a single day – for a photo opportunity. It still happens in some places. I know of an estate keeper who shoots everything that flies, no reason. Shooting is a disease. You start and can't stop. It becomes a sport, then a war, and finally an extinction.

The following scene sums it up for me. It is set in the Great Glen area, and the girl who was there told of it sixty years later. Her mother rented a croft, owned one cow, and enjoyed self-sufficiency. One day, her mother had put out the washing on the line. In the washing were three white shirts that belonged to her son. He was dead, killed in the war, but she kept washing his shirts. A shooting party rode past – *a lady* with her entourage. Seeing the white shirts on the line, she took aim and shot through them with her double-barrel twelve-bore. One, two shirts, then reloaded and shot the third one. Her marksmanship was excellent and they were all shot through the heart. Three holes in three shirts. Then she rode on, flushed with pleasure. In the morning, a guinea was sent for the lost shirts.

They aimed for the heart and called it a sport.

Black ravens perch in the frosted trees. How quickly things

are replaced! For nine centuries the sound of Gaelic echoed in these glens. It arrived in the early Middle Ages, gradually supplanted Pictish, and ruled unchallenged from around the tenth to the nineteenth century. It's only in the last hundred years that English pushed it out completely.

Pictish and Celtic clans gathered under totem animals. The clan of the Ravens. The Eagles clan. The Stags. The Seals. The clan of the Boar. Of the Bear. Of the Dolphin. I've heard that the ancient folk of Giusachan were known as the people of the Wolf. Clannish, territorial. Silver Falls was where they washed the wool and the guts. They planted oats and barley. Life was lived between high ground and low ground. The black raven watches us from above. In old landscapes, symbols are alive. It's because the land never stops moving, and *the last of the free* move with it. When the landscape fills you with moods and images that are not of your making – then you know you belong.

'That's why I fish on dry land with the detector,' Ali says. He can't sit still. His community is near-extinct but he holds on to the last freedom – to forage in the land. And if he finds a jet bead from a necklace, all the better. Or a gold coin with two fishes like Pisces facing each other, and worn in a string of status. Or a bawbee. That's a sixpence or any ordinary Scottish coin. As in –

>Ali bally, Ali bally bee
>Sittin' on yer mammy's knee
>Greetin' for a wee bawbee
>Tae buy some Coulter's candy.

A song written by a poor textile weaver in the Scottish Borders who patented his aniseed-flavoured candy, and though his candy was much loved, Coulter died a pauper and the recipe is lost. A bit like Ali, who digs up treasure but stays poor. When Ali unearths something important, he calls Rachel at the National Museum of Scotland.

Hi, Rachel, it's Ali from Strathglass in the Highlands.
Hi, Ali, what have you got for me?
When Rachel dated the jet bead, she called back.
'Can you find the other beads?'
Because it was 5,000 years old and came from Portugal. Who wore the jet bead?
'A little girl. Like my daughter. Like the girl from the house that was cleared and who died on that boat to Canada. She went in the forest to gather kindling, and coming back her string bracelet broke. She gathered it up like this, in her hand, but some of the pieces were gone and she ran home.'

Rachel relented and sent the jet bead back to him, to keep.

We walk to Silver Falls. The river is meagre. An urbane man in a shiny Range Rover passes us. His ancestor, a lord and once governor-general of New Zealand, bought this part of Giusachan from the previous lord, including the ruin and a habitable big house up the road. The family are from London and use this as a holiday estate.

He and Ali don't greet each other.

'We used to be friendly before he built his Hydro.'

A mini power station by the burn that leads down from Silver Falls. And the river is cemented by a new dam! I thought this was the last wild river in the glen. But private Hydro schemes are in fashion.

'I don't get it. He is making money and my salmon can't spawn.'

It's the Gaelic mo. My dear salmon.

Even a small Hydro scheme is big interference with the land. New and upgraded access roads, intake, power house with turbines, and pipeline excavation, which means drilling yet another hill.

Above us a raven opens its beak like a singer and utters a curse. More, more. Worse than Edgar Allan Poe's Nevermore is More.

More, until there's nothing left. We look for salmon.

'Before, I saw fifty to sixty salmon here. But there's not enough water now.'

The burn is shallow. The mechanical noise of the turbine overrides the silvery song of the waterfall.

We walk up the narrow path to the fall, lined with remnants of strange plants introduced by the Victorian owners, each plant representing a British colony. The Highlands were a colony too.

'We still are,' says Ali.

Two generations ago, the bank was washed away and with it, much of the exotica. The native trees re-seeded themselves and carried on.

At the base of the waterfall are the remains of an early Hydro. It was built by the estate owners to electrify the model estate. A sluice brought water from the larger fall above. This early Hydro scheme worked well for the estate, with minimal alterations to the land. In fact, small-scale Hydro schemes like these built by enterprising landowners pioneered renewable energy in the Highlands.

'I grew up here. First cigarette. First trout, with a worm. We came up to the falls with these wee transistor radios.'

Young men would pick a small stone from the Silver Falls and leave it at the doorstep of the one they loved. They'd check on it. If it disappeared, it meant yes. Ali presented his young wife with a stone too. The Scots Pine he planted in her memory is now thirty-seven years old.

We come to a small ruined house with two yews.

'A brother and sister lived here. He came back from the war and stayed with his sister. They spoke Gaelic.'

Neither of them married. Ali's mum came to help them out in the last years. Like everybody else, they worked for the estate.

'It was awful black inside,' Ali said. 'They looked Spanish with all that soot on them. The smoke just stayed inside.'

Because the chimney was old, not like the model-village houses. They died the way they'd lived: quietly, consumptively, together. The roof is gone but the chimney is still here and I can see where the three tiny rooms had been.

'See this pond. Me and my pal made it for the estate owners.'

Ali's detector picked up a hessian sack here, with sixteen complete pairs of leather shoes. They were all dried up and squashed. Ali went home and soaked them in warm water.

'Women and children's. Very well-made booties, with laces. Laces were gone though. The museum were delighted. Possible date, 1820s.'

Were they buried to preserve them?

'That's detecting for you. Things come up and give you a picture. But you have to decode it. Who was it, what happened to them, what was their names? Did they stay or emigrate to Canada . . .'

And the Travellers? They had their stopping places in the glens. Come summer, they brought the world with them. One family had a van called Better Wares. They sold pots and pans, combs and mirrors. Ragmen took away your old rags and recycled them. Ali's mother spoke their secret language. The Travellers brought catalogues and local women ordered clothes and better wares from them. Cabinets, pottery, cutlery, rugs, things not made in the glen. The Travellers took orders and next season brought the kist, the set of Delft china, the rugs and the smart shirts in their carts. It was a barter system and in turn they purchased the whisky and the prized leather shoes made by the glen's cobblers, and took them to sell in the cities. Booties, brogues, dandy shoes with buckles. The Highland brogue with its row of punctures became a staple. *Bròg* is shoe in Gaelic. Funny that the practical medieval Highland bròg, with its perforations to let water come out once it got in, became the British gentry's favoured shoe.

One autumn the Travellers left with their horses and never returned. Whoever had buried the shoes did not come for them later.

January.

The hills are blue-white with snow. It's a new world. Two buzzards are pulling apart red meat in Ali's garden which is big, untended, and runs up the hill. They come every winter. They're solitary birds but when they're hungry they get together.

Coming home along the shore of Loch Ness, he stopped to help two women who'd just hit a young stag. They were distraught and his legs were broken. Ali sent them on their way then took care of the poor wee stag. He lifted him into his car boot and slit his throat to end his agony. Then he took him to a stalker friend to process, so the meat wouldn't go to waste. That's what the buzzards are eating.

April.

'Do you know what the Highlanders called mid-April?'

'The Cailleach.'

'Ah. I know it as the crone's difficult week. Must be the same thing.'

A week of inscrutable weather. The Cailleach is a mistress of winter, that's why come April she bashes the ground with her hammer in an attempt to turn the clock back to March.

And especially the ground under the rowan tree because that ground belongs to her. That's why you never cut it down. Mad at the new burgeoning of life, she flies off on her foxglove with a banshee scream. And in comes Brigid, the goddess of summer.

Ali's old dad sits in the sun. He was a cattle herder. He has a genetic condition called Viking hand and had two fingers of each hand amputated. There are three very old men in the village but something harms the women of the inner glen. I have seen this elsewhere. Where the land becomes mere commodity to be bought and sold for quickest gold, the fallout is industrial enlargements, community buyouts, alcohol, depression and early death. The women leave or die young. Who is the Cailleach of tomorrow?

Ali's daughter comes out barefoot. It's midday. Young people sleep late.

'I don't feel young. I feel old,' she says.

June.

'We have a hobo in the glen,' says Ali. 'You know what a hobo is?'

A homeless person, his daughter says.

'Aye, but one who walks with intent.'

He came all the way from the west coast and through Glen Cannich where a guy has a boat on Loch Mullardoch. He had put on boat guy's waterproof clothes and was sheltering in the boat shed. You can keep them if you want, said boat guy, but the hobo took them off and gave them back. What's your name?

'Godfather,' and he walked on with intent.

Things happen in the inner glen that, unless you have a friend on the ground, you'll never know about.

July.

In the ruins of Giusachan House, the lime trees are in blossom. I fill a bag of leaves and flowers for tea.

Ali is out on the river gillying all summer, but I've come for a wee adventure by myself. I drive in-glen with the windows down. It's what you do in the ruins of the world – you speed into a glen like time's corridor and fill your face with July air. Waterfalls are magnets and I end up at Silver Falls. The turbines of the private Hydro are churning, the water is thin as a ghost. But the perfect stones are still in the river bed, waiting for the day when children and salmon return.

Chì mi

On my way out of Giusachan, I see the Iron Age dun above, where people and animals lived for generations. I see it lying empty, then recycled for a shieling. That's where shepherds lived in summer with their flocks. Then it was forgotten again until the Forestry Commission planted the hillsides with low-quality pine. I see them, planting over ruins and sacred sites, in corduroy rows. I see the post-war rush to grow the economy, trees planted the way the Great Sheep had been unleashed and the dams built, with militant expediency. Investment.

I see why the slopes of our strath look like a battlefield forty years later – because the pines planted then are clear-felled now. The trees came down and the ancient fort was revealed. Nobody knew! Archaeologists and detectorists were onto the midden because it tells you how people lived and what they kept: deer, wild pigs, sheep, cattle, fish, kale and barley. The round dun with its double wall and thatched roof is a blueprint for the black houses in which Highlanders and Islanders lived until the 1960s. *Taigh dubh* in Gaelic.

I see myself on top of the dun, with my people wrapped in wolf skins. We are the people of the wolf. The river glitters below. It's warm. The strath wears its star-studded mantle of water and sky. It's darkening but maybe I'll go down to the river and get some salmon for tea. My net is weighted with small lead weights. On the way back, it will catch on a branch and a weight will be lost – and found 2,000 years later by a fishing gillie.

I see that the bones I stand on are my bones.

The Crossing Place, transmission

A malaise crept in and dwelled in the Crossing Place with us, like a magnetic hologram of something uninvited. It sat in the corner at night. My joints and muscles ached, migraines seized my head like a vice and I'd never had migraine before, vertigo turned the world upside down. I couldn't lift anything or open a jar. A wasting fatigue, but I couldn't rest. I'd close my eyes and my eyeballs would turn madly. I'd wake in the middle of the night not feeling my legs, and wake Tony up, thinking that I'm dying, he is dying, we're all dying. Clamped inside a steel grid.

'You're like a sunflower. You need more sunshine and greens!'

Tony went to the industrial estate and salvaged some windows and over the winter built a greenhouse. So I could sit inside and be warm next to the green salads he planted. And vine tomatoes! Everything he planted grew well.

But I was still wilting. A year of appointments and vague diagnoses. We'll test for Lyme, said the GP, and give you a pill for the migraine and the vertigo, and put you through a scan to rule out the worst. It could be the Scottish climate, said the rheumatologist, there's no damage to the joints. Fibromyalgia, said another doctor, no known cause or cure. Adrenal burn-out, said my medical herbalist who usually has the last word, you need endocrine support. And warmer weather. She sent me a bottle of bitter medicine.

Was it underground water? No, the soil is sandy — that's why the quarry is here — and anyway Tony had dowsed for water and found none. Maybe it was because the bed faced upstream, which made the river run contrary to the bed, feet to head. We turned the bed around but it didn't help. Or it could be the electro-magnetic highway. It passed over the Crossing Place, the largest transmission line in the country. And lately, transmission had been amped to 275 kilovolts. We sensed it and heard it, its vibration came through the floor, the pillows, I could almost see electricity in the air. It was stronger along the river. Two years since the line went live.

'But we live in an electromagnetic world anyway,' Tony took a scientific approach.

I put it out of my mind and treated the illness as internal. As if internal and external are separate. And there was not much information about electromagnetic fields and human health.

If the grid was causing my illness, then what — I'd have to leave. How could I leave without Tony? Selling up and moving house was an upheaval we couldn't contemplate. Tony had to be close to the gallery at all times. He was wedded to the gallery. Feeding the monster, he called it. We also couldn't afford a better house. And we'd be damned if we let industry evict us!

All around us, relationships were strained. The community was stressed like the land. People fell out with each other. The arrival of *global investment* was ripping up the delicate kinship of people and place. The new line had indeed *opened up a marketplace*. A rush of wind-farm developers arrived from all over the world. Scotland's projected — massive — excess of generation was to be exported. It was going to bring billions, politicians proclaimed, but it wasn't clear where. The potential clients were not yet known, but maybe England and Norway. That meant expanding both the generation hubs and the transmission grid — exponentially. The sky was the ceiling, the ocean floor the bottom line. More underwater cables, more overhead lines, more access roads, and more battery energy storage units for the energy that couldn't be used. More. More. I saw that the Highlands and Islands were identified as a long-term target by large energy developers, that it was arriving from the top down without regulation, and that the current government and the current energy system encouraged this with no regard for nature or people. There was no bigger picture, only a rush to fulfil targets. And already, there was a great silencing of dissent. Politicians and functionaries at every level would not engage with local people because they had to be neutral, they explained. But they were not neutral — they called the energy company *our friends* and had meetings with them behind closed doors. The destruction of nature and the destruction of truth go together. And sooner or later, this will make you sick.

The winter the new transmission line went live, a power-cut struck in the glen and lasted ten days. It was cold. The first two days were cosy in candlelight by the fire. Then we started to freeze. We had the gas stove to cook on and the wood stove to heat the house. It was back to how things were before the electric. But minus the self-sufficiency, the micro-economy, the community and the life-saving animals. We jumped in the van and sailed to Orkney, just to be on the move.

We lived in the shadow of an overbearing power industry but had no power. And now we had less woodland, less peatland, less community and less health. The kinesiologist down the glen left. She said her healing work could not be done here anymore because of the expanding grid. My Chinese qigong teacher left. For a decade she ran a health centre in the Highlands. I met her when I was desperate and started learning with her the art of managing my energy flow or qi. Your qi is stagnant, she told me, it's environmental. The Earth is changing, she went on, and we must go with it, go with the Dao. That means working with the earth, following the flow of qi. The Highlands had a pure energy, that's why she came here, but the light of the Highlands was dimming. Steel was replacing wood. Industry was pushing out nature. She closed her healing centre and left, with regret.

The south side of Loch Ness became an industrial zone. Wind farms, access roads, excavation pits, barriers, and the new transmission line with its marching pylons. Back in our neighbourhood, we discovered that the forest where we used to take a small tree for Christmas had been replaced by the new line. That was uphill from the church of Talorgan. That whole ancient area was Talorgan's Place. A pylon was built very close to a couple's house there. They had regenerated a mixed woodland, but the new line ripped through it and many trees fell under the impact of construction, crushing the rest. Ten years later, he had cancer and she was a shadow of herself. But they stayed. They loved their place.

During the *stripping of the topsoil*, industry speak, old things were dug up. A Pictish burial cairn. Remains of a fortified Mesolithic Age dwelling. The energy giant dug up the bones of our land ancestors and they were put in boxes and filed away in some basement. Without a send-off by a bagpiper or a minute of silence.

There was the couple who were visited by two wind-farm developers in hipster trainers and baseball caps, one December. Their company had put in an application for a large wind farm near the couple's house. And near other people's houses. She, a yoga teacher, became leader of the local campaign against this speculative venture. 'You must stop being selfish and help us save the planet,' the company men lectured her, and told their story of working in the oil industry for years, until they saw the light and entered the wind turbine industry which was, they said, the future, and very lucrative.

Why have you come here?, the couple asked.

Your government invited us, smirked the Canadian prospectors. The couple refused to move. She continued to lead the campaign. Their house was broken into by unknown men while their daughter was alone. Her husband suffered nervous burnout. By the time the battle was won through a public enquiry which rejected the application, the couple were so traumatised, they sold their house and left Scotland. But they returned a few years later – just in time for the return of the energy giant to the Highlands with plans ten times bigger than before.

Others kept quiet because they welcomed the money. You could sell or lease land to an energy speculator and have a regular income from whatever was built there. Usually a wind farm. I couldn't believe it at first, but the turbines don't reliably generate. Sometimes they don't generate due to lack of wind, but much of the time they don't generate because the grid is overloaded and can't take the energy. Yet the money keeps coming in for those companies and landowners invested in the turbines – we're back to *constraint payments*.

A small, domestic-sized wind turbine on your land can be justified – environmentally and economically – even if the national grid covers your needs already. You get electricity for yourself and make some money from subsidies that goes back into your, say, farm. At a small environmental cost. But a large industrial wind farm owned by a remote corporation that tramples all in its way and hooks onto the mega grid just because it can – that's pure extraction.

★

We sailed to Shetland again, in the winter. Across the vast heaving ocean. We used to head north to escape industry but a large swathe of Shetland was turned into a wind farm. Vast peatlands were destroyed. By the end of it, one third of Shetland's land was occupied by the energy giant (transmission) which in fact owned the new wind farm (generation). Except that for some reason they weren't generating, or transmitting. In their first summer, the mega wind farm received millions in constraint payments. At the same time, they bullied the local small-scale wind farm into closing down. The big fish ate the small fish. Shetland society suffered divisions and ill health. The energy giant gave handouts to corrupt community councils. Mitigation. The energy giant also tried to name two of the turbines after people – an old woman who died in a state of environmental grief, and a young guy who died in an accident building the turbines. More mitigation. This time it was refused.

Tony's artists in Shetland drew, painted and etched a disappearing land. A watercolour artist lived on the edge of the island, alone. From him I bought a small watercolour of a loch destroyed and replaced with an access road to a wind farm. The loch is in the shape of a tear.

'How do you cope with this destruction?' I asked another artist who'd moved to Shetland from the Black Country thirty years ago. He lived near a long sandspit where hermits had lived. His etchings of birds, insects and sea creatures were like prophecies of an exodus. How do you cope?

'I cry a lot. And pray.' Later he left Shetland, with regret.

The sandspit was leased to a gravel company who extracted it to make concrete.

Like me, Tony had changed. He was now hyper-vigilant. The frequent buzz of helicopters and drones above put us on edge. What were they prospecting for? Which forest would be next? The mere sight of men in safety helmets driving large vehicles with the company insignia, marking parcels of land with paint, now gave us palpitations and nausea. One day we counted the vehicles passing through the glen for an hour. Over 50 per cent bore the insignia of the energy giant. Their subcontractors made up the rest, plus some actual residents.

Tony was rushing a lot, the clock was ticking.

'Electricity speeds everything up,' he said. 'And the truth is slow.'

Time was running out for the truth.

We sat in our stone circle under the geans. They were thicker and it was only now I noticed their bark – a golden silver that reflected the light like the goldleaf of an Orthodox icon. The hum of bees in their white crowns and behind it, the crash of the quarry. And the fritillaries were out! Their purple snake heads popped up overnight and always in pairs. The grass in the neighbour's field was high and full of wildflowers and yellow butterflies. The farmer in his tractor was sowing his shrinking field with seeds and a swarm of birds followed him.

We contemplated the retreating tree line. The draped wires of the transmission line, hanging like death laundry. The Crossing Place. How beautiful it was, like an imminent memory.

More and more, I needed to get away from our steel-gridded patch. It gave me claustrophobia. I wondered if I was ever going to recover my health. I'd go driving out of the glen to the light of the Firth. Or deeper into the glen, to tune into some residual truth before it was too late.

Chì mi

I see the primary school where children are happy because of the woods. I see the chickens that give eggs with yolks like the sun. I see houses like faces, each has an expression.

I see the long hill trail to Loch Orrin, dammed. I hear the ditty scribbled sixty years ago on the wall of an abandoned house. It's about the Hydro men. I see it was scribbled by one of them in a spirit of self-irony:

> Doon the glen came the Orrin men,
> they looked like ballet dancers.
> One in ten were time-served men,
> the rest were bloody chancers.

I see the house on a knoll hidden by beeches, where the kinesiologist lived before she left. It shows me one of her apprentices, the Spanish artist who left a note to a friend along with his paints, before he killed himself. *Take my colours and my hands and paint with them*, his note said, and though I never met him I am shown his dark wavy hair and his pain which wasn't really his. But sometimes the world's pain enters a body and forces the person to leave it.

At the turn-off before the humpback bridge, I see the first hills of Strathfarrar, cloud-wrapped like a Tibetan monastery. The gong of an October evening strikes and reverberates in the head of the glen brightly.

Strathfarrar

The atmosphere changes, a new purity enters the air. The river is high after days of rain and almost touches the road. Tony and I come to Strathfarrar on special long drives to the Spout at the far, far end, but now I'm alone. I've come to seek refuge from industry for a week. And Strathfarrar is one of those places where you're best alone.

Strathfarrar is the firstborn of the four glen-children – it's where the Farrar River originates. Locals call it simply the Farrar, everything here is about the river and the hills. The further in you go, the higher the hills. *Gleann Farair nam beann mora*, goes an old poem. Glen Farrar of the high mountains. The Farrar is the only major feature in the glen whose name is not Gaelic or Norse. Maybe it's Pictish: *var* is to wind, hence Farrar, the winding one. Rivers have the oldest names in any landscape, and Farrar is a remnant of that lost language.

The Farrar first appears in the writings of the Greco-Roman geographer Ptolemy. He wrote it down half a century before the invading Romans withdrew from Caledonia, having never conquered it. They retreated south to the unfinished Antonine Wall which ran from coast to coast, and had seventeen forts and 7,000 men posted on it. When that was abandoned, they retreated yet further south to Hadrian's Wall, which remained the northern outpost of the Roman world until it too was abandoned. But it is because the Romans were here for a time that Ptolemy wrote down the name Farrar, and that Tacitus wrote down the name Calgacus, the chief of the Caledonian Confederacy, *the last of the free*. If he is the first named Highlander in history, Farrar is the first named Highland river.

At some point, the words *glen* and *strath* were stuck onto the Farrar by mapmakers who had no Gaelic and didn't realise it was a doubling-up of meaning. That's how we ended up with Glen Strathfarrar.

At the entrance to the glen is a locked gate.

The energy giant comes in and out every day, because of the dams and power stations. The road is maintained by them, every fifty years or so, but their vehicles have become up to 25 tons heavy, and the road is breaking up. It means you have to go slow when you're driving or cycling. The people who complain about the potholes are the bosses of the energy company when they visit, used as they are to smooth rides.

Before the entrance gate is a lush strip of riverbank that was once a drover's stance. Cattle drovers arrived from their epic crossings from the west coast, sodden and starving, and corralled their beasts for the night before they went to the Struy Inn for a dram by the fire. Struy means a confluence and here lives a small community. Then a few houses and farm buildings leading up to the gate. The keeper Dougal, from an old family of keepers. You'll not get much out of them, I've heard, ask them the time of day and they'll keep that to themselves. Dougal is followed around by an orphaned wild goat rescued in the hills, called Suzie.

There is the young family of the under-keeper from the city who always dreamed of living in the country.

The Polish family – she is a teacher and he worked for a wind-farm company. That's how they ended up here, and now he works in a carbon-fibre factory.

A family with teenagers whose hair is rust-coloured like

winter bracken. They live in the house that was once a community hall.

Heather and Fred in the gate keeper's house.

Once you pass the gate, there is just one big white house – Chris and Rebecca live here. They own the first part of the glen. There are three more owners of three more parts further in, but they are absent. Only their keepers live on site. And that makes up the residents of Strathfarrar. It is a glen owned by five: the four families and the energy company.

To get past the gate, you do one of three things: walk or cycle, ring the gate keepers' bell, and Heather opens the gate to let your car through, or enter the code on one of the padlocks festooned along the chain of the gate like a totemic garland at the entrance of a temple. Two padlocks belong to the energy company: one for generation and one for transmission. The fact that they don't talk to each other is symbolised by the separate padlocks. The rest are used by the four estates that comprise the glen, and their guests and workers. And the gate serves variably as filter, barrier and protector to the glen. The padlocks represent an accumulation of interests over time.

GLEN OPEN

From April to October.

GLEN CLOSED

From November to March.

I have the code to the black padlock which belongs to the first estate, so I don't need to bother Heather, though she'll be clocking me from behind her curtain. Open the gate, drive through, close the gate. When you live inside, you perform this ritual every time you go anywhere. It makes you self-conscious, going in and out, as if you're suddenly on a stage. Is anyone watching? I click the padlock shut, unsure whether to shuffle it or leave it to save time for the next person. I enter the Painted Glen. It's what I call it because it is the masterpiece in the open gallery of Strathfarrar. Here is hill country with birch forests, gorges and waterfalls, rock stacks, fishing pools and a large remnant of steep Caledonian pine forest that gives you a glimpse of the distant past: this is how Caledonia looked, once. A high land of lushness buzzing with wildlife.

Once past the gate, the glen pulls you in like a waking dream. There is just one place to stay: the simple Scandinavian chalets. Chris and Rebecca had them built in 1982 and still run them on a one-pound coin electric meter. You bring a bag of coins and enough provisions for the week, because the nearest shop is ten miles away.

The days are getting shorter, the road beckons, you start walking. You want to be alone with the Farrar, as with God. The distances are great. They make you dream, then walk, then go to bed and dream of walking. Farrar is a monastery.

The birches whisper. Lightness and sadness: that's the essence of birchhood. Piles of pearl droppings from the deer. The river has been even higher than now; I see the tide mark of leaves and branches. I reach the first power station. It is underground. Its grilled maw is massive, the stone darkened by decades of damp, the tunnel in darkness. Above it is the forest and I follow a trail uphill. Something comes over me like a spell.

Here it is again – the essence of the Farrar seeps in from all sides. It gets me every time. It has not faded. The forest is full of things. There are beings among the trees, hearing and seeing, breathing. Not going anywhere, just – there. I am inside a gallery of lichen, rock, bracken and air, a painted world. So many mosses! All sorts of different mosses. On the rocks, on the birches. It's a padded land, a kind land. You can lie down anywhere and make it your bed, suck water from a mossy pad, cover yourself with a blanket of moss and sink your head into the merciful pillow of the earth. It welcomes you. The moss filters water and air. It's the lungs of the glen. I'm inside a living body, maybe that's why I feel reverence. The rusty bracken, the yellowing blaeberry bushes I try not to tread on, the noble Scots pine with its bodies twisted and alive. Like the Farrar itself. Even dammed, it snakes its way to some essential winding var. The sound of water everywhere – burns, rapids in the gorge that opens up suddenly below this hillside road in an astonishment of secrecy and growth. A gorge far from the world is ideal for the romantic – in it you will find either rapture or death. But I've only just arrived, I stick to the path.

The old transmission line marches with its pylon soldiers in a straight line across the noble land. It marches west to east, ghosted by the rivers, the drovers and the prophets. It has already conquered the land in all directions. The army of useful pylons with their special operation – where are they going, what is their final objective? They were erected by the Hydro-Electric Board seventy years ago at the same time as the dams and the power stations – and soon they will be restrung in an upgrade for energy security. Nobody knows what this means and what it will entail.

Water courses down from all sides, generous highland water reddish gold with peat. And the bellow of stags! Raw, big-bodied, it means business – the business of life and death. They have come down the glen for the rut. They fight each other over the hinds that live here. In this matriarchy of red deer, hinds live within five miles of where they are born and have the best pasture. The males live ten to twenty miles into Strathfarrar. Their gender-separate existence is interrupted by the mating season and once the rut is over, the hinds send all the males away again, except the young ones under a year old who are their children. Faces watch me in the forest. It's the sheep. Big long-legged Cheviot-like sheep live here but they are not Cheviot, it's another breed. They lie down in the rain. One looks at me without moving her head, like a marble sculpture. She looks with understanding, the way animals do. All animals. They understand something fundamental that we don't.

Every day, the colours of the tree crowns will change. That rowan! It has a red top but the rest of it is still green. My God, all the rowans are doing this. It's like a magician's act. They have red, yellow and green in their hair, in layers like poetry stanzas, and I stop as if shot by an elf's arrows. My knees almost give way under the weight of so much art. To kneel among the birches, the rowans, the Scots pines. To pray for this not to be lost. To thank the sky for being a graphite grey. And to drink in the light of the north that makes the colours of the Farrar vibrate with truth whose other name is beauty.

It's darkening, time to quit the hills and descend to river and road. The intensity of colours, the sharply serrated trees – I fly downhill, my feet hardly touching the ground.

Down on the Farrar, I sit on a rock painted with mosses and watch the river run peaty, passionate and fast. It's muggy here in the high bracken of the riverbanks, a micro-climate. The energy of the glen has seized me and it's no use trying to pretend. It won't let go until I leave. I want to merge with everything like a lover. The Farrar is a moving painting that self-creates continuously, like plasma. When I walked downhill, a rainbow appeared over the eastern dip in the hills. For the first time, I saw the truth about a rainbow: it's everywhere! Not just inside its own arch but inside the warm colours of autumn, in the brown, green, gold, copper and blackish bark of the forest, inside this entire glen which is a laboratory of miracles. Oils and acrylics, mercury and gold. The river is old as myth. The deer move through the painting but only by roar, I can't see them. I can hear syllables in their sentences. They speak to each other across the river.

Just past the autumn equinox, the stags' throats swell up and they stop eating. It's a hormone in their bodies that is linked to the diminishing daylight. The timing of the rut ensures that the calves will be born in June when the grass is at its best. By the end of the rut some of the males are so weak they die of hypothermia and exhaustion. It's the exertion of fighting and rutting, the long distance they travel to get to the mouth of the Farrar, then back to their remote hinterland, the competition for winter grazing and no shelter – their whole existence is an ordeal. In spring, the gillies start finding the bodies of stags in the hills. Huddled together for company in death.

My neighbours in the chalets are a quiet lot – fishermen and hikers, out all day.

Built on the edge of the birch forest, around a ruined stone building whose purpose is unknown, the five chalets have created a seasonal community. Chris and Rebecca have seen the same faces every year between April and November – for forty years. Fishing folk who arrive with rods, hikers in boots, couples with dogs and children who grow up and bring their own children and dogs, 'and if that's not ageing, I don't know what is,' Rebecca says in her curt way.

She and Chris are my parents' generation. Chris inherited this estate, along with his cousin. When their Scottish grandfather from Fife bought the land, it was as one entire estate. The family had made their fortune in linoleum, and would spend two months of the year here with their staff, staying in a hunting lodge inherited from the previous owners – that's the Lovat clan. The grandfather left the estate to two of his three sons: Chris's father and uncle, the third son being left out for some reason. In 1967, the two brothers split the estate in two, and Chris's father took this northern side of the river. When Chris's father died, it went to Chris who was just twenty-one. Then his uncle gave the southern side of the river to his own son who is Chris's cousin.

From the start, Chris and his cousin wanted to do the right thing with their inheritance. But what is the right thing to do with a large estate if you don't want to live in the nineteenth century? You start by living in it full-time so it's a home and not a leisure park. You return from youthful worldly travels and raise your family here and commit to running the place as best you can. You try out different things, for money, for nature, for yourself, and to avoid going bankrupt. It's called diversifying, a friendly word whose dark side is, of course, extraction. Burdened with the legacy of another era, you must hold back the tide of destruction while trying to let in improvement, but sometimes it's hard to tell the difference. The destroyers have a knack for presenting themselves as improvers.

Of all the owners of large estates in the mother glen, there are only two families who live here full-time – Chris and Rebecca, and the cousin with his family. Both families run chalets that bring people to the glen.

At night, the silence is torn by the deep-throated bellow of stags.

'Sometimes I can't sleep because the stags come to fight in the moonlight,' says my neighbour, a mild guy who works for a pharmaceutical company. They are a group of three friends and each year, they hire the same fishing gillie – and that's Ali. He arrives in the morning and rolls up his first cigarette. Then they disappear on the river and I don't see them anymore. The glen is so big, you can be alone even with others.

Every day, there is a rainbow in a different place. The colours pulse. And down the corridor of the glen is another rainbow! It's like seeing two moons. Today there is an icy wind that makes it an expedition to reach Monar even by car. Copper bracken covers the hills. Brown Hebridean sheep, gone wild, their horns like swords. Alder grows in bunches. I see a ruined shieling. The Gaelic word for shieling is *àirigh* (aari), which rhymes with 'baa'. Àirigh is full of summer. It means two things that were occupied together in summer: hill pasture and hilltop bothy. Once, dozens of place names had àirigh in them, and when you call out *àirigh* you realise that the word *is* the hills. Àirigh is full of air and light – and the air and the light have left the human psyche because the hill pasture and the hilltop bothy have left the land with the pastoral people. All I can do is wade through bracken, the wild sheep gazing at me obliquely, and say *àirigh, àirigh*, like a spell against extinction.

And snow – first snow on the peaks to the west! They rise bright and frigid like an ice palace. I am driving towards them and towards the future when there will be snow everywhere.

Two lost geese fly with effort against the Arctic front. Exhausted, they alight in the heathered moor. They're heading in the wrong direction. If they go to the ice palace, they will die. Yes, they see that now, and head back to the Firth. I'll see you in the Monks' Place! I wave and they wave back with their wings.

A cyclist from the south pushes in the face of the wind. We stop for clipped words each time we pass each other. The wind travels like a train down a tunnel. It gets under your skin and stays there. With wind like this, you're never alone. She smiles, happy and free, and we watch the wind and rain dance across the wide strath like a curtain unveiling a stage. The spectacle of Strathfarrar began a long time before anything walked on two legs. Yet the spectacle is still unfolding, out of sheer creational generosity. *Look at this*, the land is saying, *look at this until you really see it. You are here on borrowed time and your time is running out.* The cyclist pushes on to Monar.

When the trees vanish, the good feeling goes too. Then you know you have left behind the Painted Glen and you're in the exposed middle part of the glen which forms the Middle estate. The Middle estate have put up their own locked gate, which makes the road dementedly double-gated. It's dubbed 'Carrie's gate', after the keeper. The two gates – Heather's one and Carrie's one – have the same opening times but there are half-days and today is a half-day. The gate is open though, and I drive over the cattlegrid with a rattle.

Along the road are planted oaklings, boxed against deer and feral sheep and goats. Inside the boxes grow companions – birch, blaeberries – because oak creates instant community. The Middle estate is open moorland with the odd survivor tree like this lone old oak here. A giant cep nibbled by animals shelters at its roots. This friendship comforts me. Otherwise it's comfortless, being by the Middle estate's lodge. It is encased in high fence with two locked gates.

It's a shooting lodge from the second half of the nineteenth century when sheep pastures were turned into sporting estates, with luxury lodges like this. Around the house are the overgrown ruins of dwellings. The owner of the Middle estate is known as 'the Malaysian' and comes once a year but nobody knows his name, not even his employees. Under the guise of a conglomerate, he owns 71,000 acres of the Highlands, half of which is here. Tobacco empire, some said. No no, he's involved with big dams and renewable energy companies, say others, and wasn't there a British connection with some Asian deals in the 1980s under Thatcher, when a few people made so much money they had to buy things they didn't need, like an estate in Scotland? But at least the land hasn't been extracted. It could be worse, there could be a giant quarry. I peer through the fence of the lodge at the immaculate grounds mown every week by the keepers, and I recall a story heard in the glen.

There was once a guy in Glasgow who lived on the dole and liked to walk. He'd get his dole, buy a new pair of hiking boots, and start walking north. He loved the Highlands and Strathfarrar was his favourite glen. One year, he came to this lodge, no fence back then. He broke in and helped himself to the whisky. He drew moustaches on the big gloomy portraits of ancestors and passed out on the floor. That's where the police found him. I hope his sentence was light, for he only wrecked a living room and did it honestly, on his own name, not on the name of some conglomerate. After that, they built a fence so big they locked it twice and even put down cattle grids all around, like moats. You are a thousand times unwelcome.

Standing under the oak with the friendly mushroom, I'm startled by a pick-up truck that pulls over with a screech and out comes a red-faced woman in a puffer jacket and platinum jewellery like armour.

'The glen is closed, you shouldn't be here!'

'The gate was open,' I say.

'It doesn't matter. You shouldn't be here. And you're arguing with me!'

I explain I'm staying in the chalets.

'I don't care. The glen is closed on Wednesday morning. And you're breaking the Scottish access law by being parked outside the entrance of a property.'

This must be Carrie.

'Now turn your car around and get yourself out of here.'

She slams herself back in and drives back to the keeper's house on the side of the road, Hydro-built, and always for some reason strung up with bunting of the British flag, celebrating some expired coronation day. Carrie moved to the north perhaps to get away from things in the south. But things follow her. That's why she tries to keep them under lock and key.

I turn the car around. There's nothing Carrie can do if I go on to Monar. Monar is part of the third estate, she can't hunt me there. I am not breaking any law except the one in her head, but there is every chance of her pursuing me all the way in. Best to avoid another scene.

War is not something that happens out there. It's right here. All it takes is two people. Or just one – and a gate. Carrie's gate only stops those already inside the glen – that's guests of the chalets.

Yes, the deer became orphaned, the tenants left, the owners are absent and the keepers have gone mad. Carrie's locked gate is rattled by its own padlocks.

The wind is behind me now, pushing me back to the peaceful tail of Strathfarrar. Head, middle and tail. They are joined by the river but might as well be different countries with different climates and laws.

The tail is the Painted Glen. It has trees and friendly people. The head is Pait and Monar, thrashing in a mechanical cycle of generation. There are two lots there, the keepers of Monar and the keepers of Pait. They are Angie and her husband who is known as the most taciturn stalker in the glen, and that's some competition! The middle is here. Hikers climb in the middle because it has the Farrar Four – that's four Munros. The boggy ground of the Middle estate has not changed and the whole vibe here reminds me of a story about one brutal General Monck who passed through here in the mid seventeenth century, having come this far north for the Anglo-Scottish war. He was returning with his soldiers from the west coast where they'd burned people's houses and driven off their cattle. But the ground here was 'soe boggie', he wrote, that they abandoned a hundred horses laden with baggage. Peat has a long memory. The bog must hold them still.

I pass again Carrie's house with the coronation bunting. High above the house looms a citadel-like dam – a private one. It straddles like a vice the cascades that fall down the mountain wall.

The Celtic rune of hospitality goes: *I saw a stranger yestreen, I put food in the eating place, drink in the drinking place, music in the listening place.* Since the glens were cleared of their folk, there has been no folk hospitality in the glens. The last to offer hospitality were the keepers of remote glens. I know this because an eccentric Scottish scholar-priest called Ronnie Burn criss-crossed the glens of Scotland, climbed every major hill and became 'the first compleat Munroist'. He kept diaries, the diaries were lost, then found and passed down until they reached a local writer who recognised gold when she saw it. She wrote a book drawing on the diaries. It's a page-turner for those who turn the pages of the glens with their feet and their mind. Ronnie was friends with all the keepers in all the remote glens. Like the ones who lived right here, three generations ago – the Macdonalds. Out of Jacobite loyalty they always had a person or a dog in the family called Teàrlach (Charles), like the pretender prince Charles Stuart. They were Gaelic speakers but ashamed of it. So when the daughter of another keeper couple from deepest Affric came to work for them in summer, she practised her English but lost her Gaelic.

Her parents were Ronnie's friends and this girl called him 'a very strange priest' because he was like a big child himself.

It's only when I see the twisted Scots pine growing from the cliffy gorge, how they hold on to the rockfaces heroically, outliving even Cerberus at the gates of hell – it's only then that I begin to breathe again. The pines stand sentinel to the glen. It's their loyalty to life itself that makes you grateful and happy again. Then you see the mossy rock stacks like smiling heads in the late sun, and the leg-shaped trunks that look like men who've been shot and have fallen face-down on the soft forest floor, and you fill up with story again.

And here are the wild goats of Strathfarrar! They aren't always this low down, and in summer especially they avoid humans and roam the tops. I look at them and they look at me, long hair aflutter in the wind, their mineral faces intelligent. It's the intelligence of the glen. It says: *live and let live for God's sake.*

Once, shepherding families lived at Monar and Pait. When the Hydro-Electric Board built the dams and scheduled the flooding of the loch, they took their animals to higher ground and left them to roam ferally ever after.

The next day, Carrie's gate is open. This time I'm going to Monar. I pass the quiet confluence where two streams become the Farrar and where 90 per cent of the salmon come to spawn. What a trek for them! And for anyone who comes this far. Garbh Uisge and Uisge Misgeach, that's what they are called: Rough Water and Drunk Water. These streams are the origin of the long river that has brought all of us here for the last 10,000 years, starting with the people who made tools from quartz to scrape fish skins. None of us would be here without Rough Water and Drunk Water. None. Humans survived without the electric until two generations ago. But like the salmon, they can't survive without clean water.

I stop at Deanie access tunnel which goes into the hill. You can see a bit of it through the iron grille of the locked gate. It's all locked gates here, underground tunnels, a plutonic realm under the natural one. This tunnel is for maintenance workers to access the bigger tunnels. Inside the tunnel is an accidental greenhouse, warm, mutant, happily forgotten by man. Ferns, flowering plants, even a birch. You could plant a fig and it would grow. It's much greener inside the tunnel than out. The ground shakes under my feet like a quake, and the grilled gate vibrates in my hand. A terrific roar of churning water under the hill. What these tunnels hold, what the stations process, is sheer power. The power of water. There is nothing more generative and more destructive.

Water is taken from Loch Monar and another loch, passed through two tunnels (9 km and 5.5 km each), and delivered to two power stations: the citadel-like Deanie up there, and Culligran which is underground. The water runs through turbines to generate power, then it is returned to the river. But is it the same water by the time the salmon reach it from the sea? It has passed through blades and turbines up to five times. A deer that runs in these hills, then passes through the blades of the slaughterhouse and ends up on your plate, is not the same deer. It has been processed. When we die, our ashes feed the soil. Does that turn us into renewables?

I have reached the curved Monar dam. At the foot of the dam is something that used to be the Farrar. The dam executed the river like a guillotine and it's just a trickle of a memory now. The water in the loch is high, dark, and not alive. The dam is spouting excess water through a tube in its base like a catheter. The earth shudders under my feet. The wind howls like a pack of wolves past the blasted rockface, and in this enormity of elements and industry you hold on to the nearest thing. What a lonely place.

This is Britain's largest double-curvature arch dam. If you are a dam nerd like me, you'll know what this means and you'll admire it. The engineering skill that made it possible to breach gorges and eviscerate hills in such old, unyielding country of metamorphic and igneous rock hundreds of millions of years old – well, it's a stubborn land and the dam builders were tough to match.

The shores of Monar are barren. Bone-white driftwood, ankle-deep, an open-air catacomb. You wouldn't guess that Monar had extremely fertile shores. They're now underwater, like the houses. Smaller houses were set on fire and blown up before the flooding, to avoid their drifting body parts getting stuck inside the turbines. Larger houses were left entire before being flooded.

'If your home is bombed, burnt or blown over then it can be replaced. But with a dam, all hope is gone,' said the last child to grow up in Monar before the dams. He was a great shepherd and the peat-cutter we commemorate at the Five Forts of Farley.

Loch Monar was famed for its waterfowl. And for its curlew, snow buntings, lapwings, redshanks, greenshanks, widgeons, teals and many other birds that I wouldn't recognise. The Monar marshlands were destroyed by the Hydro and all their creatures are gone. Monar Dam is an ending. Yet a fork opens in the road. You can go on – either to Pait where Angie lives, reached by boat down the length of Loch Monar, or down the long road through an expansive strath where something begins, only to end with the Spout, where the surface aqueducts of the Hydro disgorge captured water in a spectacle of excess.

The remoteness of inner Strathfarrar is a dream suddenly remembered. My God, here it is, the elephant land gouged by sliding sheets of ice, and the archaic sky, like some old Earth! There shouldn't be a road here and until 1960 there wasn't, only trails, because this is drover's country made for feet and hooves. In the late summer light, the barren beauty of the strath constricts your throat. The land is used up, yet it can't stop unfolding like the beginning of creation, and it wouldn't be completely surprising to see primordial creatures with scales and heavy tails beating the ground and making it quake, their trumpeting calls and the thud of their steps the sound of land masses moving at the pace of aeons. Snow begins to fall until everything is trapped in ice, a glaciated world. Forever. After forever, huge lightnings strike, the Earth is wrapped by strange colourful auroras, the thaw begins. Chasms open, new waters gush out, the mountain slides, memory is ground to dust like the skeletons of the creatures that lived here. It's a new earth on top of the old earth.

On the way back I make another ritual stop: at the underground station of Culligran. It's a place that pulls me like a magnet. So much concrete in the river! So many gates, grilles, shafts, sluice gates and barbed wire. The water is put to work before it's set free. A labour camp for water.

Of all the rivers in the mother glen, the Farrar was the last to be impounded. By the mid 1950s, the Hydro-Electric Board had completed dozens of large schemes and the generation was enough to power all of Scotland. But they couldn't stop. Industrial momentum, cheap labour and the ideology of limitless growth drove them on. Industrial fever has a military logic, it had to burn itself out. No major river was to be left entire. And it was the turn of Constructional Scheme Number 30. That was Strathfarrar. Strathfarrar fought hard with the Board. All the residents of the glen were against it – keepers, owners, tenants and shepherds. Chris's grandfather was an active objector. But all three owners of the glen were privileged men at a time when industrialisation was synonymous with social opportunity and progress. If you objected to the industrialisation of the Highlands, you were instantly accused of being a 'scenic sentimentalist'. Today that's the charge of nimbyism.

The objecting locals were backed up by experts, including the head of Scottish mountaineering, who protested the desecration of the monument of Strathfarrar – his words. But most locals just quietly mourned the destruction of their glens, feeling that they had no say in the matter. The industrial machine was marching on.

'It is difficult to understand the complacency displayed by the press and public towards the monstrous schemes of the Hydro-Electric Board, and which, I presume, is only to be accounted for by the fact that we live in a grossly materialistic age,' wrote a local woman to a local newspaper in 1948. '. . . Putting 2,000 navvies to work in these wild and beautiful glens, destroying every familiar landmark, with all the legend and history attached . . . And yet, that is what is already happening in Glen Affric . . . the conditions there are indescribable and the destruction of bird and animal life is complete.'

And they were, and it was. Very few letters of this kind were published in the press, while industry spokespeople were given ample space. Such was the epoch – post-traumatic, post-war – looking for the future in steel, cement and convenience. Electrifying every corner of Scotland was hailed as progress.

But the real objective of the Hydro schemes was not that. It was to fuel industries in the south.

At the time of the Hydro schemes, it was victory foretold for the Board and their strong arguments: Hydro will be cheaper than coal, the schemes will solve *the Highland problem*, as the phrase went, and anyway the Highlands had nothing other than natural resources and had to do their bit for the British economy by being extracted. *The Highland problem* was the result of the Clearances, the wastelanding of the countryself by large shooting estates, and the loss of men in two world wars. Post-war industry presented itself as the solution. The Board had a well-oiled public relations machine and was embedded in government, and the Board's director and chief ideologue had started as a politician. Like him, the land surveyors, engineers and other senior staff had never set foot in the Highlands. To them, it was unchartered, virgin territory. Blank country ripe for harvesting.

And so Constructional Scheme Number 30 went ahead. The river was dammed in two places. The hills were dynamited and extracted and two power stations were built inside them. If you venture beyond Monar to where the Spout disgorges captured water, you'll see miles of aqueducts crisscrossing the land.

At Culligran power station is a maintenance van with the logo of the energy giant. An employee is inside the barbed-wire enclosure with the single transmission tower. I sit at the sluice gate and wait. These sluices and dams, tunnels and dykes are vulnerable. Building larger and larger infrastructures makes the grid less secure, not more. The concrete walls and towers are awesome because so much human toil has gone into them, yet they're already overrun with the inhuman. Organic matter creeps in from all sides. If mechanical control is lost, the explosion of water would turn the glen into a biblical flood, destroy bridges and roads downstream, and cause outages to much of Scotland. Water tends to have the last word.

A red hind appears in the birches and looks at me then vanishes in the bracken. Heavy trails in the hillside show where the stags have passed. The Painted Glen is like that – you have a kinship with everything. You belong. And there is higher ground for all animals to run to, when the waters of the glen breach their prison walls.

Odhar, odhar, the bracken whispers its own colour.

If you want to be close to God, Gaelic is better, said a church minister once. English for business, Gaelic for God. And in this glen, business hasn't yet killed God. Colour is a language. So is shape, light and sound. I can't narrate this glen, it's too great. I've walked miles of this road with friends, all writers. But I can't remember anything we said. Only the spring in their step, the hush when starlings passed over us, the swoop of an eagle, the sudden taking-off of clothes in the swimming weir, the child breaking out from the adult face. These friends are still here, walking along the corridor of the glen with all the other people and animals I can't see. It is not an empty glen.

The maintenance man is done. The plant next to the pylon is leaking oil, it needs replaced, he says. It looks fine to me, I say. Aye, that's because it's painted, he smiles. But they've lasted well, we agree, the whole lot that was built by the Hydro men has lasted very well.

'Seventy years,' he says. 'Nothing lasts that long these days.'

So why the planned upgrade to the existing infrastructure?

'Because it's seventy years old. It's due. That's the regulations.'

It's called legacy infrastructure.

The man is not up to date with all the applications for wind farms that are pouring in all over the Highlands every week, from multinational developers. And they are pouring in because of the new transmission line.

'I'm transmission. That's generation.'

Generation doesn't talk to transmission.

Like many locals, he has watched the hills get covered in industrial grids and blades, in bafflement.

'They say we need them because the Hydro isn't generating enough. That's not true. Sometimes . . .'

But he stops himself. I know what he might say. Sometimes, Hydro generation is halted or reduced, so the grid looks deficient and there is the appearance of a demand for more. More infrastructure. More lucrative contracts. This is something you hear muttered but it's difficult to verify because the energy company withholds information from the public while appearing to consult the public. It withholds information from its employees too. And the dams are elderly now. Their reservoirs are not used to full capacity anymore.

Hydro has helped power Scotland for seventy years. Thanks to the great Highland rivers, to twentieth-century Scottish engineering, and to the men who survived the war and had nowhere to go so they came to build the dams. Men like this one. His face darkens. Every time he drives somewhere – a new wind farm on a hill. More roads. More gates. More concrete and steel.

'Not a penny has come back to the people,' he sums up. 'It's all about money going higher up. And we have the highest energy bills in Europe! It's depressing. It's always been like that here. We just get used and dumped.'

'I better go and put the kettle on,' I say.

'Aye,' he bitterly quips. 'You don't want your kettle to go out.'

★

It's night. The stars shine through the birches. The bellow of the stags is close. After the windy day – a night so still that I'm sure time has stopped. Motionless, the birches look deep in thought. I can see their long-haired outlines under the stars, like women wrapped in capes, hunkering for a vigil.

I hear a churning noise. Is it wind, or water coursing down? No, it's the stags. They thud through the forest. Hooves on stone, a branch knocking on my window, or is that an antler.

The stars are not just above, they are in the birch forest like the spirits of winter. The sky is a cupola of lights. I lie under wool blankets and listen to the meter in the kitchen cupboard. It churns the coins too quickly and I am running out of coins. The economy of energy generation and consumption baffles me. It seems unsustainable. Why are energy companies more powerful than governments, and our bills so high that we go broke? How is it possible for a government to give a billion pounds in constraint payments to energy companies, while human health and ecosystems are collapsing? We are told that there is a bottomless need for electricity, yet electricity is overproduced with nowhere to go. Consuming has become a religion and electricity drives it. The grid wants to run the Earth.

In the chalet there are books. The most well-thumbed is the one about Loch Ness and the phenomenon of the monster. The details are too strange to make up. But aside from the details, what makes me dream is the relationship. The story of Loch Ness is the story of a relationship between humans and a loch. The fact that people don't see the monster anymore marks the breakdown of that relationship.

I sink in the starry night of the glen until I am at the bottom of a prehistoric crevasse filled with dark water. I dream of a powerful shape rising from it – an extraordinary event but there is no one else to witness it. I can't tell if it's a living thing like the Nessie or a mechanical thing like a giant turbine that churns water. Look, I want to show Tony, it's finally surfacing! I told you there was something in that loch! But Tony is not here. What year is it? I am alone and the morning is cold.

The meter has swallowed the coins and stopped turning. I can't boil the kettle but it's too early to disturb Rebecca for more coins. She and Chris have to deal with this all the time. Every few months, Chris must go to the bank with a bagful of coins. We have to upgrade, people need more powerful showers, more powerful everything, Rebecca says, but Chris is a traditionalist. Handling these coins makes you aware of what goes in and what comes out. The coins remind you that real things have weight, shape and value. The coins, made from non-renewable metals of the Earth, are a bracing bell in the soundless void of digital number-crunching. I wonder where all the shrapnel of the world gets recycled – the shrapnel of industry, the shrapnel of war. Whether it will remain forever in our bodies, in our land and in the waters of memory. Or come to an end one day, when things simply run out and start getting recycled for all they're worth.

I step out and inhale the mushroomy forest. Vapour comes off the ground. A badger has taken the piece of bread with peanut butter I left on the outside table, instructed by Chris, who has left a jar in each chalet for this purpose. Blue tits and robins are breakfasting on the fat balls. The fishermen and hikers are sleeping behind closed curtains.

I walk across the lawn where the stags fought in the night, to see the sun rise over the eastern hills. The sheep in the field look my way with their collective head. I sit by the ruin around which the chalets were built. Consumption walls, dry masons call this kind of medieval wall – because it consumed the stones gathered from fields and forests to make them more arable and grazable. It's a sign that this place was self-sufficient. The last woman who lived in an old cottage nearby was Dougal the keeper's aunt. She grew rhubarb in the ruin. When Chris and Rebecca had the chalets built, they left the ruin untouched so that every morning you remember to tread carefully, for you tread on your ancestors' rhubarb.

Today another rainbow will bridge the eastern hills and it's the same rainbow they must have seen. It will have all the golds of this late year – red gold, fawn gold and invisible gold that is just light, the light of an alchemical autumn.

River People

It's October again, another year. I'm staying in the same chalet. The same fishing party is here. I join them and enter their rhythm.

In the morning, Ali the gillie arrives in his old car and they all put on their waders. They become rubber men, waterproof from chest to toe. We sip our coffee by the ruin and discuss pools. There are thirty fishing pools, ten in each of three beats. What's a beat?

Ali looks at me like I'm from another planet: 'A beat is a section of the river where you're allowed to go salmon fishing. Come on, we have to make hay!'

Because it's Thursday, freshet day. Between 9 a.m. on Thursday and 9 a.m. on Saturday, five inches of compensatory water is released by the energy company for the salmon of the Farrar. Otherwise they won't make it upstream. The power stations generate most days, which makes the water levels low, because the water of the dammed lochs is diverted into tunnels and water bypasses the river. In the days before computers, a worker came into the glen each week to turn the freshet on manually. Now it's done from the control rooms 200 miles south. The freshet was negotiated between the Hydro-Electric Board and Chris's father and grandfather on behalf of the Farrar salmon, once it became clear that the river would be impounded. The Hydro is obliged in any case to release minimum compensation water, but that's not enough and under pressure from local people, the Board committed to release an extra five inches for forty-eight hours a week, fifteen weeks per year, ending in October. It was passed as an Act of Parliament. This was their meagre mitigating measure to the salmon.

Ali takes turns to chaperone his guests. Today it's a big melancholy guy. The others go off in their needlessly large cars. The pharmaceuticals guy has taken to teaching the bracken-haired boy who lives in a house before the gate, and the other one is on his own. They drive slowly down the Farrar; each chooses their first fishing pool for the morning, stops in a layby, gets his gear out and takes up position. Drive back for lunch, swap pools, and the same till dark, then the gillie goes home. Most of the day is spent standing in shallow water, hoping to glimpse a salmon. All fish are released, no salmon dinners. And in July–August – the time for Labradors and Londoners – one in thirty is kept and eaten. The main purpose of bagging a salmon is to take a photo.

'And if it's an interesting individual, we take a sample scale and send it off to the fishery board. That's Rose.'

Rose is the new river biologist, young with good ideas.

Then you remove the fly from inside the cheek and carefully release it. Is the decline in salmon that bad?

'It's beyond bad. Seventy-five per cent down in my own lifetime. Awfully sad.'

We stand under the alders by the Colonel's Pool and big guy takes his position. Yesterday you could walk across this bit without getting wet. Today, it's thigh-high. Is it because of Hydro generation? Ali sighs.

'Yes and no. The Farrar is okay. The Hydro was good for the fish, at first. Because it's naturally a spate river and the fish were happy when it rose.'

A spate river is one that goes up and down with rain a lot, but only when it's undammed.

'But overall it's not good. The biggest problem is, we've overfished them in the sea. They scoop up whole shoals and straight into the ice. Awful.'

Atlantic salmon struggle to make it to the rivers.

'They meet with predators and obstacles. Low levels when they're not generating at the bottom of the river.'

The bottom is our Kilmorack dam and station, where the Crossing Place is and where for years Tony and I wondered if the salmon will one day stop jumping.

Every child glen within the mother glen has its stock phrases, and in Farrar it's this: *They're generating*. One look at the river tells you what the power stations are up to. Intense generation results in drastically fluctuating levels. It's the principle of flooding and drought. Over time, this strips the riverbed of gravel and makes spawning harder.

We wait for two hours with no sign of salmon. They're generating a lot this week.

'The first two hours, you don't see any. Because they're still making it up the river. They wait for the level to rise.'

Salmon are strong and can travel the Farrar in just two days. They lie tight against the bank across from us because they're safe there, and rest, after the 'crappy water' they've passed through.

When you're fishing, you look for this resting fish.

'Every pool has a head, middle and tail.'

Like a fish. Or a glen.

The following story took place two generations ago. The stalker of Affric was out on the hills with the boss. The boss was getting married and in a generous mood. I say, how about I treat you and Marie to a week in London, he said to the stalker. I'll cover hotel and food but not drinks. Thinking – a Highland gillie in London may not eat much but he'll go on a bender! London? The stalker wasn't sure but Marie would love it. Aye, why not.

'And off they went. Came back and a week later, they're on the hill again. Had a good time in London? Aye, said the stalker. Good, said the boss, but Christ your food bill was something else. What *did* you and Marie eat down there?'

The stalker looked surprised. Och, just the same as here, he said. Venison, salmon and grouse.

But the days of plentiful salmon are gone. The feeling of loss is under the skin. We can't shed it. I hang around Ali who sits on the banks and smokes roll-ups. He has aged and grown even thinner. He doesn't have a rod because his role is to chaperone the one with a rod. I haven't got a rod either. We take in the light rippling in the water and the water rippling in the air, the mossed magical forest, the holes made in the birches by woodpeckers, and wait for nothing in particular. Fishing is just an excuse to hang out in places you love and remember people who are gone, not moving for hours, and everything solid dissolves. There is no form, just water.

'When I stand in the river, I forget everything. Even my own name,' big guy says. 'It's wonderful.'

On the Farrar, even salmon sorrow dissolves. You are just grateful to be here.

Driving slowly between pools in the afternoon, a car stops with another gillie and client, and the two pros chat. The other guy is setting himself up in the area but doesn't know the river. His sallow-faced client sits fully tweeded, eyes behind sunglasses and ready to be disappointed. Gillies don't choose who they spend the day with, it's like all the care professions.

'Tails are the places today,' Ali advises him gently. 'For

every ten fish, you'll get seven from the tail.' Some gillies are competitive but the folk of the glen have a habit of solidarity.

'Yesterday his client was swept down the river and he had to go retrieve his line.'

That was when the Hydro stopped generating and suddenly released the water, taking the inexperienced by surprise. This happened to Rose the biologist once. She was on a river island at the confluence, taking a sample of substrate from the riverbed. Substrate is made up of sand and silt (that's the finest), gravel, pebble, cobble (fist-sized) and boulder (head-sized). In a natural river, the substrate moves around and creates a healthy spawning habitat. But in a Hydro-controlled river, the substrate doesn't behave normally. It doesn't move around and the riverbed becomes a monoculture. No species thrives in a monoculture. Rose found healthy substrate above Monar dam and deficient substrate everywhere below the dam. You talk about fish to fish people, Rose said to me when I met her, but we need healthy substrate for *everything*. Bugs, insects, vertebrates and invertebrates.

How to fix it? Rose has an idea to use the healthy substrate above the dam. But this is a nightmare to negotiate with all the players: the anglers, some of whom are resistant to change as a matter of principle, the fishing syndicate, the landowners, and above all – the energy company who control the dam and don't care about substrate, people or fish. She would have to convince them to change their flow regime for a while. And everybody is territorial.

'We're on a trajectory,' Rose summed up. 'This means the salmon is not totally screwed, but if we want to have any left in the future, we must act now.'

The dams wiped out five strands of salmon. This is the last strand.

Anyway, Rose was on this tiny island when they started generating and the level suddenly rose. She'd waded to the island and now she couldn't get back. No boat could fetch her because of the rapids. What to do? She called Chris and he thought: the only way is to lower the level. But the dams are remote-controlled from 200 miles to the south, and no employee of the energy company who physically enters the glen has any control over the dams. In the end, Chris called the control room at their central offices and said: Hello, we have a pregnant lady on an island. Rose waited. They were pretty quick. In an hour, the level of the water dropped and she waded across.

Splashes, silver flashes in the water. Did you see that?

Yes! We jump to our feet. But the salmon escapes, a darting silhouette. Seven times before lunch and they can't catch a single one. They are frustrated to the point of tears, but at least there are salmon making it upriver.

It's two dams and two power stations they have to get past, to reach these first beats of the Farrar. Then another two dams here.

'Salmon are hardy and adventurous. Trout tend to be born, live and die in the same stretch of river, if they're happy with the food.'

In the afternoon, we go to Bob's Pool and I sit on a mossy rock – all rocks are mossy here – and watch them walk to a good spot, gillie holding guest's elbow for support. It turns out that big guy is a professional fishing instructor, he doesn't need a gillie at all – but it's a friendship. Shadows dart in the low water.

'All the fish see is movement and silhouettes,' big guy explains and shows me his cherished tartan fold where he keeps the tackle. They're feathered and the colours of the rainbow.

Red and orange in autumn. In May it's black and yellow. It's to do with how the salmon perceive colour. These colours attract them. We are silhouettes to them and they to us. How weird we must look, lumpy and amorphous above the water. Glasan, beings from another dimension.

The guys are obsessed with tackle. The tackle outnumber the fish. They change tackle, change pool, but the salmon are elusive.

Every day is the same but different. It's not really about catching fish. It's a vigil. Slowly, up and down the five miles of road with the ten pools.

Did you?

Shake of head. Did you?

Seven.

Any caught?

None.

That's worse than me. I only saw two.

Beautiful though.

How was the Gate Pool?

Dismal.

Sigh.

The water is stolen by the Hydro and the salmon are stolen by the giant trawlers at sea. And those with big stakes in the energy industry and the sea-fishing industry are rich enough to buy a glen like this and not even live in it.

'Humans are taking and not putting anything back,' Ali sums up.

Crazy that in Chris's youth, salmon were so plentiful that they would send fresh salmon as a gift to friends, placed on ice in wicker baskets and labelled on the sleeper train from Inverness to a smart address in London. Salmon were also boiled in cauldrons and sent south. Lots of exquisite things were despatched to London in large quantities. Rabbits, caught by local boys for the rabbit trapper, who packed them in hampers and sent them south by train; sixpence the pair for the boys, and fur collars for ladies. Foxes, caught alive in the glens and dispatched south – for hunts with hounds by those ladies' husbands. Many things were grown and nurtured in the glen, then harvested, shot to smithereens, processed, fed into something out of sight that is powering much, much more than kettles, never to be seen again.

Then the gillie goes home to tend to his father and daughter, throw a peat cake on the fire, reheat yesterday's stew, and watch the terrible news. At eight in the morning he is back in his maroon car. The pharmaceuticals guy has now given his line to the teenager, who by day seven will be an angler. But without fish. This is his inheritance.

I rummage in the forest to keep warm. My God, the forest is full of ruins! The mossed-up knolls and piles I thought were natural are the remains of the disappeared. And why is this Bob's Pool? Because this here is Bob's Hoosie. It's the only hoosie like this along the road, boarded up but spirited, like someone left a moment ago. Actually the last resident left over a century ago and that was the last river watchman.

I try to imagine this glen in the Middle Ages. Runrigs, mixed forest, and animals grazing upland. Cattle, goats, sheep. Before the river was dammed and became 'false', says Ali.

'This was cattle country. If they saw it today, the people of Farrar would recognise the south side but not the north side.'

The south side is the Scots pines, they haven't changed. The north side would have been pasture with some woods, but not so much birch. And wildflowers in May, bluebells, orchids. Then the cattle came and grazed, and that spurred on re-growth next season. When they're in scale with the land, grazing animals encourage diversity. It is when they stop grazing that one or two invasive species take hold. Like bracken. Bracken used to be kept down by grazing cattle, horse trampling, and cutting by hand. Where bracken spreads, nothing else grows. A bard saw it during the Clearances:

'The land of our love lies under bracken and heather,
Every plain and every field is untilled.'

Modern settlers in the Highlands like the *majestic emptiness*. It makes them feel like pioneers. The locals run away from it, it makes them feel like orphans. One year, Ali was fishing with a guest when two guys pulled over and came out. A big Pakistani guy and a smaller one, no hands.

No hands?

'Aye. I saw at once there was something fishy. Big guy sees our rods and asks: Where can I buy fish?

'In Tesco, I says.'

Ali sent them back to the gate where Heather's nose was already twitching. Phone calls were made to the police who said: Yep, we're waiting for the other two, they're setting up camp in Glen Affric. Ali called his friend, Steve the stalker of Affric, and Steve said: seen them.

Two army snipers were despatched and waited for them on two opposite hills. Four men were arrested on terrorist charges. Poor handless guy.

'The world's worst explosives maker,' Ali concluded.

Why did the wannabe terrorists set up their training ground in Glen Affric? Because they came from the south and thought the Highlands were *empty*.

But it's a false emptiness. To go with the false river. Not quite itself.

Ali shows me the 'stalker's eye'. When you don't have binoculars, you make a circle with your fingers round one eye and focus it, like an eagle's eye.

To see the country behind the country.

Drizzle. Movement and silhouettes in the forest. I tear off dripping resin from a pine and chew it like gum. The bramble is plentiful this year, which heralds a healthy cold winter. I walk and timelines appear like electricity lines. I see them the way people see when they take psychedelics, but here the glen is the drug. I long to hop onto a timeline where there is no wounding. This constant wounding of nature. I long to speak with animals and gods, for the whole world to become more like Strathfarrar and less like a quarry. This glen heals. That's why people fall under its spell and stand at the altar of the river pretending to fish.

I dream a lot in the wood-clad rooms under the wool blankets. I dream of an emerald river. It's wild like a waterfall but horizontal, and runs above the Earth like another dimension, emptying into a boundless sea. It's the river of paradise! I know it at once, the river of life eternal. It is peace itself and I am elated to be shown a glimpse of it, it is incredible, incredible.

The fifteenth of October, a solemn date in the glen's calendar because it's the last day of the fishing season. A day of goodbyes. I pick bog myrtle from a field. It's a midge repellent when you rub it on your skin. And I cut some amadou, the solid fungus with a white underside that grows on birches and that Aria makes into immune-boosting tea. Here it's traditionally used by the folk as a knife-sharpener. Or you cut a little square and stick your fly in it. Or you dry it and use it as fire kindling.

Ali informs us that a stag mounts a hind for five seconds, which even by Highland standards is short, and before he finishes his sentence a snow cloud wraps the purple-brown peak behind him. It's winter.

Rebecca and some helpers come to close the chalets.

November. Another year. The chalets have closed for the winter, just one left open for me. No rut, no fishing and no neighbours except Chris and Rebecca in the big white house across the field. It used to be two houses and the young dam engineers lived there with their families. Then it was turned into a single house, and Chris and Rebecca moved in. It's lonely on this side of the gate. Rebecca keeps busy with the chalets, Chris with his projects around the fishing board and deer management, and somehow they hold the whole thing together. Over the years, Chris has walked every inch of the land with the dogs. And he found over twenty ancient sites of special interest – duns, hut circles, field systems, round houses, remains of bobbin mills (bobbins were made from birch), graphite and lead mines, and things he could not identify, and nobody else could either. It's good to have a few mysteries left.

In their house, Chris is pulling books from shelves.

'Red deer. Very different from roe deer and the sika deer imported from Japan. Do you have this one about the dam builders? Now, fishing.'

Rebecca: 'She is not interested in fishing!'

'Well, she might become interested. Wait till you see the river in spring and summer! Have you seen the orchids?'

Rebecca and Chris raised three children here and now it's just the two of them. Winters are long. The Aga is always on and there is soup for friends, long-standing guests of the chalets who come for drinks at the end of their week, and today – me and Ali sitting at the kitchen table. We go for a walk upriver, to inspect the alder. Winter is a season for maintenance work and Ali wants to cut some alder because it grows fast and congests the pools. Chris agrees. Whatever it takes to help the salmon. It's a fine balance – between doing something and doing nothing.

If I had Chris and Rebecca's responsibility to make decisions about the land, I'd lose my sleep. They are used to it. But what is about to hit the glen is a first in two generations: an upgrade of many miles of electricity line, an enlargement of transformer stations and – who knows what else is up for enlargement.

'Two, three years of upheaval, then back to normal.' Chris is a believer in normality. But Rebecca worries about the chalets, the fishing, the deer farm, and their neighbours at the entrance. How will the crash of industry affect all their lives? A new access road will go through the hills. A parking lot for industry vehicles, plus buses, toilets, helicopters, and the sound of drilling in the hills.

Chris shows us birches with bark stripped back and blackened like black rot by caterpillars of the goat moth, Britain's heaviest moth. The larvae smell goaty, hence the name. The goat moth is disappearing from Britain, but for the goat moth to like it in this glen says a lot about the purity of this place.

'We have everything here,' Chris says. He is the kind of person who stops the car to let a goat caterpillar cross the road. 'But there's something I haven't figured out all these years. Where did the people of Strathfarrar bury their dead?'

There are no burial grounds, no graves, and no churches past the gate.

'Coffin roads,' Ali says. 'Must have carried them down to Struy.'

Chris is not convinced. It's a long way to go. But coffin roads were long. Long and steep like drover's and stalker's paths. In fact, they were the same paths. In highland communities, the same trails were made by the same people but in different roles. Today you're a deer stalker. Tomorrow you carry your beloved in a coffin.

On the kitchen table are night-sky pages from a newspaper. The stars are clear and near in the absence of electric lights, and stargazing is a way to spend winter evenings. Now Chris rushes in with his toolbox and fingerless gloves after fixing the coin meter in my chalet and produces a tin of baked beans to complement Rebecca's home-made soup. Ali shakes his head in mock despair: 'I'll never get the Brits,' and explains why his cooking is better. Yes but for all your vaunted Highland hospitality you've not invited me into your house once!

'That's because I have a father who won't come downstairs and a daughter who won't go upstairs, a cat in the living room and budgies in the kitchen.'

Chris puts the unwanted beans away. We eat beetroot soup and the snow falls.

The birches have shed their leaf and it's at their feet, they are naked.

That purple of birch against a cold-blue sky and rust-orange bracken, I can't write it. The river is dark as graphite. The same must have occurred to some opportunist two centuries ago, because one of Britain's three graphite mines was opened here and five tons of graphite were extracted before it was abandoned. Bella runs up the mound-like hills inside the birch forest which makes me notice their dun-like shape more. Who lived here, what did their laughter sound like?

The men-shaped trees fallen on the forest floor face-down

have not moved. The deer stalkers are out on the hills, on both sides of the river. I know them all now, but it's still weird to hear gunshots and to not see them.

Bella and I walk to my ritual first stop: the Culligran power station underground. The reliable purr of the generators, the churning dark depths of the river in this deepest place where round concrete columns were built in the water to slow the released flow from overboiling. The gate of the underground power station is open! A light is on. I enter with Bella. I know that at the end of the tunnel is the sunken machine hall. We advance. The rock walls of the tunnel are slimy with dripping water. It's the inner flesh of the hill, dynamited with tons of explosives. Voices echo in the far depths. I've never been this far inside.

The Hydro threw thousands of men at these projects, working around the clock at record speed, spurring them on with big bonuses. The tunnellers worked twelve-hour shifts. Sometimes, they worked a second shift outside, and even a third shift, with breaks only at mealtimes – that's thirty-six hours. Because the money was so good. 'You were in darkness all the time with a dim light,' recalled a local tunneller. Once, he and a workmate went into the tunnel on a Saturday morning and emerged on Sunday afternoon: 'like coming from hell into paradise.' Tunnellers were called tunnel tigers.

Some tunnels, but not this one, were concreted, and the concreting shift was a never-ending one, fresh workers taking over from the previous ones because they couldn't have the concrete setting inside the pumps.

The dark slimy rock drips. It's warm, like in the belly of a whale.

One foggy day, a tunnel tiger was walking to work. Over the hill came a stranger. 'Don't go,' the stranger said and vanished. The man heeded the advice. That day, a tunnel collapsed and his workmates were killed. There is no memorial for them. This tunnel is it. They died so we can *boil our kettles*. I can see how their shattered bodies were carried out by their comrades and lined up in the daylight and covered with tarpaulin. A prayer said, caps removed from dusty heads, a stifled sob.

Don't go. Don't do it. Leave things alone. Thus speaks the land.

The land sends us messages all the time. But we have gone blind and deaf. We have lost our senses. How many wars could be avoided if a higher voice is heeded instead of the low voice? Before the campaign against the English that ended in the catastrophic Battle of Flodden, King James IV went to pray at a kirk of St Michael. Inside the kirk, a stranger in a blue cape appeared and told the king he was bringing a message from his (the stranger's) mother, and the message was: *Don't do it, don't go.* The blue man made a disturbing impression on the king but he overrode the warning, as he overrode other dire omens — his tent being covered in bloody dew — and he led 10,000 men to slaughter. Legend says that the sole Scottish survivor walked back to Edinburgh.

Voices are getting closer, laughter. Everything drips and echoes, the electric light is bleary. It's eerie, not seeing anyone attached to the voices. I don't want to meet the workers because like Carrie, they might give me a row instead of a greeting. And they'll get a fright seeing me. During the construction of the tunnels, it was unlucky to see a woman in a tunnel — she might be a banshee, a spirit woman. Bella finds a dead bird. Birds get trapped in the tunnels and die. She keeps checking with me: what are we doing in this place? We turn back and when we emerge, white fog is filling the glen like gas.

On Sunday, no vehicles of the energy company enter the glen. No trade cars. Nobody, and the fog doesn't lift for two days.

The cold damp penetrates all, like an unwanted thought. The birches are skeletons in the fog, trying to tell me something. I lie with the ticking coin machine, cover myself in wool blankets, and dream of the end of the world. I dream of children being taken out of a war-torn building and laid out on the street by soldiers. I see their little faces close up. The soldiers bringing them out are the same soldiers that bombed them. Tick-tock, the war machine must keep ticking over, you can't let your weapons factory go out. The children are wounded and shell-shocked, some are dead. I wake up and weep in the white fog, and the birches weep with me.

In the morning, a hind visits, small and brown-eyed like a child. She is not put out by Bella's barks. Chris and Rebecca visit too, to check that I'm okay and to refill the bird feeders. It's all movement and silhouettes in the fog. I make a pot of soup too big for the fridge and leave it on the table outside. In the morning I find it on the bench. The key turns up on the wrong side of the door. Once or twice, I swear I see a wispy figure in the woods from the corner of my eye, gliding out of view with long birch hair. The glaistig!

The glaistig is a grey-green woman who lives in this world and in the other. A sort of banshee, but the banshee is wild and the glaistig dwells near humans. When she likes you, she gets playful. The folklorist and Gaelic church minister John Campbell tells of a glaistig that haunted a house in Strathglass. She was never seen, only heard at night. She'd put away the dishes and rearrange the furniture. Once, a hired shepherd came and the glaistig took a shine to him. She'd pull down his cover at night and chuckle like this: *Hí, hí, hí.*

Her cackle would be heard long ahead of a marriage or birth. She'd take the animals out to pasture and if you were a shepherd, you'd better be on good terms with her or your calves could stop suckling. If you were a weaving woman, you'd better take the whorl off your loom, or she'd wear it out at night, weaving her otherworldly cloth. Before the tenants of a house moved, before a funeral, before a house was demolished or flooded by appointment, she'd utter a cry of lament. We keep company – the glaistig, Bella and the hind. The hind has made a bed in the bracken. I hope she stays close to us and doesn't wander to the hilltop and get shot by Dougal.

When the fog lifts, she vanishes in the birches. The sun rises quickly and sets quickly, with six hours of light. After midday, the hilltops are illuminated but you walk in shadow. River, loch, moor. Woad blue, charcoal grey, sea purple and pine greenblack. You could eat the colours or paint with them. But it's the glen that has painted you and draws you further into its moving picture. Once you're out in the exposed monotony of the Middle glen, you begin to hear a voice, thin and windy, just a note away from *hí, hí, hí,* rising from some hinterland you are yet to reach. The banshee of Strathfarrar is calling you.

You walk past Carrie's locked gate, the crystal palace of the far hills rings in the cold sun. They called it Glen Strathfarrar by mistake, but now you see that this place is so great, it really is a glen *and* a strath.

The sun is leaving fast and you follow it to the west as if you'll catch it. It is the Strathfarrar syndrome. You follow the light though there is nothing out there except dams. No comfort, no friends and no end. But the land beckons and you walk for the land. The land saves you from despair.

The Keepers

The Gate Keeper

The phone rings. Heather picks up.

'Gate house! Right-oh.'

She puts the receiver down. Not long before the end of October, when she retires. And get some peace in my dotage, she smirks. They're looking for a small place to rent downstream in the Monks' Place. Too old for a mortgage. Will they miss the Farrar?

'I haven't actually seen much of it in the last twenty years.' She puts two mugs of tea on the kitchen table and we sit down. 'Coz I've been on this side of the gate, haven't I. And once the doorbell goes at 9 a.m., that's me tied to the gate for the day.'

Closing time is 6 p.m., but it's more like 8 when the last visitors exit the glen.

'We used to see the glen more before we became keepers,' adds Fred, who comes in and out the door. He is stocky and has a cemented face that can crack into a smile so full of fun it makes you wonder.

In my chalet is a visitors' book that goes back to the first days, and among the names are Heather and Fred. They'd come up for a week's holiday. She worked in a care home and Fred was a joiner. Heather was born in Aberdeen but there were no jobs and her parents moved to Yorkshire where her father found work as an oil engineer – ironic, seeing the oil boom of Aberdeen started soon after. Heather grew up with a Yorkshire accent but something pulled her back to Scotland until one day, she and Fred made the decision to move here. The keepers of the castle across the road had found them a cottage to buy.

The castle looks medieval and it is: built in the thirteenth century by a clan that later married into another clan who took over. With help from King James IV, the family came into possession of vast territories in the early sixteenth century and held on to them until it couldn't. In the 1930s the castle estate became property of a baron and baroness of Swiss-Belarusian origin who had it for thirty years. When he died, she sold it and moved downstream. It went to a couple from the south – industrialist (him) and politician (her) who passed it on to their son. The son had many Bentleys and few friends. He would come into Tony's gallery and demand to put red dots on paintings but wouldn't pay for them. He reminded me of the film *La Grande Bouffe*. Out of all inheritors of unearned wealth in the glen, he best embodied the paradox of owning without belonging.

'We were all set to make the downpayment and move in, and on the last day that shit turns up and says, I'm going to exercise my right of pre-emption and hang on to the house. Just because I can.'

Thus made homeless, Heather and Fred were figuring out their next move when a vacancy came up. The gate keepers of Strathfarrar were leaving. Heather and Fred decided to go for it. They moved into the keepers' cottage with the soft river behind and the hard hills in front, and for the next twenty years made it their home. Under her acerbic eye, the glen's flow of traffic was regulated. And so were relationship dynamics with the various players whose roles are archetypally fixed. Keeper, under-keeper, estate owner. Tradesman, Hydro worker. Hiker, tourist-but-not-hiker, local visitor. Chalet guest, friends, family. Over time, some of the categories fused. The couple took their holidays between November and March when the glen is closed to drivers.

'We keep up with the seasons. The lambing. The fishing. The chalets. And the stalking.'

Cars stop before the gate, someone comes out. Heather knows who they are — and if not, what category they fall into, and I learn to read them too. The body language around the gate gives away their relationship with the glen. Residents and frequent visitors are purposeful. This is the keepers, under-keepers, regular tradesmen and the employees of the energy giant who come and go every day, in the lead-up to the infrastructure upgrade. They all have their own padlock codes.

'Here comes Carrie.'

She is going out. All puffer jacket and platinum jewellery, she pushes the gate open, clicks her padlock shut, and her face.

A man walks up to the gate and reads the sign.

Heather scans him. 'Tourist but not hiker. He'll go back to the car park, drive up to the gate and ring the bell.'

This is what happens. Hikers and especially Munro-baggers are the keenest. They arrive at seven in the morning, sit drinking coffee in the parking space made to avoid a queue of cars, and wait till Heather opens the gate.

Two young hikers come up to the gate, walking poles in hands. They are walking in, so she doesn't need to open the gate. Isn't it too late to go hiking? In two hours it'll be dark. Heather shrugs: she is responsible for those who drive in. But she'll keep an eye out for this couple and if they don't show up by evening, she'll make a phone call to the Middle estate – that's Carrie. Seen two hikers with poles?

Some climbers prefer to come in winter for the extra challenge, and if you belong to the mountaineering association you are given a padlock code. But winters are dangerous and with no gate keeper to keep an eye – well, it is like everywhere else hardened hikers go. Today, a helicopter had us looking up.

'Affric estate guests?' They like to visit in helicopters.

'Nope, mountain rescue,' said Heather.

Hikers are the main worry. There have been times, like when a Dutch couple came to climb but he broke his leg on top of a hill and his girlfriend walked back to the gate, where Heather gave her tea and a tranquiliser and called mountain rescue. The weather worsened and it took hours to retrieve the man with the broken leg. Whenever a car of hikers went in, she'd wait for them to come out and if they were late, she'd wonder: have they come out and I missed them, have they had an accident, should I call emergency services?

There have only been five helicopter emergencies in the glen in all her twenty years, and one death. A fisherman had a heart attack on the river. His hat was snatched by the current and found a year later by Willie the gillie downstream. He had come full circle: his ancestors were from this glen and he was drawn back unto death.

Usually though, it is burst tyres and Heather gets a call from the keepers at one of the estates in-glen: we've a recovery vehicle coming through.

'You learn to smell trouble. I know when something's off and when to leave it alone.'

The gate keeper's house is a curiosities cabinet, an observation post, an emergency room and a depot. The postie drives to the last address, which is the two houses past Monar dam. Except in winter when the road is an ice lane and the gate keepers' house becomes a post office. Heather makes banana cake for the postie, his favourite. It's Highland tradition. Because distances are great, you feed the postie. The postie told me that some of his people are so isolated, he is the only person they see for weeks. He once found a guy on the floor, his dog yapping in distress. The postie called an ambulance, put the kettle on and waited with the stricken man.

'Ach, I've worked all me life, since I was seventeen,' Heather says. 'In a pet-food factory. Then in the old folks' home. This is the easiest job I've had, physically. But not mentally.'

You need a lot of patience.

'Worn thin over the years. And a sense of humour.'

To deal with the entitled, the hostile and the bizarre. Her worst experience has been with English-haters, who arrive, hear her accent, and see red: I'm not gonna have some English bitch tell me when I can come and go!

'I say: my maiden name is Wallace. As in William Wallace!'

But it's no use. It's also that the right to roam is ingrained in Scotland and a locked gate raises hackles. The right to roam is enshrined in law and gives you the right to walk anywhere in the country, as long as it is respectful. But this is not the same as motorised access.

'I spend a lot of time appeasing people. People need appeasing.'

More insiders come and go, open the gate, close the gate, click of the padlock. Today is quiet. You never know what kind of day it'll be – like in a shop, Heather says, except nothing is for sale. Visitors have asked: why don't you charge an entrance fee? They're all American.

A cross-stitch of animals is draped over an easel. It's how she passes the time and calms her nerves, and it's easy to pick up again when interrupted by the doorbell.

A whistle rises from the hills across.

'Wind's getting up.'

We stand at the window. It frames a painterly scene: red hinds in the field and brown hills behind them. The scene is flushed with sunset and dusted with snow. The light is never still. The light gives you the impression that the hills are gliding past you and other hills come into view all the time.

The Land Keeper

Dougal's white-washed cottage sits on a knoll near the entrance to Strathfarrar. He steps out the front door like a giant from a broch. When the great warriors who are not dead but merely sleeping awaken, the Highlanders will be a nation once again – and they will look like Dougal.

Dougal is usually seen in a tractor, moving sheep from one field to another, loading and unloading hay bales, or carrying newborn lambs, levelling ground, shoring up soil, splitting logs, mending fences, building channels against flooding, or bringing back the body of a deer in the back of the Argocat. Lambs follow him around. There are 300 sheep on the farm, freely grazing in the fields and hills. That means come spring time, he expects around 400 lambs — because of the twins. Twins are tricky, at least the deer don't have twins! In a lifetime of farming he has only seen twin calves once.

'Well, maybe twice.' Dougal doesn't like to say anything unless he is sure. He is that rare thing — a reliable narrator. It comes with being a reliable keeper.

'I was sorry to hear about Susie,' I say. 'You must miss her.'

'Och, it was a shame. I'd gotten used to her, you know. But she ate those rhododendrons and that was the end of it. She was a year old.'

He found her in the hills, tiny and stuck in a grid. He freed her up and let her run on shaky legs, let her find her mother, because wild goats fend for themselves.

'They're incredibly tough, like. They never eat the silage I leave out for the sheep. Even in the snow.'

But he returned the next day to check up on her and saw that she was fading fast — an orphan. He took her home and set her up in the kitchen and reared her with a bottle. Till she got strong enough to munch everything in sight. Rhododendron was a Victorian import in the Highlands. Where you see lots of rhododendron, you know there has been a large sporting estate. It is so invasive, it can't be burned or uprooted. It spreads and poisons the soil for others. The Victorians are gone but the rhododendron remains in the land, the way spilled oil remains in the sea after the oil rigs are decommissioned.

Dougal looks after the Painted Glen that belongs to Chris and Rebecca. What's the busiest season? He shrugs, his hands are idle and awkward on the table covered with a stag-printed cloth. It's hard to say because it just goes from one thing to the next. In winter, he feeds the wild deer in-glen. Deer blocks are kept in Bob's Hoosie. He puts them out for the stags and hinds. It just never stops. Right now it's hind season, which means he and the understalker go up in the hills to cull the agreed number of hinds.

'In the old days, you'd drag them home. We had more snow back then, so it was easy to drag them in the snow.'

The larder is here, a green shed next to the kennels, and this is where the two stalkers 'clean up' and hang the carcasses, ready for the dealer to collect them once a week. That's the wild ones. Then there's the farmed ones, 150 of them in 300 acres, on good ground. That's why they are bigger than the wild deer.

'It's like any animal. You take it from poor ground to good ground, and it flourishes. You move it to poor ground and it pines.'

The red deer of Scotland used to be bigger. When large-scale felling of trees began in the seventeenth century – for ship building and iron-smelting – deer started losing their forests and became exposed to cold wet winters. Then the wolf was exterminated. The people emigrated. The ground became impoverished. Deer numbers soared but the deer pined. The result is smaller deer who compete over pasture and starve to death.

This deer farm is the last of its kind in the area. Chris and Rebecca keep it out of loyalty to how things should be – keep animals when you have land, and they have Dougal's farming expertise. But you can't make any money from farmed deer, too much competition from all the wild venison flooding the market. And hardly any money from sheep.

Deer farms were a thing in the early 1980s. The government tried to encourage folk to rear animals that were not cattle, Dougal remembers. The first deer auction in Britain was held locally. There were subsidies for angora goats for a while too. But it didn't last. There wasn't enough easy money in it. Animals are never easy money.

I admire his yard – the Argocat, the pick-up truck, the tractor, the kennels, the forest path that starts from the back door, the graphite river running through his days. It's a practical life and a beautiful one. You flourish, on good ground like this. You've got the most magical place in the glen!

'Aye. But it's not actually mine. I was born here and my parents lived here all their lives but it's not mine. And when I retire . . . who knows.'

He grins in his unwordly but canny way. He is fourth- or fifth-generation keeper – on both his parents' sides. His father's folk come from Loch Monar and his mother's folk from Loch Ness. Dougal is the only native left in Strathfarrar.

'I don't go away. The longest I've been away is seven days. It just doesn't appeal.'

It's attachment to his glen, but it's also the work. You don't get away when you look after animals. On the archetypal level, he is a holder of the sacred fire. He is wedded to the glen.

'You can get a qualification now . . . how to be keeper. But I just went out with my father and grandfather. That's my qualification.'

Dougal's grandfather was the keeper of the Middle estate before it changed hands from aristocracy to plutocracy. Clan kinship was still alive in the glen. His grandparents lived in the Middle estate with their five boys, two girls and a resident teacher.

'My grandfather wore a kilt in the hills. They were tough then.'

Then came the Second World War. Four of the boys were enlisted, two in the Lovat Scouts. One was killed in

Italy. Another was killed in France. The three survivors became keepers in the same glens as their fathers. Dougal is one of five boys too. The runt of the litter, he smiles, and all the seasons of Farrar pass through him in a single phrase. Whatever happens in the glen, happens to him; in fact he knows it before it happens. He is a barometer. The family are caretakers of the old clan's church on the other side of the river where time passes more slowly. Even after it haemorrhaged nearly to death, this glen is still half Catholic country. Dougal's parents are buried there. To me it's luxury to live in the same countryself as your ancestors, and sometimes I envy people like Dougal. But the downside is that you can't escape the loss. When Dougal was a boy, there were thousands of sheep. Thousands of rabbits. And insects. And children. The Hydro families were still in the glen. He went to school with the Hydro kids, and with the kids of the other keepers. Then the Hydro kids left. The school closed. Dougal and the remaining kids went across the river to a tiny Catholic school run from a house. The old faith is what is left when the old language is gone. Dougal's grandparents spoke Gaelic but by the time he was born, Gaelic was lost.

'Just the odd word we still use, like.'

What a load of trok. And – what a burach! And the place names.

'The way things were named . . . When you know the place and the place knows you, like. When there were people here, every little hill had a name, maybe not on the map but for us it did.'

And all the ruined shielings on top of hills that only he knows.

'They all faced south. A shieling faces south.'

Sheep have always been in his life.

'We're the only ones left with sheep in the glen.'

There are others, but they're hobbyists with indigenous breeds. And indigenous breeds are a hobby because they don't make money. He is right! This is the only sizeable sheep farm in the glen, once a country of sheep. In summer, contractors come to shear the flock and cut the grass and bale it.

'We used to do everything ourselves. Your neighbours come and help out and then you help them out.'

Animals and crops bring people together.

'It was just more fun. There was craic. More like a ceilidh than work. You got on with it, and you were in it together. We had community.'

After a day of hard work, they'd go to the inn or the hotel and someone would pick up the accordion. Or the fiddle.

'There are more houses now than before, in the glen. But you never see anyone!'

Houses don't make a community, just like roundabouts don't make journeys.

The kitchen is tidy and bare. He must cook for himself since his mother died. A geranium sits in a deer-painted pot. The wall clock is an hour ahead. Maybe Dougal waits for the changing of the clocks to naturally catch up with it – because he deals in permanence. When the energy giant arrives to hack an access road through the deer farm, all the heavy vehicles will pass his house. For three, four years. He knows it'll be hard, he knows it'll bring the end of the deer farm, the noise will stress the pregnant sheep and he'll move them across the river.

'We'll have to get on with it. But . . . I don't know.'

Nobody does. What will happen to our precious glen?

'Change just happens, like, whether you want it or not,' Dougal says in his lullaby accent, and out of nowhere I see – I see why this English spoken in these glens is so singsong, so soft and mellow. Because it's infused with the ghost of Gaelic. When you go south, this Highland English vanishes.

Dougal has picked up my geographic thought.

'You go south, say you go to Edinburgh, and you see all this good arable land turned to roads and houses and factories. It's like they don't want farming at all. They don't want animals. They're rewilding arable land. Building on good farmland. To create jobs, they say. But – what doing? And importing lamb from New Zealand across thousands of miles. I don't mean to sound anti-anything. But that's not green. And we could grow everything we need here. We have good ground.'

That we have. Fifty per cent of young Highlanders want to stay, not emigrate to cities. But they need jobs, and more than just any job they need a relationship to something alive. Something from the ground up. Not to be minions in some big corporation that arrives top-down to level their country.

What will happen to animals? Will sheep disappear from the land?

'I'd hope not! But in a way they *have* disappeared. When I was a child there were thousands on the hills. And shepherds, farmers, kids. You know that Brahan Seer prophecy . . .'

Dougal goes into a room and finds the book of the Brahan Prophecies. Confirming that every Highland home has a copy, like a Bible. We find the prophecy:

'The day will come when the sheep will vanish and when a man stumbles on the jaw-bone of a sheep, he won't recognise it.'

But that, too, he takes in his stride. He closes the Prophecies and his hand covers them from view. It's like the book contains his own life. Transparent yet hidden.

I come out of the keeper's broch. The glen road is flooded. Even flooded it's beautiful. And none of this belongs to Dougal. But it doesn't matter. He would keep taking care of it no matter what.

The Memory Keeper

Before the gate was locked, local families lived in the gate house in exchange for doing jobs on the estate, unpaid.

On the other side of the small Struy bridge lives Margaret who grew up in the gate-keeper's house. Margaret is expecting me in her doorway. The stove is lit.

'I'll put the kettle on.'

Her house is so tidy, even the book piles on the table are aligned.

'Now, I don't know that I can help much,' Margaret says in her musical voice, a Highland voice very different from Heather's. We're straight into the heart of the matter – the glen.

'The main change is, there were more people.'

Margaret had lived in the gate keeper's house with her mother, and when she came of age, she worked in the inn.

'But not on Saturdays. On Saturdays, the fellows from the camp came down, and – well. Time to go home. Or in the snug with the other girls.'

The snug was a small room in the inn where the women gathered separately. The builders of Monar dam lived in a makeshift camp deep inside Strathfarrar, in what is today the

Middle estate. There were over a thousand workers sheltered in military-style Nissen huts. The keepers of the Middle estate live in one of the houses built by the Board for their headmen. Nothing is left of the camp. The workers lived as single men during their years in the glen. There were fights over women and gambling. The engineers and managers, on the other hand, had their families with them and enjoyed proper houses, like British Army officers. Eighteen houses for special workers, Margaret recalls. The Board brought their own police – two cops in the camps – and their own industrial chaplains. The cooks were important because food was the only pleasure. But the food varied from camp to camp. Here, many of the cooks, canteen and admin staff were women – locals and displaced persons who'd washed up from Europe.

Then there were the ceilidhs in the community hall before the gate. Margaret riffed on the piano.

'Ach, I wasn't very good.' But she was.

Because so many men stayed in the glen, notices were pinned in the city hospital for nurses and other staff: Saturday dances in Strathglass, free transport.

By the mid 1960s, everyone was gone. The head engineers with their families were posted overseas. Wales, Nigeria – to build more dams.

'Monar was a copy of a bigger dam on the Nile. Or vice-versa,' Margaret says. 'I looked up the big companies from back then, and they are still going but under other names! And much bigger!'

Still going. Building oil rigs, dams, ring roads, turbine blades and artificial cities in the desert. More, more.

'Some say there are community benefits,' Margaret says with doubt. 'Grants.'

Ali the gillie's daughter was put through college with one such grant, while the energy company built a giant storage battery behind her school and two of Ali's friends living next to a transmission tower and unable to move away died young of cancer.

When the Hydro schemes were completed, the glen emptied again. It was in the 1960s that the population of the Highlands reached its lowest of many low points since the Clearances. That's why there was still talk of the *Highland problem*. This offensive phrase was first coined during the Reformation period to tar the Highlands with the accusation of lawlessness and banditry and engineer a negative perception of the north by the south. It has been successful. The phrase took on the hues of each subsequent historic moment, and never was there a moment without a perceived *Highland problem*. Depopulation, lack of jobs and the cultural diminishment in the long wake of the Clearances – that was the real problem of the Highlands. Its perpetrator was empire with its extraction of resources for leisure and profit, and its view of the country as commodity rather than an entity with its own life force.

The last dramatic loss of people before the Hydro had been in the 1920s when a generation of men was wiped out by the First World War, and many of the survivors stayed away because there were no jobs for them. Before that, the Highland Potato Famine (1846–54) had contributed to reducing the people of the glens, not on the scale of the Great Irish Famine, but enough to change the face of the country. Three quarters of the previously self-sustaining crofters in the Highlands and Islands were suddenly without food. Arable land had been given over to sheep. The rotating-crops system of the runrig was almost defunct and in its place was put the enclosure movement which controlled all production. Over-reliance on a single crop (potato) made Highlanders vulnerable to blight, and mass emigration to Canada, Australia and the Lowlands continued, encouraged by the British government and sometimes funded by landlords. The potato recovered but the Highlands didn't.

Fast forward to the 1980s when the Forestry Commission left, and a few years later the power stations went automatic. Thirty families left the inner glen, which half-emptied it. Margaret was born on the eve of the Second World War and grew up without a father because he was at the front. He survived a desert crossing in Egypt where he and his comrades were saved from starvation by locals who gave them dates and water. Returning with malaria and finding no work in the glen, he went to work in Aberdeen and once again, it was just Margaret and her mother. Once a week, her mother received a parcel of clothes to launder and send back. Her mother worked in the hunting lodge, now gone, which belonged to Chris's grandparents. She'd get it ready for when they came up with their half-dozen staff, including a cook, in the familiar master-servant set-up that pretty much made up the local economy. Many Highlanders had become servants to the prosperous Lowlanders. Margaret hadn't seen much of her father when he died of malaria complications at fifty.

The castle is just down the road, and as a girl Margaret's future mother-in-law was a maid there. It was still the seat of the clan chief, the last years of it.

'Two of the ladies took to their beds and never left their rooms. She would bring them trays of food and take their laundry.'

The ailing women of a family in decline. The clan chief once owned 125,000 acres of land here, more elsewhere, and a plantation in Trinidad. By the early 1800s, most of the clansmen were evicted and large tenancies (called tacks) were given to fewer numbers of people. This increased the rental income of the estate threefold – for a while.

We can't see it now, but up across from us there is a hill pass like a carved step in the wall of Maol Bhuidhe, the Yellow Hill.

A band of sheep speculators came over from the Great Glen and said to the clan chief: you gotta clear the land of tenants and get sheep. That's where the money is. That's what the chiefs of neighbouring glens were doing, which is how 20,000 of their people ended up in Canada, while the chiefs cashed in from sheep and held lavish parties for their guests from the south, showing off their sheep walks and deer forests and posing in full clan regalia in their ravaged fiefdoms.

You have to do the same, said the sheep men to the clan chief.

And gullible as most clan chiefs were, he was about to agree – but his daughter the Gaelic speaker climbed out of a window and let the people of the glen know. They came, a thousand of them – to plead with their chief not to sell them out to the sheep men. For they had nowhere to go.

'The chief relented and they carried him up and down the strath in a ceilidh, piper and all.'

But up on the carved step of the hill were the three sheep men on horseback. They'd been run out of the glen this time, and would be the next time too, but the third time it was another clan chief, and the good mother and daughter were gone. And the chief did clear the people from the land. In the first wave, a thousand folk from this strath boarded an emigrant ship. A few years later, the chief's land agent advertised the land to sheep farmers from the Lowlands (6,000 sheep were invited) and another lot of people were forced off this 'once happy but now devastated valley of Strathglass', wrote a witness. In the next purge, half the strath's population was made homeless.

Today, when an energy company wants to evict you or encircles you in an industrial ribbon and state policy backs them and not you, this is called a *compulsory purchase order*. What wretched little bureaucrat makes up these words? In the Clearances, the compulsory purchase order was a sailing ticket to Canada, if you were lucky.

'Well, some chiefs were more humane,' Margaret tries to balance.

But they were few. A bard from Glen Affric called Angus the Blacksmith was forced to board a ship in his old age, and as he stepped on the ladder he uttered a curse:

'May a shroud be spun for the chief who runs after money!'

His curse was fulfilled. Some would call it karma.

The heads of the haemorrhaging clan declined, son after father. The one remembered fondly was the daughter who stood up for her people to the end.

The carved step is a doorway. Drovers and reivers, traders and speculators, bodies in coffins and refugees, Cailleachs and horsemen of the apocalypse came through that pass and didn't close the door so a cold wind still blows through it.

'The biggest change came after the Second World War. Until then, the estates all had farms and gave people work. When a boy or a girl left school, they could find a job locally. And now they leave. However!'

She won't let her sentences end on a downer.

But the crux is this: person and place lost each other. The school closed. The church will close on the last day of the year – hard for Margaret who holds the keys, and whose grandfather-in-law helped build it.

The last ceilidh in the hall was held in the 1960s, then the dam workers left and it was declared unsafe and converted into a house.

And the Affric Hotel? Drovers and shepherds, stalkers, gillies and dam workers, administrators and teachers, travellers, labourers, cooks and crooks swapped news of the world and gossip from the glen, made telephone calls and danced the tango on Saturday nights.

'The Shepherds and Stalkers Dances and the Steak Suppers were so popular that if you hadn't booked – well!'

That was fifty years ago.

And I remember the Glen Affric Hotel in its last year. It was a handsome Art Deco building, always closed. The young woman who owned it couldn't run it, nobody could. It was too large and leaking to bring into the twenty-first century, and she dwelled inside with fifty cats and a horse. Sometimes you walked past and the horse poked his head out of a ground-floor window to say hello. One day the hotel wasn't there anymore. Just a stain in the shape of a legend.

However – Margaret counters brightly, that girl is now looking after horses near Corrimony cairn, where a Norse woman is said to be buried in a crouched position, and to get up and roam at night. Sometimes she, the girl, and maybe the Norse woman too, can be seen walking down the road between glens – one of the last moving people who walk for no reason and sing forgotten songs, followed by cats and dogs, and horses, their hair wild and their clothes unmatched, and are called crazy by the sedentary ones who double-lock their houses. And gates. They sing:

When the yellow's on the broom,
when the yellow's on the broom
Take me on the road again,
when the yellow's on the broom.

'There was one other fellow who walked a lot. Geordie Coat. His grandfather had the Struy Inn. Back then it was an ale house.'

He lived with his mother in a cottar's house, no electricity, just paraffin lamps. Cottars: people without access to land. When his mother died, he moved to a static caravan.

'He used to go round villages in a van, selling mutton. Short, red-faced, wore a raincoat that had never been cleaned. That's why he was Geordie Coat. A loner. But people would pay him to go and find them a good sheep.'

The world needs people who walk and have an eye for a sheep.

Margaret is widowed. Her joiner husband was from an old local family. When I ask about second sight in the glen, she says at once: 'Yes. There were two brothers. They had the sight. My husband had it too. He sat on that couch, and he'd say: in three days' time, there'll be a funeral.'

And there was. A classic of Highland augury is when in the night you hear the banging of nails or the sawing of wood for a coffin shortly before someone dies.

We are so lost in conversation we forget the boiling kettle. Margaret remembers the full names of all her pupils at the local school, their parents' names, and where they went when they left the glen. She remembers the orphans who lived in the glen – boys and girls whose fathers were maimed or killed in one of the two world wars. One woman next door fostered fifty children.

'They had hard lives.'

And Margaret catalogues their names: those who stayed and married here, and those who left for the cities, unable to find a job on a farm. Because the estate farms were already in decline.

Her windows frame the hills across the river on the mysterious, slow-flowing side. The hillside is recently razed of its commercial conifers. They were planted by the forestry men of Cannich when Cannich had the biggest forestry training ground in Scotland.

'They started planting between 1947 and 1949.'

Each time a single crop monopolises the glen, the long-term effect is the same: the native species shrink and diversity dwindles. In time, that crop stops being lucrative. But the land cannot be restored overnight. The weave is torn.

'They've cut them down now, but they're replanting with broad-leaved trees.'

That's good, we agree.

'Monar forest was one of the first to be felled.'

I thought she meant by the dam builders. But she meant the first big felling. In 1791.

'Then Cannich in the early 1800s.'

The glens were stripped of their forests and people at the same time. The whole of Strathfarrar was given over to two lairds from the same clan. They wanted to bring in sheep farmers from the Lowlands.

'The forest of Monar is fit for 4,000 to 5,000 sheep,' in a 1792 newspaper advertisement. The trees were felled but the word *forest* remained in the land, like a ghost. If you see *deer forest* on a map, it tells you that once there was a native forest here. Then the forest was cut to make way for something more useful.

In addition to Cheviot sheep for wool, some crops could be grown in Monar: wheat, broad clover, lint. Lint? Hard to imagine flax growing in this exposed terrain but maybe it did. For the linen industry. And the sheep – for the meat and wool industry. A few decades later, the dominion of the Big White

Sheep was over, and the glen fell into sporting estates. But all along there were people on the land, subsisting.

'Strathfarrar had sixty smokes. My father-in-law remembered them.'

One in the community had the task of counting the chimney smokes every few days. If a smoke had gone out, something was wrong in that house.

In what is now Margaret's garden used to be the blacksmith (her father-in-law), the cobbler, a horse stable, and then a petrol pump with a shop operated by Margaret's mother-in-law, a formidable woman from whom Chris and his sister at 'the big house' came to buy sweeties, with trepidation. It was a rest-point for travellers. Carriages and horse riders would stop here to have their horses re-shoed by the smiddy. Men refreshed themselves at the inn, and ladies at the comfort spot in the field backed up by a drystone dyke, behind Margaret's house. Soon after the glen was electrified, an electrical fault sparked a fire and everything went up in flames, doused by the petrol pump – the blacksmith's, the cobbler's, the stables, the house.

Such things happened in the early days of electricity. The inexperienced sparkies would install new kits in old houses, but sometimes connected the wrong wires or didn't connect them. People were used to paraffin lamps and candles, and there was the glowing hearth. The hearth was the heart of the ceilidh. The electric arrived and the ceilidh left the glen.

'Now, you must visit the lead mine,' Margaret suggests. 'The lead had a trace of silver in it. It was used for bullets. It was sent down the glen, then shipped south, who knows where. Aha.'

Who knows where those bullets were taken and who they killed in the war that never ended, those bullets made from the lead of the glen, extracted by men of the glen who died young or emigrated to the new world only to be enlisted in the world wars and die in Gallipoli or France, and sometimes came back to die here. Like the sister of the blacksmith brothers who went to Saskatchewan and were very successful in the logging business – that is, extracting the indigenous forests and people of Canada just as they and their forests had been extracted – yes, the sister came back to die in her native glen.

If you can't live here, at least you can die here.

The names of her brothers are engraved in a small glass pane at the back of the Giusachan Hotel that's closed. That is where the lead bullets with a silver trace went and that is how they came back to the glen.

Aha, Margaret nods. 'It's a shame I have this pain or I'd come with you.'

So I go alone, on a snowy January morning. The track starts behind her house but it's lost in the snow. A mile and a half, it's quite a trek into the hills. This is still Strathfarrar but on this side of the river it's rougher terrain. Even in summer. You go past a silage tower that always looks like it's weeping. Past some pigs who forage happily. Past a static caravan with a young woman and her horse. She helps the estate keeper – a cheerful guy with a moody brother who is under-keeper of the Middle estate. After that, all landmarks are gone. I wade through creaky snow. The silence is like an afterworld. I begin to feel like the last woman on Earth. A familiar feeling. How often have I walked remote trails like this, and not unhappily. You find companions, at least for a while. I love pushing through snow or water, or any wilderness, getting lost in a white desert. It terrifies me and enraptures me. But sometimes you don't know when to stop. The concealed entrance to the lead mine is hard to find and I am crazy to look for it in the snow. It goes 600 metres into the hill. Is this it?

The mines were abandoned not long after they were dug. Just like all the other failed ventures that squeeze blood out of the land.

Soon I'll be frozen and lost and it would be a relief, to be gone from this beauty and pain. I've been pushing through the snow with some force. Where will I go if I leave the Crossing Place? The thought of leaving Tony and the Highlands is bleaker than death. It makes the world into a wasteland. Without Tony I am anchorless. And I've been having homeless dreams lately. Somewhere in a town with a suitcase, looking for a room. It's an old refugee dream. I've moved houses many times, I've had many separations and new beginnings. I sit in the snow for a while. I begin to drift.

Then I wrench myself from it and turn back to the chimney smokes and the rest of my life.

One, two, three, I count the smokes and my faith returns and I cheer myself by cackling like a banshee: *hí, hí, hí*. I've learned the trick of cheering myself from Tony, who regulates his sadness by getting on with things like planting the next salads, or doing something for an artist. Or just going – *hí, hí, hí*.

I report back to Margaret who takes one look at me and puts the kettle on. Nothing can shock her. We sip sugary black tea by the lit fire and gaze at the snowy hills.

Seventy years after the dam builders left and the community hall closed, men would ring the bell of the gate keeper's house and Heather's face would greet them. Old men with their grown-up children, come to show their life's work: Monar dam, Culligran power station. With mixed feelings.

Pride, nostalgia, doubt, worry. 'They're not looking after things properly!' fretted an engineer. 'They want to upgrade everything, but they should look after what we built.'

Upgrade means replacement or enlargement, which means disposing of the old when it's able-bodied. Like the dams, the old electricity lines and the Hydro power stations. Because there's no profit in maintenance. Caring for something is not lucrative. It is merely – sustainable.

'Oh yes,' Margaret would say down the phone line, when Heather called to tell her: we've got visitors from the Hydro days. 'That would be the Baxters. I'll put the kettle on.'

The dam engineer and his family would cross the little bridge over the Farrar, and there would be Margaret standing in the doorway, stove lit and photo albums ready, her face bright and remembering.

At Heather's farewell party, Chris and Rebecca present her with a golden padlock that makes everybody laugh. The party is held in the only gathering place left in the mother glen – the Cnoc Hotel, across from the castle. The Cnoc, like the inn, changes hands every few years, business is seasonal, people move on, others come and try their luck but the dream gives way to reality. The Cnoc has just been taken over by a young couple, good news.

It's a long building on a *cnoc* (mound), the forest at its back and the river at its feet. Once it was part of the castle estate. Here the factor decided on legal matters, held executions and issued tenants with tax and eviction notices. In the 1980s it was converted to a hotel. And in the forest of rhododendrons is a spooky ruined manse (last inhabited in 1966, Margaret notes, and put up for sale to no avail). Tony and I broke in once, but some ruins are best left alone. Ghosts and hedgehogs need somewhere too. And local kids grew up being told by their mothers: don't go to the manse, the green lady will get you!

A green lady here, a Morag of the spring there, a keeper on every riverbend – thank God a few folk are still around.

The bar is filled to bursting. It's a struy of people rarely seen together because they live far apart, along tributaries and schisms, but most of all – because this is the only place left for ceilidhs. Garrulous faces and introverted faces. Margaret is sleek in a knitted dress, the postie and his wife the deaf teacher are here, and the Polish family that helps Rebecca with the chalets. Rose the river biologist is here with her girlfriend. Rose is about to give birth and the hospital is thirty miles away, but she's been stranded on an island before.

And the keepers in their chequered shirts, thick trousers and wind-burnt faces. The keepers of the castle are here – that's Dougal's brother and his wife. The castle owner with the Bentleys died, the inheritors are absent, but the keepers are holding the fort. Laughing Lachlan the handyman too. He's been in the grounds for thirty years doing odd jobs and fixing the glen's broken appliances. His workshop is inside a gloomy stone byre full of lawnmowers, engines and chainsaws. It's where the cattle were kept when this was a working farm under the baron and baroness, and there were grazing animals on each side of the river.

If you visit Lachlan in winter, figure-skating your way over the river of ice that leads to the castle cottages, with fish-like leaves and coral-like branches trapped inside it, you'll go up some stairs past a just-delivered box of wine, past three monkey sculptures (hear no evil, see no evil, speak no evil), and knock on a steel door.

'Come in, I've been expecting you!' and you'll find him

with an ashtray of fags, cat Google by his side. The carburettor on the coffee table drips oil onto a newspaper spread over an old Afghan rug. Paintings and arty photographs on the wall, a bohemian scene. His eyes are kind and watery.

'Sit in that chair and throw a stick in the fire, will you? Hahaha.'

A cough-cackle. He'll fix the hopeless cases and charge too little. Forever googling obscure parts. Lachlan used to be a forester but injured his back and became a handyman in the castle grounds, in this flat with hand-painted wallpaper and cupboards that open into secret stairways. How come all foresters get injuries?

'It's the angle you hold the saw, is what does it.'

It's cold in the flat. He's looked at installing air pumps but he's a tenant. He could be booted out any time.

'Och, I had a soft spot for old Robbie,' he says of the late castle owner.

'You must be the only one.'

'Hahaha, you've got that in one. Old Robbie liked his orange juice in the morning full of vodka.'

Laughing Lachlan has seen different owners, factors, guests and farming tenants. The rent hasn't gone up, a small mercy. Has it really been thirty years?

The old sequoias are frosted with the magic wand of winter. The Druid's sacrificial stone is just out of view. He offers me a cigarette and I smoke by the crackling stove, rocking in his chair.

'It's like the castle clock has stopped,' I say. 'It's waiting for you to fix it.'

'You've got that in one!'

But Lachlan is not at the party. He prefers to snuggle up

with Google and a bottle of wine, because 'no one else can put up with us. I mean, with me.'

Dougal is at the party, standing in the same spot all evening with a placid eye. This family are like a row of oaks still standing when all the other trees are cut.

Everyone here has a practical life that revolves around the seasons. And it's not often you have a chance to get out of the wellies and dress up a bit. All these people are stoical and reserved but the same passion runs through them. That passion is the glen.

Heather and Fred are on the brink of change. In a few months when they are settled in their rented village house, I'll run into Heather. I'm not used to seeing her out of the glen and for a moment, I'm disoriented. She is too. She misses having a role and she misses Strathfarrar. No stag roar, no daily film of moving light, it's nothing but hairdressers in the village! You can't replace hills with shops. And Fred? Fred spends most of his time in Strathfarrar. Helping with the animals and other bits and bobs. And when there is no work, he walks from the gate to Loch Monar and back. It takes all day. I've never done that.

'I need my fix!' and his cemented face cracks into a smile.

And something else: in the Monks' Place, cars keep reversing into their rented house. Drivers get out, inspect the damage and apologise to Heather, who stands in the door with her pixie face – nothing can shock her.

'It's on a corner,' she comments.

Once again they are on a threshold, gate keepers forever.

Back at the farewell party, I realise there are different types of keepers. Those like Dougal and Margaret who are wed to the glen. Those like Heather and Carrie who fuse with the glen for a time and stamp their personalities on it.

The Middle estate, Pait and Monar are represented by their keepers or under-keepers. Monar's keepers are a young family. Their children are driven to school every day up and down Strathfarrar, through the two locked gates, past the dam and the power stations – and these kids' self-confidence is striking. They remind me of Gypsies, growing in the outdoors when other kids are potted house plants. The last of the free. In the old days, all Highland children were free and tough. Now it's down to the children of gillies, keepers and farmers. Remote schools, shops and pubs remain open for them, without them the hinterland would empty.

Angie, the keeper of Pait, is here with her taciturn man, but they have left Pait. They now live above the Monks' Place.

'You adapt,' Angie says, and her man says nothing. They have no small talk in them. He has spent half a century talking to the wilderness in its own language. Nothing can match that. Angie too is a woman of few words, with that contained look of the keeper, but with a generosity. Cooking is what she does for a living. They left Pait after it changed hands for the first time in half a century, and anyway glen politics got too hard. What with Carrie's gate.

Carrie and husband are not here. But the understalker of the Middle estate is. I've never met him before. He is young with an old face, silent and moody – it's the prerogative of the deer stalker to be silent and moody. His is a timeless face of the Highlands. In him I see the understalker of Neil Gunn's novel *Second Sight*, a rare smile 'flowering in his face like a dark rose'. I've seen this face in the Bulgarian highlands. A face of an old indigenous world where people and places know each other like friends, river and hill are your home and mountain springs have watchers, and poachers. Teeth are stained and manners unpolished, but everything is a true story.

The moody understalker's brother is the keeper on the other side of the Farrar where I looked for the lead mine in the snow. Their father is a river bailiff and his coffin is being banged together in the fairie silence of the glen: he will die at Christmas. When Carrie and husband leave next year, the young under-keeper with an old face may step into their shoes and become full-time keeper of the Middle estate – no small thing to manage 40,000 acres. Everybody hopes that he runs a lighter regime and loosens the padlocks of the second gate.

I look at his moody back in chequered shirt and realise I have accidentally seen this shirt draped on a chair in what must be his room! That was a few weeks ago, when you could still drive to Monar, then Carrie locked her gate for the winter. A bleak, grey-harlinged house by a ruined sheep pen, it was built by the Hydro. Two control engineers stayed here before moving closer to civilisation in the 1980s. The isolation is extreme, exposure to the elements too. Through the curtainless window I saw a stark room with a bed and a chequered shirt flung on a chair. No phone signal for miles. In summer the midges wait for you outside – a black cloud at your window. That's why he likes winters best. No midges, no tourists. Just him, the deer and the eagles. The odd ceilidh in the mother glen, maybe a woman to catch his eye, but he leaves alone, unlocks and locks the first gate, drives many miles in the teeming darkness, unlocks and locks the second gate, drives more miles, and finally enters his cell, sits at the foot of the bed and takes off his boots. Maybe he'll have a roll-up before sleep and look at the scythe of the moon, how beautiful it is. Sometimes he doesn't know if he loves it or hates it.

On a hillside opposite his house – a memorial cairn to a piper. Bella and I lean against the cutting wind to reach it. All is air and water. No fire. It makes you waterlogged and groundless at the same time. Next to the cairn – the ruins of the clachan (settlement) where the piper was born in 1878. That was the last year of the Russo-Turkish War which changed the face of the Balkans. Bulgaria became independent after five centuries under the Ottoman Empire. Imperial Britain supported the Russian Empire, but then suppressed the emerging Balkan states, and in this way provoked the fierce revanchist battles of the First World War. On the Macedonian front alone, 10,000 British soldiers perished. Among them were many Highlanders. As if the Highlanders were born to be harvested by empires, pretenders and speculators. My Macedonian great-grandfather fought the British invaders in his land. He looked like the young under-keeper with an old face. A wild and vagabondish look, a look that's disappearing from the land. Industry is killing it. And here I am, blown by the gales of history.

On the piper's memorial cairn is an inscription:

Thig crìoch air an t-saoghal, ach mairidh gaol agus ceòl.
The world will come to an end but love and music will endure.

The boy Willie was raised here and learned the pipes from his parents. He joined the Scots Guards, became Pipe Major William Ross and taught two generations of pipers in Edinburgh. He died soon after Monar dam flooded the glen. The stones of his abandoned clachan were recycled for Hydro houses.

Every year, kilted men and women pull up at the gate and ring Heather's bell. One glance and she knows why they're here. They drive to the cairn, walk up the path with their bagpipes and play for Willie Ross, piper of pipers. The glen picks up their tune and takes it away. They play military tunes. But that's false. The original pipers and bards, fiddlers and fairies played from the land, with the land, and to the land. That's the definition of ceilidh – when everything plays together. The pipes had an animal-human, story-telling voice. Their music is called *piobaireachd* (pibroch). It was only in the dismantling of Gaeldom that Highland men, renowned for their marksmanship and toughness, were conscripted into the Crown's armies and began to murder and die in Empire's wars – only then that, festooned with medals, the bagpipe became a martial instrument instead of a human one.

I hear the lone piper. Tears freeze on my face and the wind blows them away. This glen is the world and the lone piper is its ghost. The walls of the strath rise, curved like a singing bowl. The bare hills of Monar are awesome, even without their forests, animals, humans and birds. Their shape fills me until I become the hills. I swallow them and disappear in the land. The sleet grazes the faces of the land, and mine. Bella realises the sleet is alive and chases it but it's everywhere. Water comes down black glistening rocks like mercury.

Out west, the snowy curtain opens and a blue sky chimes against the icy peak of Red Birds, then the peak of Black Iron. Ping, ping! The land is having a brilliant revelation. I love this place and all the people who have felt what I'm feeling for 5,000 years. In this place you could see anything, even plesiosauruses that, before they are submerged again in the loch of the psyche, drag their dragon bodies at the pre-Cambrian speed of crag, beinn, cnoc, stob, tom, dun, meall, sròn, òrd, drum and sgùrr. So many ways to say a hill! So many sounds the wind makes.

When even the sheep vanish and stumbling on the jawbone of a sheep we no longer recognise it – still there is light and shape. Still the wind and the water play their piobaireachd for the deer and their young keeper with an old face.

Chì mi

You can't drive to Pait (pronounced Patt). You reach it by boat at the far end of Loch Monar, six miles. Its lodge is one of the remotest dwellings in mainland Scotland. Pait is a large estate and Angie spent twenty-eight years out there as keeper. Twenty-eight for her, forty-two for her man. Before they got together, it was just him and the dogs. She'll never go back but she can see it in her mind's eye. Always with dogs, anywhere between seven and eleven. She grew up in Cougie. Grandfather was army, father a keeper, mother a housewife. When Angie was ten, she went to school in the city and stayed in a hostel. The other girls were from the islands. Right! She learned the Gaelic. She missed the hills of home but it taught her self-sufficiency, and then she returned to the glen.

It was just the two of them out there. A household at the end of the world. It's not for everyone. Och aye, we had fights but not often and everything's weather dependent. Not much point storming off if there's an actual storm. When the weather's good, I'd head for the hills. The dogs came along. Off to Meall an Buidhe or Meall an Odhar. Between those two passed the coffin road west to Kintail, did you know that? And the drover's road. By the time you get back your mind is clear.

One time, her dad was ill in Cannich but there were high winds, no way could they get across the loch. Right. She walked around the loch in the face of those high winds till she reached the truck. When the loch froze solid, the same. They would go round it, making a trail in the snow by walking, the dogs close at heel. It took hours. Another time, when a dog got poisoned by eating autumn crocuses, it was a mad dash across the loch, then a drive down the glen to the vet in town where the dog stayed for ten days. Angie visited her every single day. Across the loch, down the long glen road.

Life at Pait revolved around the seasons. Summer: the main purpose is to keep the midges out. Before guests arrive, a big shop. Shopping took a whole day. Boat, truck, supermarket, truck, boat and mule – that's quad bike. Load and unload groceries in the kitchen. The Aga was the boiler. Angie cooked, cleaned and laundered for up to fifteen people. No tumble dryer or heating, no hoover; a dustpan did the job. Three-course meals and cooked breakfast. She enjoyed it when people were well fed. Early autumn, shooting parties arrive. If a guest has a bath, the hot water runs out. Right! Heat water on the stove. Late autumn, guests leave, close down the guest lodge, turn off water. Bring coal, car fuel, deer blocks before the glen road froze. Blocks are deer food. It's heart-breaking to find dead deer on the hill, you have to keep an eye on them. Winter: maintenance and long walks with the dogs. And before you know it, spring again.

No, never travelled. Couldn't be away from the dogs. And the hills. I went to London once but couldn't take the noise. Then I understood how some guests from London can't sleep in Pait. They can't take the silence.

We've left Pait and we'll never go back. It means too much, we don't want to see it changed. I want to remember it the way it was. Have you been yet? When they're generating, you can see the old jetty and submerged houses. You can see where there used to be a pait. That's a sand spit. It's how people and animals crossed between Pait and Monar, before the Hydro flooded it. We were happy there. It was a privilege, to be the keepers of Pait.

The Crossing Place, gravel

It turned out that the quarry was not leaving but expanding. We just hadn't caught up with it. The local authority had approved this years ago. But the scale of its expansion dawned on us in the spring of the pandemic. Most of the Crossing Place would become a quarry! In two more phases: phase two and phase three. While the glen was in lockdown, subcontractors to the big gravel company cut down a large section of woodland. It was nesting time, which made it illegal, but there was no one to point this out because everyone was locked down – except us because we lived next to it. The local paper came out to photograph it for an article, and that was it. An art-photographer from the Monks' Place came to record the remaining forest, the one marked up sickeningly for phase three. He wanted to document the beauty of the woodland before it was destroyed.

In phase one, the quarry had destroyed Pictish cairns with carved stones, and extensive hut circles. This had been a large Pictish settlement. Our ancestors had lived, died and called this the Crossing Place. A beautiful carved stone with an eagle was salvaged by the local archaeological society, and quietly taken away.

I contacted a young naturalist in the nature park in the glen and he came out to record the residents of the wood marked up for phase three. He sent me his notes.

'Notes from a soon-to-be destroyed woodland to make way for a quarry.'

When Scots pine plantations are left to mature and are relatively open like the one at Balblair, they begin to revert back to native woodland, he wrote. The tall Scots pine have an open canopy and that means the light can reach the forest floor. Some broad-leaf trees have taken advantage of this — many birches and rowan but also oaks. Some mammoth oaks can be found in this wood. Oak is a rare sight in this area because they were all felled in the past, for timber. Oak is a miracle. More invertebrates live on oak than any other tree species, and they only become more diverse the older they get. The tree diversity is pleasantly surprising in Balblair, wrote the naturalist, and a great example of what diversity a native woodland should have. These are the species he found in only two hours of walking in the woodland, before it was destroyed.

Bumblebee
Early bumblebee
Common carder bee
White-tailed bumblebee
Bluebell
Chickweed wintergreen
Blaeberry
Ling heather
Tormentil
Wood rush
Wood sorrel
Common polypody
Honeysuckle
Holly
Willow
Bramble

Bracken
Wild mint
Oak
Birch
Beech
Rowan
Speckled wood butterfly
Green-veined white butterfly
Roe deer
Red squirrel
Badger
Pine marten
Bat
Scorpion fly
Snipe fly
Click beetle
Ichneumon wasp species
Common heath moth
Bordered white moth
Great spotted woodpecker
Wood pigeon
Robin
Crow
Bullfinch
Goldfinch
Goldcrest
Coal tit
Buzzard
Chaffinch
Pipistrelle bat, three varieties

The company went on and completed phase two. A large section of forest was cut down. They worked long days. Then the diggers arrived. Every day, for weeks, we listened to the sound of –

'Rape,' Tony said.

Wastelanding is deliberate, systematic, it's happening everywhere. It looks more and more like a policy and an ideology. It looks and feels like war. War and big industry have the same results: wasteland. War achieves it faster, with instant death and destruction. Big industry takes longer. Together, they sustain the economy of destruction.

All the woodland creatures went homeless. Our garden filled with hundreds of birds looking for food and new nesting places. We were overrun by refugees. Tony bought fifty kilos of birdfeed. The deer whose sleeping places in the forest were gone ran across the road and were killed by lorries carrying gravel. Or timber. The trees were going to be pulped and turned into biomass, which is considered a 'green fuel', and it is but in a sickeningly inverted way – it is the burning up of living forests like this one. This green fuel comes at the price of wastelanding the Crossing Place. Commercial vehicles increased in size. The thunder of industry was everywhere. I closed my eyes at night and saw diggers. You wake up and you don't know what else will be gone by the end of the day.

Whose land was it anyway and how had it come to this?

The land was leased to the quarry by the landowners, a legendary clan who had owned large stretches of the Highlands for centuries. They still do. It's crazy how much land a single family can own in the twenty-first century. This kind of feudal possession has always looked to me as absurd as the entire British class system.

This clan has Norman roots from the Middle Ages. They

fought and schemed their way to the top of the heap in the usual way of clan chiefs. In the eighteenth century, one especially colourful lord was dubbed the Fox for his opportunistic genius. He inherited entire glens and maintained political clout, switching allegiances with dizzying speed. Ending up on the Jacobite side in Culloden by fatal chance, he was imprisoned in the Tower of London and condemned to death, and this Highland Houdini joked all the way to the guillotine, coining the immortal phrase 'to laugh your head off'. Later, the clan became known for their scouts – an elite military unit of Highlanders that was initially part of the Black Watch. Every day, I walked past the field where the Lovat Scouts had bivouacked in the First World War with their horses. Now there were salmon fisheries in the field, for spawning.

The land owned by the family was managed by the young lord. He appeared one day after years in London and moved into the Dutchman's house by the river. The Dutchman, who'd been the fishing tenant and reputedly Scotland's richest man, had died. New gates appeared and new signs, river paths were blocked off. The lord was a withdrawn man hollowed by something. In the glen were mutterings about the family curse. But they were loved, these fixtures of Highland aristocracy. They were one of the last big clans to have stayed and remained close to the folk. The previous generations had been gregarious and open and had kept to the last the spirit of kinship in the glens. But in every family is a fatal flaw. A decline had set in. Large debts had been run up by the male line. Business ventures failed. The land was sold to pay death duties. That's why the quarry was spreading, the sins of the past catching up with the present.

The clan's one-time castle was the one I contemplated from the roofless church of Talorgan. Built in the late nineteenth century but looking like it belonged to the eighteenth, its turrets were so high they served as an orientation point. I couldn't help but see a symbol: to be one foot in the past while borrowing from the future makes it hard to inhabit the present.

The current lord's grandfather was decorated as a war hero, having led multiple battles accompanied by his personal piper. He'd had a heroic war, but peacetime was tricky. Entire glens were sold, a large bet on a racing horse was lost, the quarry moved in and the castle was bought by a business tycoon. When fireworks went off, we knew she was here. It was heard in the glen that a small forgotten Monet painting was found in the basement by the new owners. If only the old owners had appreciated what they had, they could have sold the Monet instead of the castle. A parable if not a fact.

In the space of ten days in the mid 1990s, two of that lord's four sons died in hunting accidents. The youngest was mauled by a buffalo in Tanzania. Three days after his funeral at the family church deep in the glen, the eldest went hunting on the riverbanks, setting off on horseback from the castle with his party. It was in a corner of the sloping field that holds the forgotten tomb of Talorgan that he died of a heart attack. A year later minus a week, the old lord passed away. One of the middle sons played the bagpipes at all the funerals.

The oaks planted by earlier clan chiefs had seen it all and a few of them still flanked the river, hosting a thousand species each. The quarry spared the oaks but nothing else. The oldest abandoned quarry ground was planted quickly with cheap spruce, not a single bird in that dead forest. The active part of the quarry was pits with ground water and mountains of sand. They were in a hurry.

We stopped buying gravel for the driveway. I'll never buy gravel again!

'If we don't get new gravel, we have to make use of the old gravel,' said Tony, and he found a way: he power-washed the compacted gravel and that got rid of the dirt and mud that kept squashing it down and making it look like it needed more, more. But we found that we could do with less. The washed gravel was like new.

Either we recycle or we get swallowed up by the quarry.

The quarry had originally been opened up to provide sand for cement, needed for the building of our dam. Fair enough, but it *created a marketplace* and now it's the size of an airport.

And the dam builders? They seemed completely forgotten. Of the thousands of workers who had passed through the glen, there was just one left.

'Jonny the Pole,' said Tony. 'But his name wasn't Jonny and he wasn't Polish.'

The dam builder had come into the gallery when Tony was still doing it up. He lived in the old sawmill by the railway station. He died, but his son is still there.

Chì mi

In the months before the dam builders arrived, and without knowing what was coming, several women in Glen Cannich heard things. One of them, an estate keeper, heard hammering noises and men's voices by Loch Mullardoch. She rushed back home, not wanting to meet these men. But they were not there yet. Years later the dam breached the loch in the same place.

Another woman heard an eerie sound that moved over the glen like witches singing, she said. Years later, the buzz of transmission wires mimicked what she'd heard.

The glen would change forever with the blasting of the hills, the impounding of rivers with thousands of tons of concrete, the ticking power stations underground, the churning of turbines, and the racing of high voltage through pristine atmosphere. So great was the pressure of the future against the present that these women sensed it before it arrived.

The power schemes went ahead and were completed. But for decades, lone workers on night shifts heard sounds. Laughter, voices in the tunnels. They'd feel all the hairs on their head stand up. Because the tunnels were long empty.

The Dam Builders

The longer you are in a place, the more territorial you become, like a dog. You have your trails. You pass the wooden shack by the railway and wonder who lives in it, but out of habit you don't stop and knock on the door. A rusty pick-up truck sits outside. Years pass. The shack leans to one side and the books in the window shelf lean with it.

The Monks' Place has expanded in all directions but the shack has stood its ground, an island surrounded by fields.

One night I lay in the cottage in the Crossing Place under the buzzing electricity lines and dreamt that I went to the shack, but it had leaned too far and been flattened by one of the bulldozers that are flattening the forest to make way for the quarry. I woke up and walked the two miles from the Crossing Place to the Monks' Place.

It was a warm pandemic Easter. The sap rose in the trees just before they were cut. Fear smothered people like fog. A woman jogged with a mask on. She saw me coming and nearly threw herself under a timber lorry to avoid contagion. My feet bounced off the tarmac. Everything looked abandoned. I sang that old Travellers' song:

When the yellow's on the broom,
when the yellow's on the broom
Take me on the road again,
when the yellow's on the broom.

Broom and gorse lined the road where the quarry had once excavated. Where you see them in abundance, you know the land has been extracted and left.

Rural roads are dangerous for walkers now. But when the children of the dam builders were growing up, not many people had cars and you walked, cycled or bussed. To school and the farm and the pub and church and back, not always sober but singing old Travellers' songs.

I walked on the grassy verge and ate the yellow blossoms of broom. They smell of vanilla but don't taste of it. Travellers ate them in salads and sandwiches. When you walk, an instinct awakens: to meet things in the flesh, sniff them, chew them, spit them out, and be delighted. Everything is a tonic when the yellow's on the broom. Where have the Travellers gone?

Before the big bridge was built over the Firth, there was a great Traveller ground on the southern shore. Horses, caravans, women in long skirts, deals and dealings. It survived for a while after the bridge, but in the 1990s the camp was disbanded and something more useful put in its place — a stadium. I don't know where the Travellers went. A few still camp on the fringes of the industrial lot and there is the odd horse grazing gorse and broom among the mounds of excavated earth that were just left there after the construction. The stadium is big and ugly and plastered with advertisements for energy drinks.

Some of the Travellers were descendants of navvies. The navvies, short for navigators, were hired labourers. Irish and Scottish, English and Welsh, they were called navvies because one of the key industrial infrastructures they built was the navigation canals. Another was the railways. The last one was the Hydro schemes.

The navvies travelled from scheme to scheme. This went on for over a century, interrupted but not completely by two world wars. Some couldn't go back to their poor farming communities and stayed on the road. At the Hydro schemes, the most itinerant of them were dubbed long-distance kiddies. That's because they couldn't stay in one job. They had to move on, criss-crossing Scotland in search of bread and adventure, shunned by the settled ones whose roads and sewers they built.

Gypsies of labour, that's what they were called by the Irish writer Patrick MacGill in his autobiographical novel *Children of the Dead End*. He was one of them, the army of youth that poured their hot blood into the cold pits of British industry.

In the wake of the Second World War, the gypsies of labour were joined by British prisoners of war already on British soil, plus a hotch-potch of displaced Europeans. Thousands of the 11 million people displaced in Europe were shipped to Britain to work in new industrial projects like the dams. These men and women were called European Voluntary Workers. Most were refugees with no way back. Many had spent years in forced labour camps in Nazi-occupied territories. Some made up biographies for themselves in a place where no one knew what they'd been through. Sometimes there were no words for what they'd been through. Silence was best and living in a foreign country is like silence.

They became Jonny the Pole. Johnny Foreigner. That's what the parochial locals called them, unable to pronounce their names or grasp the complexity of where they came from. It was the first time the glens had seen so many new faces. European workers like these made up between 10 and 20 per cent of the labour on the post-war Hydro schemes.

The rest were Irish, English, Welsh and Scots, half of those Highlanders.

To reach the Monks' Place, I walked down a concrete lane skirting a field. It was built by the quarry after their *phase one*. There used to be a path through a grove. The quarry felled the grove, poured concrete on the path, and put steel railings to protect walkers from falling into nature, plus automatic street lights. Large companies that invade small places and extract them before they move on call this *community mitigation*. We will poison your soil and your ground water for the next three generations, but we'll put a bench outside your school. Say thank you.

Ravens and blackbirds blacken the fields. Their feathers glow. Everything glows. The oat field ripples in the breeze. The clouds move fast through the air and through me and I can't tell if time is speeding up or that's the effect of walking fast. Daffodils bloom a freakish yellow. The light of spring, the rapture of the land, it's newborn every May!

On the door of the leaning shack is a faded name plate:

W. OKSENJUK

I knock. A man in blue overalls comes out and blinks. He has bushy eyebrows and a reclusive face.

'What is this about?'

He is wary. I might be one of those people that go around offering to sell you faster broadband, or to flatten your house and put something more useful in its place. But his wariness falls away when I mention his dad and he comes out to stand in the sunshine. His name is Stas, short for Stanislav.

'But nobody calls me that. Except – the other day I was in the supermarket and this lady called out Stanislav! I nearly fell over.'

An old friend of his parents. Stas's father was Ukrainian and his mother Scottish.

'Everyone called my dad Walter coz they couldn't pronounce his name. His name was Wolodimir. Wolodimir Oksenjuk.'

Wolodimir had worked on one of the dams but Stas didn't know which one and what sort of work.

'Not a tunnel tiger, that much is sure. I wish I'd asked him more about it. General labour, I'd guess.'

After the war, the Hydro-Electric Board became the biggest employer of men in Scotland. Work on the Hydro schemes was up to ten times better paid than any other manual work like farming. Poles, Ukrainians, Italians, Czechs, Germans, Lithuanians and Belarusians joined the Irish, English, Welsh and Scots in the sprawling makeshift camps that mushroomed in remote glens. Many of the displaced Europeans were still in a state of traumatic shock or denial. There was the German who displayed a swastika over his bed, thinking the Nazis had won the war. The Pole with an invented war-hero identity who had in fact spent the war in Scotland, hiding with his wife. Many of them had burned their bridges. The only way was north and west. Many sailed to America, others stayed in Britain.

Wolodimir Oksenjuk came from a farming community in eastern Ukraine. He was nineteen when the Germans arrived in his village and started rounding up young men for slave labour. He would never see his parents or homeland again.

Years later, labour prospectors turned up at the camp for displaced persons in England, where Wolodimir had ended up. 'Do you guys want to make good money in Scotland? There's lots of work up there!' Wolodimir travelled to the Highlands with some friends, all refugees. Up here, they were put up in a recently disbanded camp for German prisoners of war.

The camp was set in a large private estate called Brahan. That's where the Brahan Seer had lived, working as a manual labourer. That's where he had lain in the woods and looked through his stone with a hole in it that his mother had received from the ghost of a Norse woman. He belonged to the clan who owned the Brahan estate – the Seaforth MacKenzies.

The prophesies of the Brahan Seer have survived but the true identity of the seer hasn't. Many prophecies attributed to him came from other seers, making the figure of the Brahan Seer a repository for the collective psyche of the Highlands and Islands. And whoever he was, the Brahan Seer likely spent his life moving from job to job. A gypsy of labour.

In the Brahan estate, two memorial stones are found. They are seemingly unrelated, they're far apart, and you have to search for them. One stone quotes the Brahan Seer:

An déidh latha an daimh duinn
Thig latha a' mhathain
After the day of the stag
Will come the day of the bear

The Seaforth MacKenzies had the stag as their crest. And the bear? It's the crest of the current owners.

The other stone is a carved Ukrainian trident in the forest, a reminder of the hundreds of Ukrainians who gave their best years to the Hydro schemes and other heavy industry that enriched Britain and in exchange gave men like Wolodimir a place to belong.

In Nazi Germany he had been a slave labourer. If he went back to Soviet Ukraine, he would be tortured and shot as a traitor by the NKVD (precursors to the KGB), or sent to a labour camp. This is what happened in the Soviet Union to returning prisoners of war or displaced persons who had been held by the Germans. During the Soviet repatriation campaign, Soviet citizens were forcibly deported from Germany and one survivor who managed to stay on and ended up in Scotland like Wolodimir saw a Cossack woman jump from the speeding train with her child. She knew what awaited them on arrival: a state orphanage and a labour camp. Better a quick death.

'Dad never said why, but he didn't want to go back.'

That's why. We blink in the soft Scottish sun.

'Dad said the Ukrainians and the Poles and Irish got on quite well, on the schemes. But the local Scots didn't want them.'

They fought over women. There were too many men.

'When Brexit was going on, it really brought it home to me, what it must have been like for him.'

Stas chuckles briefly, he isn't in the habit of laughter.

Wolodimir had left behind two brothers. They exchanged letters, even though Soviet censors read all correspondence. What was it like for his brothers and parents? Perhaps they were singled out as the family of a deserter, or maybe they did okay, seeing as they'd fought in the Red Army. Stas has no idea. He kept himself from asking too many questions while his father was alive. It was all too much for him. And now it's too late.

In a framed photograph, his parents glow in fur-collared coats in the spot where Stas and I stand. Their little boy glows between them, the apple of their eye. His father has good-humoured eyes with wide cheekbones and bushy eyebrows. His mother looks kind and solid. They met at a party.

'A bit of matchmaking, I think,' Stas grins.

He has the fated bachelor stamped all over him. His love for his parents is obvious and undimmed. The very fact that he has stayed in this shack and left things as they were at the time of his father's death, not even fixing the fence – it speaks of loyalty laced with pain.

'Aye, there was pain for sure. My mother had a difficult life. And he did too. Though he never complained.'

By the time they met, they were in their forties. His mother had been engaged to an Irishman but he'd gone back *beyont the sea* and vanished – maybe he was one of the long-distance kiddies. She worked as a cook in a big house. Meanwhile, Wolodimir worked long hours at the sawmill in this field. There were several basic wooden houses like this, for the workers. The boss gave him a patch of land and he did up this shack and when he brought his Scottish bride, they stayed on. Even as the sawmill folded and he moved to another one up the road. These were the last of the Highland sawmills, and he spent his working life among the sawdust, shattering noise and iron cutters that maimed men. He was already deaf from his years on the dams. One day, a log splintered the wrong way and nearly severed his arm.

'They grafted skin and flesh from his leg to save it. But he was back to work.'

Stas too ended up working in forestry.

'Dad was desperate for me to become a teacher or a doctor, but by fourteen I was done with school. I didn't want to sit inside all day.'

He went to Forestry School. A log split the wrong way and hit him in the eye. He was lucky not to lose it, but for a while the eye closed up and half his face went black. He took time off and, arriving back home to his father, he discovered that the Ukrainian relatives had arrived. A long-awaited visit.

They had bought a flight as soon as the borders opened. The two brothers came with their families. It had been fifty years.

'Aye, Dad was emotional, like. He cried when he saw my black eye. My boy, my boy! My mum had just died.'

It was nice enough, but Stas only had a few words of Ukrainian and they had no English. And they never visited again. I wonder what they made of the wooden shack, the widowed Wolodimir, his forester son with the blackened eye who wasn't a teacher or a doctor like their own children. Perhaps they'd imagined something more. Didn't people have more in the west? But Wolodimir had less. He and his wife liked it here and didn't want to be crammed in a city flat. Either way, Wolodimir had somehow remained a gypsy of labour. A happy, settled one on the edge of the Monks' Place. Something of the open road lived on in him, and in Stas. Stas has spent a lifetime imagining Ukraine. It's funny, he said, I've been to all the countries in Eastern Europe, but not Ukraine. Though I always wanted to. Maybe I was afraid it wouldn't live up to my expectations.

He preferred to keep his expectations close, like a talisman. He preferred to look at the map and browse photographs.

Arty the cat wanders in the back garden planted with native trees, in casings against the nibbling sheep that come in from the field. Rowan, birch – that's what he plants in the estate that he works for – and Scots pine.

It's a large private estate. There are grants for *rewilding*, which means planting trees, and the owners of large estates can't say no to a grant.

'I like planting trees instead of cutting them. I was into felling for years but got depressed. Now at the end of a day, I feel good.'

Those native trees will never be cut, he says. But on that estate Stas and his workmates also plant commercial pines. To be harvested in forty years' time.

'When I'll be long dead. I hope.'

And because there are also grants for having wind farms on your land, the estate has taken a bite of that pie too. It's win-win.

But Stas — he would not give up this place for anything. He's had offers from developers.

'I've never felt like moving. I like it here. It's private.'

And very public. The world speeds past the leaning shack. He is visible and invisible. I am the first person who has ever stopped to talk to him. We stand facing the railway.

And the railway bridge is where, coming back from school one day, aged five, he held his mother's hand when she lost the use of her legs and fell softly on the pavement. It's his earliest memory.

'Multiple sclerosis. It's common in Scotland. They say it's the Vitamin D lacking.'

Though she lived another twenty-five years, she was confined to a wheelchair.

'But her mind was sharp as ever,' Stas says gently. This is how he grew up — his mother in a wheelchair inside, looking through the small window to the field with blackbirds, sheep and April daffodils, his father working long hours at the sawmill in Talorgan's Village.

'He cared for her. Every day, he'd save up his tea breaks to make up a whole hour at lunchtime and he cycled home to make sure she'd had her lunch.'

I give Stas three yellow-dyed Easter eggs.

The next time I stop at the shack, it's Easter again. A freezing Easter four years later. The military machine is working overtime. The industrial machine is working overtime. These are two things that never sleep. I bring Stas a dyed egg again and stand in the cold with him. Any news of your relatives in Ukraine? He shrugs, hopes they're alive.

The fence is collapsed and he hasn't touched it. Don't try to improve, it's pointless, better hold on to what's here and try not to rock the boat. Without him, this place would be turned into a battery storage plant or a parking lot.

'I love it here. Last night me and Arty sat out and looked at the full moon. What a beautiful place.'

Stas promises to find a suitcase of photos for next time but never does. Maybe the house is holding together because of all the stuff that props it up.

Wolodimir worked on Mullardoch dam which was part of the Affric-Cannich project completed in 1952. Mullardoch is the largest mass gravity dam in Britain. If you are a dam spotter, you'll know what that means. It's an engineering feat, especially when you see where it was built.

Once upon a time, Mullardoch was a beautiful loch in Glen Cannich. One of the most biodiverse glens in the Highlands, with many smokes. And now it's a place you need a reason to visit. Maybe if you're a dam spotter. Or a Munro bagger. Locals call it the Empty Glen and this is where I'm going today. If nothing else, I can gather kindling in the birch wood.

Further in-glen, I stop to see Margaret who tells me her mother used to dye Easter eggs with beetroot powder. Before the manufactured chocolate egg, all Highlanders used to dye eggs. Now the only people who dye real eggs are the odd East Europeans like me.

Margaret has had pain in many places. It started just after the Hogmanay service. That was the last service in the last Presbyterian church of the glen. She was the precentor and has lived across from it all her life. I went to that service. Margaret in her tartan shawl presided with composure while the minister read from Ecclesiastes – change and decay in all around I see – and comforted the gathering that Our Lord Jesus is the same yesterday, today and tomorrow.

The congregation was made up of the glen's faces. The last of the old Highlanders like Margaret, with their stoic fatalism. The odd keeper with a ruddy face, awkward hands in lap. The more recent settlers from the south.

'It's the faithful who are the church of Christ, not this building,' the minister reminded the largely faithless congregation.

The building was constructed 130 years ago by local masons with money from the community. Now the community is too reduced to buy its own church from the Presbytery. For a while Margaret couldn't find the deeds and when I suggested she kept it that way – no deeds, no sale – she said: Well, I could be amenable to suggestion! But the deeds were found and the church went on sale. Margaret's body aches began at once.

'It's like selling the family loom,' Margaret says. 'However.'

And she gives me the good news: the church organ has found a home – a music school. Few music students learn to play the organ now, an instrument that will fade with the church.

'Aha. And did you hear about the new gate keepers of Strathfarrar?'

No!

Yes. They have just moved into the keeper's cottage with their dogs and parrots. Margaret can't come to the Empty Glen because of her pain but tells me where to look for ruined settlements. It's where Ali the gillie found lots of bawbee coins.

Ali Bally, Ali Bally bee
Sittin' on yer mammy's knee . . .

Time is ticking. I pass the postie's house. He promised to take me on a postal round of the glen with him, but he is terminally ill. They are one of the last old Highland couples. They are like everybody's parents. Without them the glen will be orphaned.

In Cannich, a gentle alcoholic points me to a row of houses where I look for the house of Steve the stalker of Affric, to drop off an Easter gift for the venison he gave me, and spot it at once – it's the antlers above the door. The village is scenic, stoic and sad. All the terraced houses are from the Hydro and forestry era. It's a worker's village. They are well built. In the Cannich store, Ali's daughter is serving coffees to German hikers. It's quiet. Too early to drink out, I say. Yeah, she says, people are drinking in. Lots of people on disability benefits. The large warehouses of the energy giant hum behind the village.

From the ghostly stain in the shape of the Affric Hotel, I climb the steep road and Glen Cannich receives me and Bella with mixed feelings, or maybe that's just me. Enchantment and sorrow. The high road and the low road. Longing and already, farewell. Birch and alder and even old beech at the entrance to the glen. Where there is woodland, there is soul and birdsong, there are whispers, movement, story. But no people. No people.

The forest ends and a sadness creeps in. I sit by the Cannich river *of the bog cotton*, open a flask, munch an oatcake, lie in the bracken that is rousing itself from winter brownhood. Bella swims after a twig. The river is low. They're generating. The Mullardoch power station generates 8 million units per year, which sounds a lot but is less than others. By comparison, Culligran produces 57. Monar dam at top capacity can produce 63, once its water has passed through the four power stations downstream.

The footprint of Hydro is big. By the time it becomes really productive, like Fasnakyle power station, which generates 223 million units, hills have been drilled, lochs breached, rivers diverted, roads hammered in, and all inhabitants gone. This happened in every major glen of the Highlands where the rivers have their heads resting on the edge of the Atlantic seaboard. But Hydro energy has been reliable, at least. Not so with wind energy, whose footprint is even larger.

A few houses stand along the river at great distance from each other, but just two households live in the Empty Glen – a keeper's family and a family at the old mill house where sheep graze in the ruins of farmhouses and three glamping pods have gone up. The young family bought the place and did it up, to run as a subsistence croft with sheep, chickens and basic crops. I must give the good news to Margaret!

The keeper's house has two flags – the Saltire and the British. That's because the son of the keeper was in the army but quit after serving in Afghanistan the second time and took over from his father. But the old couple still live up here. The keeper's wife has spent forty years in this windswept emptiness, without driving. She must be lonely. Or wild at heart like Angie.

There's Blind Freddie's hoose too. Blind Freddie had two Rottweilers who walked him down to the village and back. Six miles! When Blind Freddie died, his daughter moved in but isolation and booze *got to her*, which means it killed her, and now Blind Freddie's hoose is a holiday let.

The land is bare. Two cyclists on a bridge. The sign STALKER'S HOUSE has fallen in the wind. Black shiny cattle in the field. Their pensive faces and muscular trunks make them look like minotaurs. Newborn calves run across a bog on shaky legs. Two hunting lodges.

The road ends at the dam and the dam blocks the horizon. It is 700 metres long and 50 metres high. Three hundred thousand cubic yards of concrete were poured in the Cannich

River to make it. You don't have to look at the dam for long before you start feeling like something has gone wrong here. I know how the local women felt when their river was stolen and their birds disappeared. I know it because I live in the shadow of the electricity grid and next to the quarry.

Within a couple of years of Mullardoch dam being put to work, an engineer came to measure things again. And he was shocked to find that the dam had moved by a fraction. The floor of the glen had slightly sunk, causing less than an inch in the wall to tilt to one side, but even that was significant. A reminder that the land is tectonically active.

We walk the lochside track, Bella looks for something and can't find it. She stops, quizzical. Where is it? She runs down to the shore of the loch but the shore is all blasted stone and concrete where the debris was disgorged from large wagons on rails seventy years ago. She runs up the hill but there is nothing there either.

Beyond the dam there's no birdsong. Mullardoch dam is the death of something. The oystercatchers, blackbirds, thrushes and warblers are gone. The shepherd's houses are underwater and the last Caledonian pines on the other side, where only dam employees have access, have a wasting disease like heroes dying on their feet. It's an ecological Culloden.

No insects either. When I see a red-orange caterpillar crossing the track, I stop and almost cry. Bella doesn't touch it, it's too precious. Something survives!

There is heather and bog myrtle. Myrtle to repel midges, heather for thatched roofs and for rinsing food, like a sieve. But there are no faces to rub with myrtle. No edible plants, no mouths. The flooded loch is 15 kilometres long, twice its natural length because it's two lochs in one. The vanished loch at the far end is Lungard, and nobody reaches the far end except the guy with the boat where the hobo took shelter. Here's the boat. And there was the hiker who found a mysterious cupped stone at the far end where nobody expected to find druidic stones. But since then, the track has been blocked by landslides. The denuded banks don't have a chance to recover because the water levels vary too much. Flood and drought. Today it's low.

And yesterday, does anyone remember yesterday?

'Yesterday, today and tomorrow, Jesus is the same,' intoned the industrial chaplain for the Hydro workers, their faces sceptical. Or just tired.

I see the chaplain standing on the shores, in his black shirt and white collar. Labourers with caps in hands and clean shirts. It's the weekend. Friday is pay-day and the weekend is the only time they are not covered in mud and ash. Among them is Wolodimir with his Cossack cheekbones and bushy eyebrows. It's not that they are all religious, it's a chance to reconnect with something familiar from before the war, before the industry, back in a land they'll not see again.

It is Easter and zero degrees. After half an hour's walking, sleet begins to fall like razorblades. We can turn back to the warmth of the car. Not the dam workers, they never stopped. The only time that work here stopped was when the entire construction site froze solid, like a giant silver waterfall.

I see Wolodimir walking in his torn boots along this track, whistling to cheer himself. He is single. A forced celibacy – the gypsy of labour lives in male-only camps where the religion is work and the entertainment is gambling, fighting and drinking, and even if you settle in the same glen, like Wolodimir, you don't have much to offer a prospective bride except your broken English. At least the Irish spoke the same language. Not that it helped them. Wolodimir is surprised by the bad blood towards the Irish whom he likes. One of them told him an old ditty, composed a generation before by an Irishman at Kinlochleven – that was the first of the big Scottish dams. A precursor of what was to come. That Irishman was the writer Patrick MacGill.

> Though up may be up and down be down,
> Time will make everything even,
> And the man who starves at Greenock town
> Will fatten at Kinlochleven.

But gypsies of labour never fattened. They moved on to the next construction scheme or stayed on and kept working like Wolodimir. Turnover at the Hydro camps was quick because the labour force was unstable. Nine thousand men worked in the Glen Affric scheme. At one point, skilled tunnel workers had to be brought in from Lithuania because Britain didn't have enough of them. The Scots especially disliked working inside the tunnels, even though some of them were coalminers, and would often decamp after a week. The toughest Scots were those from the Hebrides, like Harris and Skye.

Bella and I push into the sleet. The Empty Glen sounds a monotone. It is not a song of the road anymore. It's an epitaph and walking here is a funereal act.

At the far end where Loch Lungard used to be, there lived a shepherd. He was a brilliant piper but very lonely, and sometimes of an evening, when the stalker of Affric would come over the bealach (pass) for a dram, he would hear the banshee wail of a bagpipe. The shepherd was playing to the hills.

Wolodimir too heard the wail of pipes in the months before the musical shepherd was booted out by the Hydro-Electric Board. And on weekends, a chap in the camp played the accordion, in particular 'Gloomy Sunday' which was so sad it emptied the hall. Wolodimir remembered the title in Hungarian – '*Szomoru vasarnap*'. That chap made some extra money playing in the pub on Loch Ness.

Sleet is worse than snow and rain. Sleet is an eternal gloomy Sunday. Come on, Bella. That's enough. Even the homeless man didn't hang out at Mullardoch, once he'd spent the night in borrowed clothes inside this boatshed.

On the shores of the dam is an anvil-like clan stone. It is very old. This is where the chief held meetings and collected tax from his clansmen. When the dam is high, the stone is submerged.

A cairn next to it holds a small plaque. It affects me every time.

TWO CENTURIES AFTER THE DIASPORA OF THE CHISHOLMS FROM STRATHGLASS, THEIR DESCENDANTS RETURNED FROM FIVE CONTINENTS TO THE LANDS OF THEIR ORIGIN, NOW DEVOID OF THE CHISHOLM NAME, TO CONFIRM THEIR HERITAGE.

I suddenly get it. A question has plagued me all these years: why did Highlanders remain enamoured of the selfish Bonnie Prince Charlie who brought catastrophe to their country? Why is every second cave Charlie's Cave, making him the clandestine hero he wasn't? Why did exiles from these glens remain loyal to the very clan chiefs who kicked them off the land?

The reason is the land. The clan chief was the ancestral head of the clan, synonymous with country. *Clann* means children *and* strands of hair. The folk were strands off the land's head. When the paternalistic chiefs turned to money-counting lairds and predatory landlordism gutted the lives of the folk, the land itself could not be blamed. It was loyalty and love for the land, lost in the mist of a departing ship. *Oh chì, Chì mi na mòrbheanna*. That's what the folk of the glen kept seeing. The countryself could not die. They held on to the memory of hills and lochs in their mind's eye. And they wrote letters – from Canada – to their vain and treacherous chiefs, pledging loyalty once again.

The dams of Scotland are dwarfed by those in North America and in Asia, still being built now, destroying life in river deltas, evicting indigenous people and enriching giant companies. The devastation is the same everywhere. It is to scale. The Chinese government evicted 1 million people to build a dam on the Mekong.

Maybe it's the sheer size of it, and the total absence of birdsong, but every time I come to Mullardoch, I see the fact of death. The death of nature and the death of men. Hydro workers suffered extreme cold, poor diet and exhaustion, and were maimed and died in these glens, but there's no record of those deaths. The company didn't want their reputation stained. No record of the men who died building Britain's railways and perished in the coal mines. In 1850, there were a quarter of a million navvies, *tramping* from job to job, living in squalor and working on the most dangerous sites. They lay 3,000 miles of railway. They outnumbered the Army and Navy put together. They also died more often, received no respect, and were given no credit for their epic toil. Those given credit are head engineers, politicians who enabled industry, the names behind companies, and eventually all that's left is – the names of the companies.

The face of the industrial world order is here. It is this dam.

At one point in the late 1800s, navvies died in accidents at a rate of 500 a year. The railway company did nothing to improve their living conditions and safety or slow down the pace of labour. Productivity was everything. *Industrious, not rebellious*. The schemes couldn't be stopped. There were targets.

Accidents were gruesome. During the construction of the British railways, men were crushed and decapitated. Later in the Hydro schemes, there were diesel-operated locomotives used for carting spoil from the tunnels, and these occasionally went off-rails or lost their brakes and crushed anyone in their way. The most deaths were caused by explosives, which tore tunnel tigers to pieces. The tunnel tigers were experts in explosives and they blasted and fortified the tunnels – the most dangerous job on the dams. The writer Patrick MacGill witnessed every kind of accident because he worked on railway and Hydro both. He saw the crushing of English Mickie, mourned by his brother. And the 'little tragedy' when English Bill was impaled through the throat by an iron pick ricocheting from an unexploded dynamite charge in the rock. The workers' camp at Kinlochleven had its own proverbs – 'He would gamble on his father's tombstone and play banker with the corpse', and its own graveyard where the unlucky went directly after their last-ever shift. The concrete stubs that mark the graves are still there.

> Bury him deep in the red, red muck, and pile the clay on his breast,
> For all that he needs for his years of toil are years of unbroken rest.*

Before they were buried, they were stripped of their boots because boots along with luck were the top commodity. Most workers were so poor, they had just one shirt. Some had no

---

* *Children of the Dead End* by Patrick MacGill

shirt at all and stole one from sleeping comrades. These are the people who built Britain's industries and enriched bankers, politicians, industrialists and speculative traders. Some were still boys. MacGill was 'a man of twelve' when he hit the road.

The isolation of the workers' camps was doubled by the deliberate ignorance in which they were kept by company bosses. Sometimes not even the gangers (leaders of work gangs) knew what the scheme was actually for.

'All that we knew was that we had gutted whole mountains and hills in the operations,' writes MacGill.

The first large-scale Hydro scheme in Britain was in fact commissioned by the North British Aluminium Company, founded in 1894. North British stood for Scottish in the colonial phrasing that came into use after Culloden. It found an ideal place for its smelting needs on the south banks of Loch Ness. A lot of energy was required to process raw bauxite ore into alumina, and then smelt that to obtain aluminium. It took 19,000 kW of electricity to process 4 tons of bauxite into one ton of metal. Construction on the quiet shores of Loch Ness started in 1895, the next year British Aluminium was already producing 10 per cent of the world's output, and thanks to the abundant waters of Loch Ness, by 1900 it was producing 1,000 tons of aluminium per year. Demand for it was growing worldwide. Why?

Because aluminium is a prime metal in the manufacture of aircraft and weapons.

The results were so lucrative for the company that they decided to expand. More. More. They had expanded as much as possible on Loch Ness, and now turned their attention to the generous waters of Loch Leven to the south of the Great Glen. An industrial hub was built and called Kinlochleven, and it had a workers' village next to the new smelting plant. The Black Water Reservoir built by the Kinlochleven men between 1905 and 1909 was then the largest in Europe: 914 metres long and 27 metres high, the water tunnel 6 kilometres long. And in that pre-mechanical age, all was done by hand, wielding impossibly heavy hammers and axes.

'We turned the Highlands into a cinder-heap, and were as wise at the beginning, as at the end of the task,' wrote MacGill.

Only after completing the Kinlochleven scheme and descending into the town did the workers understand what they had been toiling for. They read about it in the newspapers. This was going to be the first major Hydro plant in the British Isles.

Built by industry and for industry. Not for people.

To this day that power station fuels a large aluminium smelter plant, selling the surplus energy back to the national grid in the usual lucrative set-up. And aluminium is still used for the manufacture of weapons.

The completion of the Black Water Reservoir must have felt like the end of an era, and it was. But it was also the beginning of a new, more dangerous one. Extractive industry enables war, the ultimate extraction. And war requires more extractive industry, in a cycle of production and consumption, whose dead end is extinction. The industrial age manufactured an ideology, an economy, and a vision of mechanical supremacy over nature. It dehumanised humans and denatured nature. The fever of the First World War was fuelled by the successes of European industry, built by the desperados and mercenaries, the slaves and famine survivors, the gypsies of labour and nameless navvies, the children of the dead end.

And by 1942 the United States of America was frantically

building major Hydro schemes to power aluminium factories, to build military aircraft and bombs. Britain couldn't be left behind. A politician and industrial zealot canvassed government and persuaded them that Scotland had enough lochs and hills to provide power for the war and beyond. In 1943, the historic North of Scotland Hydro-Electric Board was founded, and ambitious plans were made for the Highlands. That politician became head of the Board.

Without the war, there would have been no post-war boom in industry manned by people like Wolodimir. The power industry wouldn't have built its mega-infrastructures. It would have built smaller schemes, locally operated and serving people, with less damage to nature. This is how the Highlands had run, until British Aluminium arrived: on small-scale harvesting and processing of local products. Fish, grain for whisky, wool for tweed.

The Hydro-Electric Board aggressively pushed through with the final schemes. The real reason was that a change of government was looming and the company bosses wanted to make sure their projects were completed before they came up for scrutiny.

They knew what the public didn't know: that the last of the schemes were not really needed. The Strathfarrar-Kilmorack scheme, completed last in 1963, was not needed. The national grid was already over capacity. It was clear, early on, that the power generated in these glens would serve consumers in the south, and in particular it would serve large factories.

The very remoteness of these rivers made them more vulnerable. Industry could get away with murder. Like building two dams next to each other. When Monar dam was built, it turned out that it was not enough to hold the banks of the loch and a second, subsidiary dam was built to the west of it, a mass gravity one, but not arched – to do the job that should have been done by a single dam.

It is as with shooting-as-a-disease. Once started, it's hard to stop. The momentum heats up until it burns itself out, like a war. There is the manpower, the resources, the fever of zealotry. The natives can be brow-beaten, silenced and bought out, nature is defenceless, and the mass population has been persuaded that this security upgrade, this special operation, this phase one, phase two and phrase three is necessary. For the growing need of consumers. For the security of the national grid. For economic growth. For the war effort. For the solution of the Highland problem. And to keep your kettle on.

To leave a river undammed that could be dammed – it was too late for such restraint. The global energy industry does not fuel our kettles. It fuels consumption and war.

How I long to taste the essence of Glen Cannich! Is it still possible? Only if I don't go to the dam. Only if I stay close to the birch woods where there is birdsong and moss. It's an Empty Glen not just because everyone is gone. It's because the land is brain-damaged, as after a lobotomy. Its coherence is gone. It has no countryself. The garden has been turned into a machine.

The dams did not bring prosperity, jobs, people or cheap electricity to the Highlands. They devastated the human ecology of the glens. They opened the floodgates to industrial land grabs on an unknown scale. That's where we are now.

A question echoes in the Empty Glen: what did we learn from this?

One of the estates here has just been sold. A selling point was: *potential for a profitable Hydro scheme*. I heard it was bought by a big company which will use the glen to *offset its carbon footprint*. What does this mean? We drill for oil here, extract cobalt there, cut down forests for biomass fuel everywhere – but we build *another* dam and Hydro scheme on a Scottish river and our employees drive electric cars.

At the base of Mullardoch dam, I lose Bella. Where did I last see her? I whistle and call. The thud of turbines churning water is all I hear. I run to the top of the dam with its locked iron gate. The earth shudders under my feet. The sleet comes in gusts. Anguish chokes me. Then I see her – sitting by the car: it's time to go. I cuddle her and cry with relief, and we set off.

And the women of Cannich who heard the banging noises and the witches singing?

I can see them walking in the whispering birches. They serviced the big houses of estate owners and lived in cottages in the lower part of the glen, now empty or gone. Their quiet land was invaded by thousands of men and machines. The noise of industry was constant, for years. And they couldn't get away from it. I know how that feels.

And that man walking down through the birch forest to Cannich village, whistling a tune I almost recognise? He wears his better clothes though his boots are coming apart. Wolodimir. He hopes to get some fresh eggs and milk from someone because the food at the camp is dire. Spam (slices of processed pork), tripe soup that made him retch, powdered eggs, powdered milk, stale bread and not a vegetable in sight. Some of the lads strike deals with the local stalkers and get fresh venison, but he can't afford it. The tunnel tigers are the best paid. The Mullardoch boys broke a European record for most rock taken out of a hill in a single week. They extracted 3 million tons of rock to make the tunnel between Mullardoch and Benevean in Affric. Two hundred and fifty-three tons of gelignite were used for that.

Two local lads, tunnel tigers, went and bought a car with their wages but got drunk and drove the car into Loch Ness. They survived and bought another car the following weekend.

He peers through the birch trees. A fresh egg and a woman's face would be nice to see. The old mill maybe? There is a light on. He crosses the small bridge with hope and takes off his cap.

Many years later when Wolodimir walked home from the sawmill on a spring evening like this, he would stop and lean on one of the old oaks. The sunset blazed over the braes of the Monks' Place. The braes were a patchwork — here's corn, there's tatties, there's the black cattle, and the creamy oats. How could he explain to anyone, anyone other than his one or two friends that had travelled the same road, but nobody in this world had really travelled the same road as him. Starting on that day when the Germans arrived and went from house to house. Of the three brothers, Wolodimir was picked, maybe because he was nineteen and seen as a good work horse. His uncle tried to stop them and the Germans shot him. Wolodimir can't forget the scene. It cut his life in two.

I walk in Wolodimir's steps, I put my foot down and touch his, and something of his impulse travels to me like a frequency. Another day. The sun is setting over the Five Forts of Farley. Wolodimir is walking home. His wee boy cooking dinner for his mother in the wheelchair. They'll be there. Nothing is sweeter than having someone you love waiting for you at home, nothing except winning the war against the bastards. His back is sore but to have your hair stroked by the May wind and know that life's not over yet — what is greater than this?

The May wind is benevolent. Sometimes, he really felt the

presence of a guardian angel. Just as he'd felt the presence of absolute evil. How evil walks the Earth. He could not bring back all the lost people – the ones he'd known and all the murdered strangers. But the guardian was there. How else to explain that day towards the end in the German camp, when the Allied bombers passed overhead and everybody knew it was the end of the war and any day now they'd be free. That day the Allied bombers passed overhead, there were the usual shouts – Shelter! And normally he would, like everybody else, but that day Wolodimir heard a quiet voice say to him: *Don't go.* He stood nailed to the ground. The next moment, a bomb fell on the shelter, killing everyone inside. All the men and women he'd gotten to know. He was alone in a ruined world.

What was it all for? All this savagery, this separation. All this improving, removing, clearing, erecting, constructing, enclosing, drilling, dynamiting, burning, extracting, all these clean solutions that were filthy. So much toil and torment. Sometimes when he looked at the site of the dam in progress, the river severed in two and the hills gralloched of their viscera, and the hundreds of men moving around like grey ants on a heap, he imagined they were building the pyramids. Their names would not survive but the pharaoh's would.

The dams were progress, he was helping build the future and he wasn't unhappy, but he couldn't help what he saw. The dynamite, the concrete, the iron, the shafts, the miles of tunnelling, the poor bodies covered in perpetual dust like souls at the gates of hell.

Eighteen men were killed in the building of Mullardoch dam. There is no memorial: the Board didn't want to leave a record of human death. Their names and faces are gone but Cannich remembers the number: eighteen. The tunnel tigers who were blown up in Mullardoch, Wolodimir can still see the clean rivulets of tears down the dusty faces of their mates.

For a few weeks he worked as a powder monkey. The powder monkey was a guy who sat all day at a table and handed out explosives to the tunnel tigers. It was a boring job and he gave it up and went back to shovelling and drilling again – at least there was craic to be had there, and he enjoyed craic. Both the word and the thing.

He can't help but wonder, when he sees the new dams now. And each day, on the way back from the sawmills, he walks past the gravel pit. He remembers when the gravel pit was opened up. The idea was to quarry gravel for the Kilmorack dam. He remembers when work started on that dam, the shock on the faces of people, his own shock. What, another one? It destroyed the cascades of Kilmorack. The dam was completed but the gravel pit kept growing. All the promises made – thousands of jobs, prosperity, more people in the glens – they were false. He can't help but notice that only a few of the Hydro boys have stayed on like him.

Soon after the Kilmorack dam was completed, the Kilmorack church had its last service and was locked up. He went in once, to look at the stained-glass windows like a time capsule.

When it opened its doors again, he was amazed. Has it really been thirty years? He walked in and looked at the stained-glass windows and smiled. The guy his son's age who was doing it up had holes in his jumper and moved quickly up and down dangerous home-made scaffolding.

'Bravo, my boy,' he said to him. 'You have to give it your best.'

He too had given it his best. You have to. Then –

After all the miles you've covered and all the lives you've lived, well, you think you aspire to some ultimate purpose.

But maybe all that you need is this, and this is the secret rapture of gypsies and long-distance kiddies, of Travellers and desperadoes who face the open road, even refugees. To walk back from the horse betting in town, along the Firth that glitters like a gateway to heaven but it's the Highlands and maybe that's as close as you get.

    To walk back to a place you can call home, and for the May wind to stroke you like an angel's wing.

The Crossing Place, loss

We sit on the patio. It's the weekend, the quarry is not working and the silence reminds us of how things used to be. We have adapted to the ring of steel and the electro-magnetic radiation. But we can't get used to the crushing of gravel next door, the noise is like machine guns. *Ta-ta-ta-ta-ta-ta-ta*. They're excavating the floor of the forest where 150 species used to live, nest, walk, nibble mushrooms and hibernate.

We have been living inside with closed windows, avoiding the garden all summer. I work with headphones on or go for long walks but the noise carries everywhere. The noise is in my head. Tony escapes to the gallery. But in the gallery, you can hear the *ta-ta-ta-ta-ta* of the private quarry up the glen where our dream croft sold to an extractor.

I dream that I am moving across a furrowed battlefield. Diggers like tanks are moving along the furrows. Trenches of suffering, a desert of the mind, a mechanical world without end. If I stay, they will drive over me. I survey the land for a scrap of green, but there is nothing left. Open graves waiting to be filled. The sky is cut into pieces by wire. I run inside the open graves and disappear from myself. I wake up and weep in the night. Tony holds me.

'If you leave, I'll just get on with things here,' Tony says. 'Because I can't leave. I have duties. I have the gallery.'

He flips a barbecued mushroom on my plate.

'And I accept that everything goes south and we die. But I'll still love you if all your hair falls out.'

My hair has been falling out. I feel Tony's pain for him. You have to, when you live with a stoic.

Tony used to be a peaceful soul and now he is rushing to get artist shows up and running, rushing to plant trees, pushing through the crash of industry, getting up in the dark before industry traffic starts, to get some quiet time. We are under siege.

I too will still love you. I put salad on his plate. But I am drifting away and can't stop. Something has been eroded, a landslide. I can't see the way forward from here anymore. I need to get away and return to myself.

It has been ten years. I am leaving the Crossing Place where I learned that peace is an inner garden you cultivate. That to love is to see. Chì mi. And that when you stay in a place, you begin to resonate with it. You see things and hear things that belong to the place, not to you.

Our mission here will go on. We inherited it from our land ancestors. What happened to us, last time we were here?

Maybe we went on a droving expedition and were lost in the fog with our cattle, and our bones were picked clean by ravens. Or in some wretched famine when we bled the cows and mixed the blood with gruel, and watched our kin wander in search of something to eat until they lay in the heather and died with relief. When we picked them up they were light as seaweed. We have forgotten the details but brought the unfinished mission with us into this lifetime.

I moved to the Monks' Place two miles away. Tony brought a pile of paintings by my favourite artists and put them up on my blank walls.

I bought a house, the first house I'd ever owned, but I was unmoored. For the first time I felt disconnected from Scotland. I roamed like a ghost. Should I leave the country? I went back to Bulgaria for a time, walked forked roads, took dangerous turns, slipped into the skin of other lives imagining that I belonged there and I did, for a season. But I returned to the Monks' Place. I straightened the paintings on my wall. Tony had bought me a new fridge and plugged it in! The dust of the road settled. I accepted my new reality and planted up my garden with herbs and roamed the river of the Monks. I witnessed the fall of the oldest inhabitant of the Monks' Place: the Wych elm, 800 years old. It was ceremonially carried out. People thought it would last forever. I'd walk past it and wonder who had planted the sapling. Someone like Tony, with long hair and a hemp robe, barefoot and selfless.

At night, the outline of the ruined monastery looks like a forest. It was all woodland here, once. The monks were the first to clear it for pasture and cultivation. My neighbour is a Celtic witch. She makes voodoo dolls of people she doesn't like, which is most people, and puts them in the freezer. Better to make friends, so I make her herbal teas but she takes a dislike to me and I'm sure there is a voodoo doll in the freezer with my hair. And there's my other neighbour, the tree surgeon, waving from his campervan. He is off to Bosnia for the first time since the war, to make peace with the land and himself. I give him a small bottle of elderberry syrup for the road.

It suits me well, this monastic existence. Me and the creative daimon and nothing between us. The faces and places from the book of my life never leave me.

My bed points downstream, and my feet to the sea. Estuary dreams pass through me like seasons. Sometimes I close my eyes and see the Firth frozen over and snow drifting inland:

an Ice Age has come to the Highlands but I can't tell if it's past or future.

I like it in the doorway of the sea and I accept my need for solitude. But a sadness remains like a background hum: our world, our glen, our Crossing Place, what will become of them? *We get on with things* in our separate homes yet Tony and I remain each other's person. The seasons reseed themselves. Like the flowerhead of a chive. I miss the chives of the Crossing Place but Tony brings me a pot of them.

Tony feeds the birds and tends his flock of artists. He witnesses the lives of his client-friends who come into the gallery as to a confessional. Most conversations now revolve around the environment and how we are losing it to energy hubs. The one thing that unites all across social class and nationality is the love of art and the love of the Highlands. Tony continues with the lifting and moving, transporting, packaging, fixing, and writing about art.

The garden in the Crossing Place remains strung up with Tibetan prayer flags, to which you add a fresh one in the spring and let the old ones rot away. As a reminder that everything that is born dies. Even the Earth will die. Only love is unborn.

Chì mi

On my way to visit Rowan in her hilltop farm, I stop in Corrimony to see Ciara.

Corrimony is folded away from the world. It's a glen-within-the-glen that runs like a magical corridor between our glen and the Great Glen. So many rivers! Even Corrimony has its own river and waterfalls. It's famous for its big burial cairn with standing stones around it. I see people approaching and asking the keeper to let them in. The keeper is a spirit but that doesn't mean you shouldn't ask her. I see myself crawling through the stone corridor of the cairn, scared of getting trapped, and there's the burial chamber like a round house holding nothing, long plundered of bones and treasure, but the stones remain where hands put them first. Who was Mony? Nobody knows. A land ancestor. Maybe she was the woman buried crouching inside the cairn. Or maybe she only passed through here and left behind her name. Over time the cairn became fused with Mony. Many cairns contained the crouched bodies of women. The Picts were a matrilineal society and their richly pictorial view of the world evolved into Celtic design. Its central form was the spiral. Nature is round. Mony's cairn is round, inside this round corrie. The old Christian graveyard is round. And the Clach-an-Tullan is round. That's the baptismal font which survived the complete destruction of the church by Reformist zealots.

Corrimony is a bowl, says Ciara in her west-coast Irish that makes her sound like a perpetual poet, and we are on the lower edge of the rim. There are two houses along the lower edge – the old shepherd and his wife the Gaelic teacher, and the keeper's house where Ciara lives with the keeper and their son.

Ciara is a gardener and keeps a big garden in a house owned by a man who is not here, but at least he hasn't sold out to a developer. Others have. Industry's foot is already in Corrimony's door. When the first wind turbines arrived, the blades were so big, a road was built for the lorries. It cut through a farm and chipped the bowl of Corrimony. More are on the way. A new application has come for another fourteen turbines, 149.9 metres high, plus pits, access roads, substation and hardware.

Ciara used to live in the city but the river and hill pulled at her. Now she's river bailiff. That means if you want to fish, you ask her – and from the chipped rim of Corrimony's bowl, she will answer you. Six people own that stretch of river. She's been here twenty years like me, and it still staggers us both that so few own so much. Does it matter? It does. But what matters more is the relationship.

I'm a Gypsy, I kept moving till I came here, says Ciara, then I fell in love with this place and stopped. I've never owned a house. I tell myself it doesn't matter, but maybe it does?

I don't know. But if you didn't keep the garden alive, this would be one sad and empty chipped Corrimony. You fill the bowl with food, I say. The keeper is a tall Highlander with a beard. All he does is work. There's no shooting here, just odd jobs. They have no neighbours. It's quiet in Corrimony. You get to know the trails to the waterfall on the high edge. It's an undammed waterfall, a miracle! But the river is dammed.

We climb above a private Hydro station on the river, another one! It belongs to a wealthy charity organisation for the protection of birds.

'The destruction of the land is so far gone, I don't know if there's any hope,' says Ciara. It's winter and she's blue like a Cailleach because she's away from the garden. The waterfall thunders, the trees are bare, the garden is mud and we climb to a place where all you can see is wind farms in every direction. I used to walk to Giusachan that way, Ciara says, but they have wrecked the trail. There are applications for more wind farms – on that hill, and that one. It means more forests cut down, more hardware brought in, an access road by the cairn. Maybe the developers will level the cairn too. The *homes of the silent vanished races** are not profitable.

The ruins of a large bobbin mill sit on the higher lip of the bowl. Bobbin mills were in vogue once, they made quick money for the textile industry.

'The only way to protect the land is to uncouple it from money,' Ciara says.

It's August. The centre of the bowl is a field of pumpkins and flowers. I see a gleaming machine moving through the field – it's a robot picking pumpkins! Weird to see this tech body harvesting living things. The old couple drive past and wave.

> * From 'The Whaups' by Robert Louis Stevenson:
> *Gray, recumbent tombs of the dead in desert places,*
> *Standing stones on the vacant, red-wine moor,*
> *Hills of sheep, and the homes of the silent vanished races*
> *And winds austere and pure!*

They have gone past the sadness of being the last Gaels of Corrimony. The crowns of trees are in rapture. The gnarly oak by the keeper's house is so ancient it might be left from a Druid's grove. It was struck by lightning like a stroke, but it's leafing again! We're all leafing. Ciara's hands are busy, everything is growing in her garden that isn't hers, she is herself again. The land is itself, I am myself, it's impossible not to be happy, and the only thing in Corrimony that is neither happy nor sad is the robot picking pumpkins.

Back to the Land

Rowan's farm sits on the upper rim of an amphitheatre-like valley not far from the bowl of Corrimony. You can't see Loch Ness but you can see the steely light above it. Every time you look, you catch the hills thinking of moving on. If you turn your back, you've missed it. But up here you can't turn your back to the hills, they're everywhere. On every hill there are remains of standing stones, cairns and hut circles. They are dots that join up to form another country above the country, closer to the sublime.

We climb through heather to the nearest hilltop above the house, and the Great Glen opens up below like the interior of the Earth. Stargazing becomes second nature. Air-traffic gazing too. This is the route of passenger planes to the islands. You track the sky and notice every change. For example, there have been more jets lately and they aren't scheduled flights to the islands. Military exercises? Lots of dirty white streaks that don't dissolve for ages. Rowan looks at them every day and wonders. Walking up here makes you want to sing to the peaks and valleys at your feet. But there is another, mechanical song now — many of the hills are *hosting* wind farms, their blades harvesting an invisible crop.

'They look like they're advancing. Taking over the land,' says Rowan.

Rowan is one of the new friends I've made since leaving the Crossing Place. It's a bright winter. She has been clearing the Stone. The size of the Stone is not known. You have to do it gently not to damage it. You can become obsessed with it, peeling back the mossy soil to reveal more of the Stone's surface, like uncovering details of a prehistoric painting. One day, the dots will join up into yet another ghostly map.

In places, there are large crystal intrusions.

'Quartz and garnet. Otherwise the generic name for this kind of stone is hornblende mica schist. It's quite common in this area.'

It has taken years to reveal a bit of it. First they cut the gorse that choked the dark woods. Then the layer of earth, inch by inch. Volunteers help with it. All sorts of people come. The family in a campervan who weren't practical but built decorative stone rims for the pond and talked to water sprites. The girl with green fingers and inherited trauma who decided to pilgrimage to her ancestral homeland, while she was here. The guy who enjoyed digging up the old well, and after that we dowsed with rods for the stream. The nephew who built a fence for the goats Rowan will accidentally acquire in the spring. People are drawn to the wood, and in the wood is this stony outcrop, like the floor of a ruined palace. The air is different among the trees. The wood inhales and everything exhales with relish. *Aaah.*

You stand in a submerged world on top of the world.

Many of the volunteers are souls in search of something. Something that looks like this farm.

'People looking for a better way to live. With less material things and more nature, more passion. Lots of creative types. Mostly in their twenties and thirties.'

Everybody finds something to do while they stay. It's always been this way in the Highlands. Travellers and peripatetic visitors would stop on a friendly farm and camp for a while in exchange for odd jobs and making things. Wicker baskets from willow, with a rim of rowan or hazel. Horn spoons – you soften a ram's horn in hot water and shape it into a spoon. Pot scrubs from heather. And heather ale from the purple flowers, made in big pots with golden syrup and hops.

Rowan and her husband used to travel. Then they settled here and their daughter Evie arrived. Now the world comes to them.

Rock rose and thyme grow well, even from the Stone. It's surprisingly fertile for such an exposed hilltop. As if growth is accelerated.

'The farmer who sold us this place did say: your sheep will have lots of twins. It's this place makes everything double. I'm still waiting though.'

Rowan is planning to milk a couple of sheep next season. She has never done it and I've only milked goats but I'll give it a go with her. You learn on the hoof.

'I call it intuitive farming.'

Yes, but informed by twenty years of working in human ecology. Rowan studied geology, travelled the world and worked in conservation. She lived in Tanzania for a time, carrying out research into the biodiversity of remote mountainous forests. Once a year she ran a nature tour for visitors, to fund her studies. And her studies became more and more focused on the impact of misguided management in a new national park aiming to conserve orchids. But it did much more damage than good for the people of the land.

'And the orchids!'

The research became too expensive and too political. So she ended up focusing on taking people to enjoy the flowers and raise awareness instead. The biodiversity, the purity and the way people were still close to animals and plants – she found there what she couldn't find here. But the time came to leave. Leaving the highlands of Tanzania was hard but that is what it took to return to these highlands. Her ancestors were from here – until life was nibbled to a desert by landlordism and they started leaving for greener pastures, south.

To get to Rowan's place, you cross a footbridge. When Rowan and her man came to see the old cottage with land for sale, she sat in the wood where she and their future daughter Evie and future friends and animals would spend happy years.

'And when I closed my eyes, I was in a time vortex. My two grans were there. My English gran and my Scottish gran. I knew then that the place was speaking to me.'

By then, the couple were coming up against the same thing in their conservation work: the western approach to land management is not working. They were frustrated. The only way to restore a piece of land to balance is to work with it over time. They bought this place. Rowan quit her job and took on the management of the land. It happened bit by bit. They tackled the lifeless Sitka spruce plantation where birdsong was rarely heard. They cleared the invasive gorse from where the old field road had passed. The forest was clarified by a woodsman called Dylan and his horse Nomad. He cut the Sitka and let the light in and the horse pulled them out. The forest floor came to life. Mushrooms, hedgehogs, juniper and blaeberries appeared. Native trees self-seeded. The trees he felled have been used as fuel and to make fences, sheds and a little bridge for the pond which breeds more wildlife. Ducks are coming next: they are low maintenance and give eggs.

And the birds returned!

Once the forest was tackled, they got a few horned sheep. Soay and Shetland, native breeds that are densely woolly and tough. Rowan felts the wool and makes rough covers with it, used around the house and on vegetable beds.

We visit them on a sloping field. They spend the whole year outdoors, munching their way across the hillside. The density of animals (low) versus plants (high) is ideal. This means it's not overgrazed. The pasture has time to recover as they circulate. They greet us with interested faces.

'Hello, Breaches, my love.' Breaches looks at Rowan with devotion. She has one broken horn and smoky-tinged wool, so dense you could shelter next to her in a storm. They remind me of the Karakachan sheep I spent a summer with. All indigenous grazing animals are perfectly adapted to their environment. Here it means exposed hills and rugged coast. They like seaweed and Rowan collects it from the coast for them.

There were twelve last year and now there are twenty. Two went into the freezer. Rowan couldn't catch them because they ran amok, crazed by the mechanical noise of diggers, and they were uncooperative boys anyway, poor boys.

Before the Clearances, a typical Highland community was made up of families that each had a cow or two, some sheep and some goats. Grazing animals were small and semi-wild because they lived outdoors and had no fencing. They roamed the hills together and gave milk, wool for spinning, and occasionally – meat. It was a subsistence economy, as in all pre-industrial rural societies.

Rowan grew up in the country where England and Wales meet. Her happiest times were summers with her grans. Her English gran had a huge garden and goats that she milked. And her Scottish gran lived in England but always talked in a wobbly voice about Glen Gairn where she grew up. Glen Gairn has no people anymore.

Her Scottish gran's uncle was green keeper of the royal grounds in the Balmoral estate. A green keeper looked after everything alive – fish and deer, river and hill. One time, the green keeper was ordered to shoot the otters in the river – they were eating the fish that King George VI wanted for himself on his Scottish holidays.

'My great-uncle loved those otters; he saw them every day. They trusted him. He shot them and it broke his heart.'

The memory has stayed in the family. Then the family was *encouraged* to leave their enchanted Glen Gairn, under the pretext that the house was infested with woodworm. But other tenants were installed. And later, when someone came into the abandoned house to look for that woodworm, there was none and it seems that the land was later cleared for military exercises. The farm was abandoned in the 1950s and the glen fell into a grouse-shooting estate. The green keeper's family moved south. Rowan's gran married a man who was big in the flower-and-garden world.

'They had a big house and a life of parties and hosting. But she wasn't cut out for it. She always talked of Glen Gairn. That's where she had felt free, before marrying and playing this role.'

Rowan's mother too was estranged from her family's homeland but brought Rowan to Scotland for holidays.

'You know it in your heart when something's right. And Scotland always pulled at me.'

Every year on her Scottish gran's birthday, Rowan travels to Glen Gairn. It's quite far. Next time she will take Evie, who is ten.

'Any excuse to visit. The ruin of Gran's house is still there. I visit the leopard's bane. My flower.'

I love leopard's bane's sun-like heads! In herbal medicine it dispels congestion in the chest. Rowan learned about herbal uses in Tanzania. For example, how mugwort is used on people and animals for de-worming and malaria. So she makes a blend: mugwort, turmeric, garlic, nettles, thyme, sage and molasses – and mixes it in with the oat and pea feed. The sheep like it and they've never had worms. I would quite like it too.

'I won't have chemical dipping and inspectors manhandling my sheep. That's why we don't take subsidies.'

Plus she doesn't agree with the mindset of taking subsidies for everything. It encourages dependency. When there is easy money, people breed, plant, extract and erect the same thing all over the land. Great white sheep. Corduroy forests. Wind farms and battery storage systems.

The farm was de-crofted by the previous owner, who made it into a commercial farm. Crofting and de-crofting is about practical things. You can't build on a croft, for example, and you can't run a commercial venture. Historically, a croft is a piece of land dedicated to agriculture, and it's protected. This protection was bitterly hard-won by the Highlanders in the long wake of the Clearances. In the late nineteenth century, the crofters revolted against the continuing affliction of landlords having every right and tenants none, and their revolt culminated in the Crofters Holdings Act of 1886. A basic justice earned through centuries of injustice. It gave small-scale farmers and subsistence growers the right to remain on the land and in turn, they committed to working the land. For a while in the twentieth century, the croft embodied healthy land stewardship. Then people started buying crofts simply to own land: a future asset. But they were alien to the culture and craft of it. The croft became another speculative investment, a picturesque attraction. The absentee crofters – a contradiction in terms – undermined the cause of the Crofters Act. Today, it's a suburban affectation to call your house Croft this and Croft that, even if nothing edible grows and the ground is all gravel. This is what happens when the real thing disappears from the land – only its name remains.

And for those who want to run real crofts, crofting has become a procedural maze. A friend of Rowan's with sheep on her croft had a visiting inspector who told her to sell off her lambs quickly. But I want to keep them longer, she protested. Yeah but if you sell them now, your carbon footprint on the croft will be reduced and we'll tick that off and you can get some money for carbon offset. But these lambs will still be somewhere, the friend protested. That won't be your problem, said the official.

'That's why we want to be free. And this is where I want to sow my oats and barley next year. And I'm thinking of sowing calendula and leopard's bane. We can make tinctures and teas!'

A cold and gloomy spring. We need more sun. It's been a long winter. The war machine hasn't stopped. The industrial machine keeps it company. We lie in the moonlight, she on the hilltop, me by the river. How to stop the destruction?

There are new plans for three massive Hydro pump schemes on Loch Ness. That's on top of the existing one which was completed in 1974 and remains the largest in the country, processing 200 tons of water per second. These Hydro pumps involve drilling at least half a kilometre into the hills, pumping the water of the loch uphill, storing it, and then using it to generate power. The construction phase would involve workers' camps, huge dams, tunnels, new roads, decades more of mechanical noise and machinery, light pollution, and us watching industry smash the face of the Great Glen. And the *operational phase* would involve the continuous extraction of Loch Ness accompanied by a constant maddening hum.

Why? For the same reasons as the other energy hubs: to export energy at great distance to the south, down gigantic new transmission lines – and the water needs to be recruited for the times when *the wind doesn't blow* and *the sun doesn't shine*.

'Loch Ness is a living organism. We have to remember this or we're screwed.'

A year later, Rowan and her husband set up a citizen group to raise awareness of the impending industrial takeover of Loch Ness. It's the magnitude of the ecological destruction that has spurred them to action. If just one of these new schemes went ahead, the level of the loch would fluctuate by 73 centimetres. That's drastic. Tampering with the levels of a loch whose ecosystem is on the brink, whose salmon are endangered, and that lies in a tectonically active fault – you don't have to be an ecologist to see that it is wrong. It is dishonest to talk about *decarbonising the grid* while destroying the fragile ecosystem of Loch Ness. It is immoral to boast about the billions of pounds this will generate (for big companies and their shareholders) while destroying nature and displacing people and animals. It is a delusion that *pumped storage Hydro schemes can help tackle the issues caused by climate change by releasing water during dry periods and storing water to help flood management* – this from the developer. It's a lie that pumping, drilling and impounding Loch Ness will offer *a range of benefits including better water management, substantial carbon savings, improved energy security and a boost to local jobs*.

Where have we heard this before?

We have some hope about zonal pricing, which is being discussed. It is not the innovative technology that's needed. It is just a regional approach to the existing technology. It offers an alternative to grid gigantism. Zonal pricing means energy is generated closer to where it's needed. Instead of one mammoth grid that spreads like a cancer across the whole of the country, we would have smaller, stabler grids where every wind farm is accountable for what it generates. No *constraint payments*. No battery storage systems. A much smaller footprint, less wasted public money, more agency for communities and less nature destroyed. It would also mean lower electricity prices. It seems like common sense.

Will decision-makers put common sense before the interests of a global fleet of water-mining, air-mining, sea-mining, gas-mining, oil-mining, rare-mineral mining, space-mining, pocket-mining and health-mining corporations?

Rowan is dubious. From up here, she sees things with painful clarity.

'They are destroying the land from the top down. The uphill peatlands, the sources of the rivers. It's where all life starts, and that's where they're building these hubs.'

Then the toxic chemicals trickle down from the top. Into the soil, into the ground water.

We look at the gorse. It's blooming like crazy. And there's some primrose to keep us hopeful.

And – the sheep are lambing and it's all twins this year! They are immediately on their feet. The births are all easy. Rowan would get up in the small hours, make a thermos of tea and come out to look for newborns on the hillside. And watch the sun rise, wrapped in a blanket. Then go to the house and make breakfast. Parenting and being on the land are a full-time job. There's no money in this kind of small-scale crofting. The aim is to not lose money. But the payoff is self-sufficiency.

'And it feeds your soul! To see the land blossoming. I'm constantly learning, no two days are the same.'

When a sheep has to be culled, Rowan calls a local guy who used to be a deer stalker. He comes and shoots the sheep with a silent shotgun. He showed Rowan how to disembowel the animal. The meat is frozen and used to feed the family and the volunteers. Evie doesn't eat meat and her parents rarely.

'I thought I'd do the slaughtering myself because it's more honest, but it's too much. And I can't send an animal of mine to the slaughterhouse. But death is part of the cycle.'

The deer stalker-cum-butcher told Rowan that he often lies about his job in polite company. There is a stigma.

'Yet they want the pack of chops in the shop.'

Once a year, the same guy comes and shears the sheep. The excess wool Rowan gives to another small farmer who makes rugs from the raw fleece. Small-scale living has always involved barter and sharing. Rowan has been looking into sheep feed. How do you get feed that's not genetically modified? There is just one supplier in the country of non-GM oat and barley.

At one end of the sloping sheep field is an old plough. The sheep scratch against it. That's where Rowan wants to sow oats and barley, the two traditional crops, because it's cheaper and sustainable to grow your own. Barley broth was a staple for centuries here. She asked the supplier of non-GM feed to sell her some seed. But they don't sell it. We keep it safe, they said.

'And organic feed without soya isn't on the market at all! But my ancestors had free access to organic seed. Where's that seed now? Has it disappeared off the face of the Earth?'

It is the same with human food.

A farmer on an isle off the west coast has organic oat fields, oat growing in the family for generations. Rowan and Evie visited them.

'They're still eating the oats of three years ago because oats go a long way. He uses a salvaged threshing machine.'

Oat is the Scottish crop. It has endured. People sowed it by hand and some still do – out of reverence. You have a canvas creel slung across your shoulders and you dip one hand, then the other, in walking meditation, and throw the seed in the warm land.

But the oat sowing will be delayed because Scottish Water will arrive to upgrade pipes around the fields. This stresses the sheep who bolt from the diggers' rattle, and by early autumn Rowan decides not to stress them further by milking them. This is not the year for oats or milking. Or for the garden.

'Last year we had lots of veg. This year, weeds. So we eat the weeds in salads.'

It's been wet. Slugs eat your leafy veg. But even without slugs, a vegetable garden is unpredictable. No two years are the same. This is why if you grow a single crop and it fails, you starve. You can forage but it's a full-time job and you get skinny fast. You fall back on your preserves but did you make enough jars? Pickles and syrups, dried mushrooms and winter onions go quickly. And the winter is long. Living off the land is constant work.

Robots can pick a monocrop from a field of even rows. But can robots forage?

Scotland's most voluminous crop is the potato, exported as far as Israel and Iraq. But before the potato arrived and took a monopoly, it was barley, kale, cabbage, turnip, corn, pea and oat. Oatcakes, oat bannocks, oatmeal. When people said bread, they meant oat bread. A typical daily meal for a subsistence household was this: porridge and milk for breakfast, potatoes and milk for dinner. It was because milk and cheese were so precious that the family animals were slaughtered only as a desperate measure.

We're on the Stone.

'These rough patches are called calcareous outcrops.'

I sit in the special spot. When you sit here, you sense a force in the earth. It's like a vibration that comes through your body.

And here come Pickles and Nyika. They've pushed open the little gate of their enclosure in the woods and bounce up to Rowan with puppy-like devotion. Although they're quite big now.

'Hello, my love.' Pickles rubs his head on her thigh. His horns are impressive.

Rowan built this enclosure because they'd break their tethers and come up to the house, looking pleased with themselves that they'd found her. They knew she'd saved them. She got them off a sheep farmer. They were badly neglected, waiting to be shot like pests – not even for the slaughterhouse. He'd castrated them first. Castrated billy-goat kids means no milk and no babies. You only need one for insemination, the rest are meat or vermin. That's the industrial mindset. Rowan brought them home in the back of the pick-up truck, with no plan.

'I thought we'd re-home them but they've become part of the family. Pickles is a bit of a pain. He's quite strong and won't stay put.'

In the first few weeks Pickles followed her everywhere. Useless goats, her husband muttered, we can't afford more pets. We have two dogs. Maybe we should get them a nanny goat at least, for milk. Then they'll be working goats.

Rowan takes them out in the morning and evening. It's a lot of footwork.

Goats are much more like dogs and not at all like sheep. Something I'd noticed during my season with pastoralists in Bulgaria. Sheep have a collective head but goats have a mind of their own. We take them for a walk down the hill on long ropes.

Pickles! Nyika!

Pickles is neurotic and butts at Nyika to dislodge him but also puts his grazing head next to Nyika's. Nyika is confident and tolerant. Pickles was skin and bones when she picked them up, maybe that's why. Or just personality.

Six months later, Pickles is a changed man. He is relaxed and still so happy to see Rowan, he hops and smiles. A third goat has joined them: Lily. Lily came from the neighbours and has sweet floppy ears and is more independent than the two guys. She likes her own space in the generous enclosure and only joins in when we go for a walk.

'Come, let's show Kapka what you've done to my young rowan trees. But we've made peace with it, haven't we!'

They munched the bark. Rowan was annoyed but then read up on it and it turns out rowan in this kind of mixed wood should be coppiced every five years. Well, the goats coppiced it. The older rowan that hadn't been coppiced had been slowly dying among the dense Sitka spruce.

Now that Lily is here, starting a small herd is inevitable. Except the guys are castrated. A buck will be brought for a few days, so the quest begins: where to get a buck. A few weeks later, Rowan notices that Lily is in kid! The castration of Pickles had not been successful, hurray. So there will be milk.

Pickles, Nyika and Lily graze as they please and won't be moved. We have to move at their pace. The pastoral clock is different. You become part of the scene and disappear from the industrial world.

'The other day I was walking with these guys when I suddenly remembered that my great-great-grandfather used to walk his sheep. From Glen Gairn to the west coast! He was a pastoralist! It brought tears to my eyes. I had to sit down on that trunk. I'd completely forgotten. Then I remembered something else.'

When they bought this place, there was a clause in the deeds about some common grazing ground above the house. That's the hills where Rowan walks with the dogs. They had good pasture once, before the grazing animals disappeared and heather took over for grouse shooting. Where heather and bracken have taken over, the soil is poor for growing anything but it's fine for grazing.

Let's not bother with that, the solicitor told them, you won't be needing grazing ground.

'But now I do. I'd like to take these guys for a walk, together with the dogs. And maybe the sheep. To graze upland, like they're meant to. But do I have legal access to that common grazing? Or did we forfeit our access to it with a light hand, not realising what we'd lose. Did he *encourage* us to give up grazing commons just as my ancestors were *encouraged* to abandon their land?'

Something to pursue with the solicitor.

The goats are having a go at the young birches planted by Rowan and we pull them away. That's why they can't be let loose for too long and must be walked.

The sheep graze these flower-rich areas from November to March. And their grazing encourages hundreds of new orchids to come through. But goats eat everything and this is where Pickles ate my greater butterfly orchids, the little shit, says Rowan.

Last week Rowan and Evie were goatwalking to the boundary of the neighbouring field. The neighbouring field is vast and owned as a holiday place. The owner gave her a row once, when he was here for a week and saw a sheep go onto their land. Their field has no animals, crops, or anything else that moves other than high grass in the wind. He wore tweed from head to toe, in some lairdish Highland fantasy from another century.

'He totally looked down on me. My hands were covered in soil. I guess I was spoiling the scene for him.'

Anyway, Evie and Rowan were goatwalking here when Evie said:

'Mum, there is a woman.'

Rowan couldn't see a woman. The woman wore a long dress and walked across the field towards them, Evie said. Rowan knew what this was. Evie's second sight is place-specific.

They crossed into the neighbour's field after the goats, who had jumped over the fence, and the woman followed them.

'What is she saying, I asked Evie, what does she want? It was making me jumpy.'

But Evie was totally cool.

'Nothing, Mum, she said. She is just sad because she says the land is not used as it should be anymore. For the people. Like it was when she lived here. She is sad for the land.'

Then the woman was gone.

Evie's special sight revealed itself gradually. Once, Evie and Rowan were hanging out at the top of the hill. There is a big rock there. Evie put her hand on the rock and told Rowan what she saw. Two men fighting with swords and a lot of blood. One was well dressed and armoured. The other was in rags and he was killed, horribly. These hills were in fact the site of a medieval clan battle known as Blàr na Léine. Battle of the Shirts. None of us knew this until I came across it by chance in a history book. Hundreds of men were killed on both sides, just thirteen survived. The day of the battle was so hot, the clansmen took off their plaids and fought in their shirts.

The poor man looked like a peasant, said Evie. And that's what clansmen were – peasants indentured to fight for their chiefs in clan battles, in exchange for the right to subsist from the land. They could be chucked off it without notice, with their families. Which is what happened when landlordism replaced clan chiefdom.

You don't need to be born of the land to read the land. Evie is adopted. Her ancestors came from the Caribbean. Her birth mother lived in the Highlands the years leading up to her early death, but Evie was already separated from her and stayed with another family – until Rowan came along. The decision was made soon after – that Rowan would give up her paid job and be fully available to her daughter. And the land.

'It's strange how things return in a different form,' Rowan says. 'It all takes careful nurturing. I don't want to make a big deal of her gift. But I don't want her magical qualities blunted by the education system either.'

It's time to go back. Pickles, Nyika and Lily are happy to go in the pen but give us a loaded look: don't forget tomorrow's walk!

It's Beltane. A few of us are by the small fire, all women and girls. A small ceremony is held to welcome the fire season of May. A two-faced mask is used – one side is the Cailleach, mistress of winter with her white hair, and the other is fertile Brigid, the Celtic Mary. The summer passes.

It's Equinox and a full moon. The last volunteer of the season is a woman studying to be a herbalist. She's been having long chats with Rowan; in fact Rowan has become a full-blown therapist. Listening to life stories and dilemmas, trying to be present for them all without interfering. She and her land change lives. It's girls only by the fire, again. The moon is round, white and polished like a sphere of pure selenite. The Pleiades are very clear. We count all six of them.

'But there were seven once,' says Evie.

'How do you know that, my love?'

Evie shrugs.

'Once upon a time, there were seven sisters,' begins the volunteer in her French accent.

Her voice and the hills rock us into remembering. We are star seeds. In Gaeldom, the seventh child had special gifts. Spells and prayers were repeated seven times. Evie is a child but the Cailleach of tomorrow is here, and I am glad.

Chì mi

I see the mouth of the glen smashed by thugs. I speed past it. I want to see something beautiful and true and alive. Without it I will die.

And so I see the Crossing Place, what's left of it, full of pecking blackbirds.

I see Tony's gallery like a treasure chest with its bell tower pointing at the sky with hope.

I see the hermit's horse chestnut leafing. What will happen with us, *mo ghleann*?

The Crossing Place, endurance

Four years since I left. Tony and I are sitting inside our stone circle under the geans. It's overgrown. The birds are singing their hearts out. That's because of the quarry. They have started phase three. Men with diggers cut what's left of the forest after phase two, four years ago, which has now been fully extracted.

Ta-ta-ta-ta-ta-ta. The soundtrack of the Crossing Place. The gravel crushers in the quarry have not relented their machine-gun rattle. The quarry will only stop when it reaches the river. Tony loads up the birdfeeders but the birds are everywhere – in the field, flying into the house, and grouse and partridge walk into the gallery and crane their necks at the paintings like clients. I look for words to console us and can't find any. We photograph the pits but it's too upsetting, and the media are not interested. It isn't the lockdown this time, it's war. It's everything. Fear has enveloped the glen like a fog. *They'll do it anyway.* People feel disenfranchised and big franchises are getting bigger.

And now there is something so big looming on the horizon, we cannot get our heads around it yet. A new wave of contractors and subcontractors for the energy giant is sweeping across the Highlands. Men in fluorescent jackets and safety helmets are popping up everywhere, travelling in company vehicles. They pop up in fields, on hills, in people's gardens. They measure the ground, set up recording equipment, mark up roads, bore into the ground, conduct tick-box surveys of wildlife and water probes.

This spring, the energy giant unveiled their next big plan for the whole of northern Scotland, sea and land. They now wanted to build *a holistic network* – on top of the last one from ten years ago. This network would clamp the north in an industrial grid. It would require the construction of three or five new transmission highways, dozens of new switching stations in quiet places like our glen, and *asset improvements*, which means everything they already have will quadruple in size. Our transmission line will go up to 400 kV.

This chaotic new transmission grid was meant to invite waves upon waves of *generation*. That means more Hydro schemes on lochs, and more wind farms. More. More. The grid that encircled us already would look small compared to what was to come. Hadn't the energy giant and the government thought of this ten years ago? They had. They always intended to enlarge – without end in sight. If their *holistic network* of transmission lines and its accompanying fleet of wind farms, battery storage systems and Hydro pumps was built – then northern Scotland would become an industrial mega-park, a giant energy-producing factory, with pockets of organic life surviving here and there. The country would be wastelanded – sea, soil and air. The lynchpin of their new steel web would be on the other side of our river: Talorgan's Place. All the way between the Firth and Loch Ness is an open-air archaeological treasury, and Talorgan's Place is an integral part of it. On every hill a hut circle, burial cairn, a loch with nesting birds. It is a land alive with past and future. This is where they wanted to build a massive new substation. It is only a mile from the existing one.

Along a narrow road in Talorgan's Place is an industrial

building with the insignia of the energy company which uses it as a storage yard. But it used to be a mineral water-bottling plant. The land here belongs to the old clan of Lovat Scout fame. The bottling plant was a commercial venture of the clan chief's family. A mineral spring had provided their estate with water for three centuries: why not bottle it and sell the water. So they had this built at great expense, but within months of the fatal hunting accident, the venture went into receivership. A large food company took over and kept it going for a few years until it failed. They said the spring dried up. But springs don't dry up except in times of drought or when you over-pump them. A series of new ventures was started on the premises – one was making botanical cosmetics from Highland plants, another good idea that should have worked – tapping into a local natural resource with minimal footprint. A guy with a strimmer and large bags harvested the myrtle of the hills. Investments were made but that too failed, because of corruption. I used to walk past it and see a little light inside – one guy was left on site to switch on the light, and off. Into this void swooped the energy giant.

It is known in the glen that the first thing they did was to pour cement over the site of the spring, but since they closed the visitor centre you can't go in and check. It is also known that the houses next to the bottling plant are haunted. An exorcist was quietly brought in to clear the place, but the ghost remained.

It is this ancient, fertile and symbolic Talorgan's land that is marked up for the construction of a new transmission hub where an unknown number of new transmission lines would meet in a mega switching station. Its size is undisclosed, then they disclose it: 68 acres. That's big for an industrial hub with power lines branching off it in every direction, mirroring what's already happening on this side of the river. Then they revise their plans and overnight, the size changes to 868 acres.

It takes a moment for that to sink in. How big is that? No, that's impossible. There must be a mistake.

They use out-of-date maps. Like colonisers with rulers, they superimpose their plans over the map. The whole point of the desired upgrade is to provide a highway for even more speculative wind farms. And the applications are pouring in. Every week a new application for a wind farm on a hill. The wind-farm speculators have never set foot here. They don't care. All they care about is: Scotland is an open shop. They come and loot it.

The largest owner of wind farms is the energy giant itself. By rolling out its new grids all across the north, it wants to weave a steel web where it can lay its own eggs – and continue to hatch profit for its owners and shareholders. And when it doesn't generate, or transmit, taxpayers pay out of their pockets to keep the company in profit.

'How can you sleep at night?' someone asked a rep.

'We have a loyalty to our shareholders,' he shrugged, depressed.

Eight hundred and sixty-eight acres is the size of Glasgow Airport. Mature woodland, houses, farmland, peatland, burial sites – they would all have to be ripped out and replaced with industrial junk. Four hundred workers are to be put up in temporary camps. The work would last for nobody knows how many years. People would be forced to sell their houses for half the value. The reason why the energy giant wants to build a new switching station there and not expand the existing one is the quarry. The quarry has extracted all the land next to Scotland's largest switching station. The extraction is so comprehensive that it has reached the base of 'our' pylon. If this pylon fell, it would fall into the quarry pits, which would be apt. They have dug so deep that ground water was reached and the land made useless for another extractor. So the energy giant has looked for good land that hasn't been raped to death. And they found Talorgan's Place. It would take them two years just to *strip the topsoil* of Talorgan's Place. This information brings people to tears.

Behind closed doors, the energy giant, hand in hand with the government, tries to negotiate with big landowners and small landowners, in their bid for more land, offering deals, buyouts and other delights. The couple who are a shadow of themselves since they've been living under a transmission pylon are not negotiating. And they are not leaving. Like many people in the area, they have strung up a banner on their gate: WE ARE NOT YOUR COLLATERAL DAMAGE. But they are. We all are.

All this is excellent news for wind-farm developers, who are being invited by absentee landowners with castles, mansions and lots of good green land to make them money in the easiest possible way – by handing it over to an energy developer.

The combined electromagnetic radiation of all these transmission highways crossing over our area would be a health hazard for people, crops and animals, but strangely, health has been left out of the application. This means that human health has not been considered at all. Other things that are left out are environmental impact, land use and agriculture, electric and magnetic fields (EMF) and radio frequency interference (RFI), major accidents and disasters, air quality and climate, disposal and recovery of waste, and decommissioning.

At the same time, the Isle of Skye has eleven new wind farms planned. In the Hebridean Isles 187 square kilometres of sea would be occupied by a wind farm that already calls itself Spirit of the Sea – in Gaelic too, to appear to be working with the natives. And when the real thing is destroyed, only the name remains. The wind turbines want to be 360 metres high, each blade 100 metres long. One third of the landmass of Lewis would be occupied by this developer for their own logistical needs. This is where the transmission line going west from our trashed Talorgan's Place would be linking up: with the wind farms extracting the Hebrides, to transmit that energy hundreds of miles to the south. If the south needs this energy at all, but that is not even discussed. The energy industry is not driven by need, but by targets.

The Highlands and Islands are bombarded. Yes, we are a colony — not to another country but to a ruthless, faceless industrial capitalism, eagerly placed here by our government.

It comes from the top down with its own map and a long column of abnormal-load vehicles to redraw the boundaries and the rules. It is a law unto itself. It commits ecocide at every turn.

There is still a fork in the road, away from the economy of destruction. A sustainable model is still possible. How do you recognise it? It appears from the roots up and is smart and small in scale, all its parts interconnected. There is no waste of resources. There is no destruction of life. It builds an economy of creation, invention and interdependence.

'Land is the key to the future of the Highlands and Islands,' wrote a historian a generation ago, and its truth holds. 'History has shown that the region can support forms of land use which approach an ecologically acceptable compromise, where natural resources and the human element exist on a common plane for the assured survival of both into the future.'

It is the definition of resilience.

Tony is in the gallery. He has curated a mixed show called *Borrowed Land*. The paintings and sculptures express the intimate relationship of the artists with their place. The show is inspired by the adage: *We don't inherit the land from our ancestors, we borrow it from our children.*

The hermit of Kilmorack has gone into hospital. We know she won't be coming back. That'll be another custodian gone. Who will take her place? We worry that the energy giant will buy her land, a subcontractor will come in an abnormal-load vehicle, pour cement into the spring, flatten her bungalow, and build something more useful.

'We have to come up with something,' I say.

We sit in our stone circle under the geans and peel dyed Easter eggs. By the time they are peeled, they're covered in fine white dust from the quarry, like everything else. We swallow them like swallowing our souls.

We survey the Crossing Place, how beautiful it is, and how shrunk. The compost heaps are doing well, at least. The lushest nettles and gooseberries grow here and attract bees and butterflies.

'These days when I sit here, I start chanting like a native American,' Tony says.

Or a Gael in the ruins of a cleared village.

When a coloniser arrives with extractive machinery and new maps – that's not borrowed land. That's stolen land.

Some are telling Tony to cut his losses and sell up. If the new substation goes ahead, all the industrial traffic will pass over the bridge of the Crossing Place. For years.

If he stays here, it will kill him, said to me the yoga teacher who fought the Canadian developers and doesn't mince her words.

But Tony loves the Crossing Place. He has put so much into it. And if he sold it, the new owners might *develop it*. The new owners could be the energy giant. Transmission. Or generation.

And he can be very stubborn.

Will there be people here, after us? Will they dig up our compost heap and study our way of life?

Tony has planted two juniper trees next to the old bedstead in the field. And 200 saplings in the neighbour's field. That field belongs to the clan that owns the quarried land. And Talorgan's Place. They must be making a fortune. But the young lord looks more haunted than ever.

Tony has started putting little kami figurines under trees and on branches as an offering. And more Tibetan prayer flags. Because you have to not just fight against what's wrong, but show what's right.

'Am I going weird? I just don't want the spirits of the place to be driven off. I want them to know that someone is still here.'

No, you are not going weird. I am crying. Tony holds my hand. We have always consoled each other.

'You have to not think like a human. Can you imagine a time when all of this is engulfed in greenery!'

His dream, to green up the world and for everyone to have a painting. A new technology will be here soon. Pylons are a hundred-year-old technology and steel is criminally unsustainable. Wind farms are falling into obsolescence already, shedding toxic fragments in the water and the soil. The renewable-energy industry as it looks today is not a solution to a problem, it is part of the problem. To keep the global renewables industry going, the non-renewables industry is happily working overtime. They have each other's backs like Janus twins. One body, two shop fronts. Together, they trash the Earth.

'There's got to be a new technology on the way!' Tony tries to soothe me, and himself. 'With a small footprint. Back to Schumacher's "small is beautiful".'

Yes, a truly green technology that works with nature and people instead of ripping their guts out. I hope it comes before Talorgan's Place is trashed. And the woods of Aigas gorge.

The dam will be gone one day, we know it. Our friendly hideous dam that imprisoned the falls of Kilmorack to serve kettles, fridges, bottling plants, aluminium works and weapons factories, and is still holding up.

'What do you think we'll eat, when we return in the future?'

'Hopefully not soylent green.'

We sit under the geans and cherry blossoms fall on us.

Chì mi

I see the top of the braes where the blue-landscape artist lives with her ex-oil rig man with the million planted trees, now a mature woodland – but the *preferred route* of the planned new pylon line passes through it on the map, and if it goes ahead it will make a sterile zone of their wood.

I see Loch nam Bonnach the Cake-shaped One, where I walk and swim with Bella and pick mountain cranberries, and which too is in the way of the *preferred route* so the energy giant might drain the loch to put in an access road. The thought of this causes me pain in many places. The blades of the wind turbines that are already here cast long shadows on the moor.

The Good Woodsman

I untie the farmer's gate like a trespasser and step in. For years, Tony and I have wondered what he's like but have never caught sight of him. He is the one who brought light to Rowan's wood.

In a small clearing – neat log piles and horse dung. A car wreck recycled for parts. A German shepherd on a long rope doesn't bark and is glad of the company. A static caravan with a porch. The feathered skin of a grouse hangs – roadkill. Pinecones on the branch, picked up for their beauty or maybe as kindling. Drying clothes, a worker's safety helmet. Baskets woven from willow branches, the kind of thing you need patience for. Everything has the gossamer touch of someone who speaks the language of the woods. The tap-tap of falling acorns. The latrine is all wood, a door made from branches, a grass roof. A log table with trunk-chairs. In the caravan – kitchenette, bunkbed with cushions, a shelf of books on birds and shelter-building, a framed photograph I can't make out. A mug with a dry teabag. The dog has food and water but has been alone for some time. Birds everywhere. A cuckoo song rises, clear and calling to some absent mate. A goshawk hangs above the green mirror of the river.

I remember when a hand-written FOR SALE sign appeared on the gate and disappeared. A guy called Dylan moved into the forest. Years passed. He's in forestry, works with a horse. Quiet guy. I returned in another summer. The roads were empty. The only sound: the crackling of pods on the yellow-flowering bushes of broom and gorse.

The woodsman was busy. He was building a house over the gorge: foundations and two walls. He knew what he was doing – it was immaculate work. But still he wasn't here, only the German shepherd – hello. Hello you, she said. Her face was greying. She was growing old.

I sit in the cuckoo flowers – like pink-white orchids, delicately veined. They were once called fairie flowers, because the fairies were all around. They still are in Aigas gorge. If I tune in, I hear the flower voices. The bluebells are always tinkling. The blue-green Glass river catches the summer light like the thickest glass made by humans, and my heart trills with a yearning that sinks me into the warm ground. I am surrounded by invisible friends and children. Today, a woman walked down the empty road, her long black hair suddenly lifted by the wind like a raven's wing, filling the world with beauty.

A force is moving through the air but hasn't taken shape yet. Things are about to change but I don't know how. For me, for everybody. Except perhaps for the woodsman. I watch the glass-green water for signs but it is a cloudless day. I want to untie the dog but she is asleep.

On the other side of the river is Dun Fionn. It means Fort of the Fair One. Fionn is fair, fresh, limpid, chilly, and when water is fionnar, it's spring water. Something sad seeps in like moisture. Is it simply that here is a way of life that accepts our fundamental nature. We need very little. But we use an awful lot. And when we're sated, we throw it away and replace it with the same but bigger, but don't feel better for it. Then we die and are composted with the worms.

Big industry rips wholesale from nature with casual violence. Big industry extracts rocks, earth, oil, wind, water, gas and air to keep our gridded industrial habits abuzz, night and day. Like cocaine addicts. To keep us lit up at night and anxious in the day, never enough, always more, more. To keep us consuming-discarding-replacing. That's the sadness. The madness. The badness. Industrial civilisation makes us into users, and uses us back. The caravan in the forest is a reminder that there is another way.

I leave Dun Fionn and stumble into remains of an old drystone wall. And an old road gobbled by the forest. Secrets lie close to the surface. Old roads followed the river if they could, or climbed high above the river if they had to, and were wide enough for animals and humans, no wider than two haybales. The new road was built to lead from one power station to the next. And now it isn't wide enough for the new industry vehicles.

When you emerge from Aigas gorge, the light brightens and the future is blank. So many roads when the yellow's on the broom. You drive out of the glen in search of another journey. Up at the Five Forts of Farley the moor is brown with heather. The future is blue-peaked with distance and I speed towards it.

September. The light has reached that tipping point – summer and winter in one. I didn't come to Aigas gorge anymore because I was living in the Monks' Place. My daily trail did not follow the tributaries of the glen. It followed the glittery mudflats of the estuary. I had other patches of wild garlic, mint and nettle. Different birds too – geese, swans, and this year the kites and buzzards are everywhere.

Then one day I heard on the grapevine that a subcontractor of the energy company had visited Dylan, and informed him that the next *preferred route* for the new transmission line passes through Aigas gorge. Aigas gorge may be destroyed.

I drive into the glen, past shuddering lorries loaded with pines, and signs: STRATEGIC TIMBER EXTRACTION. Every few miles, a new road hacked into the hills, a fence, a sign: RENEWABLES.

I untie the rope of the gate. The horse is here and he looks at me without surprise. He is a heavy-load breed, caramel-coloured with a blond mane and chilled manner. The house is completed – a stunning cabin in the woods with a porch, of perfect proportions. Every larch trunk was cut by Dylan and shaped on his sawmill.

Two static caravans put together, that's the size of a wood cabin you can get permission for. He had to jump through bureaucratic hoops to get permission for the cabin, the kinds of hoops that industry doesn't have to jump through before it flattens entire islands for its hubs.

Woodland crofting is getting more popular in a small way, and each decade it's easier to get permission to build something like this. Tools and ropes, and a lump of pink salt on a rope for the horse. A simple fence of mildly electrified cord plugged into a generator. And something I've never seen: a logging pully, for moving logs along steep terrain. It's like a cable car but without a car, just a big hook, and it runs a hundred metres downhill towards the grey-green river of the gorge. The horse is relaxed, unshoed, no bridle or saddle. I scratch his head through the thick hair and he tolerates it, in that way horses have – of hanging out and tolerating.

A pick-up truck drives in, loaded with bales of hay. Dylan gets out with a limp. He is tall and not the rustic type I expected. There's something refined. A cobweb of wrinkles around his eyes but he is not old. I confess I've called on him before, that I'm interested in glen people, and – you're one of the unusual ones.

'Am I?' Dylan half-smiles, not in the habit of considering himself, and limps to the open kitchen to boil water for tea.

'Those are for birds and that big box is for the pine marten, but don't tell anyone. People are funny about pine martens. You're not supposed to build boxes for them.'

The nesting boxes are affixed under the roof. He built all this on his own.

'Well, with Nomad. And all the equipment. There are ways.'

The cabin is classed as a temporary dwelling. The ingenious way he built it is part of the woodsman's specialist craft. Dylan practises intelligent forestry — a re-emerging approach to logging and reforestation. It combines the traditional horse with the latest understanding of how woodland systems think. The technical term is Low Impact Silvicultural Systems. Which conveys nothing of the hard toil and bright joy of the actual work. It's a way of life. Sleeping and waking in the forest, breathing and eating with your horse, cutting down trees that suffocate other trees and opening space for light and growth. The smell of damp soil, the sunshine trilling tunes through leaves, the chorus of birds that rises at that time Gaels call shadow of the day.

'People think regeneration is about planting, not cutting. But you need both. It's just that it has to be done differently now.'

For a hundred years, there was a wholesale mechanical felling of forests. No thought for the future. We must return to a smarter way of harvesting and replanting. Smaller scale, with technologies that are sympathetic to the environment.

'You have to think like the trees. Trees live in a different time.'

In the clearing – a forward trailer, a bogie wagon, the horse box and a pile of logs. A circle of deciduous trees hugs the clearing – all rescued saplings he planted.

After years of conventional forestry work, Dylan saw the damage done to forest floors by heavy machinery and senseless logging.

'I saw that the industrial approach is a thing of the past.'

He learned about horse-logging from an old guy, and bought Nomad. This breed comes from the Jura region of France and there is only one other like Nomad in the whole of Scotland.

The harness is of the Canadian type, a padded ring of leather and felt placed around Nomad's chest and attached to a soft body harness, which in turn is attached to the wheeled trailer with the logs. It's a well-balanced contraption, and the woodsman's task is to walk behind with a long rein, and guide the horse. This method is especially handy in steep and remote terrain. It is widely used in Scandinavia but fell into oblivion in Britain. Dylan now employs a few men on these highly specialised jobs and they travel together in the north of Scotland. It's seasonal, irregular, and there are two types of clients – individuals and organisations. The individuals are landowners who want their woodlands managed in a good way. There is a woman on a croft out west like that. He gets a few tons of firewood for her at a time and, while doing that, cares for her trees.

A few tons! He and Nomad can shift up to fifteen tons of timber a day. I can't get my head around this.

'We're getting there,' he smiles. He has that freakish Celtic fairness of white gold, and something tragically handsome that makes me think of Lancelot.

'But you can't make a living from this. It's too niche. You

do it for the love. And to educate. Show people what's possible. I don't want it to be just a hippie thing.'

There's nothing hippie about it. And anyway, the hippies of the 1960s were the first ecologists of the industrial world. They tried to do things differently. They saw the looming Silent Spring and to avert disaster, they recommended relationship instead of rape.

As a boy Dylan had a horse and a few sheep to look after. It was a happy, free childhood in the hills of Wales, then his parents divorced and something fell apart. He dropped out of school, left home, drifted. But quickly gravitated back to nature and did an apprenticeship with an arborist, then went to university and studied sustainable forestry.

How to live? Already in childhood, he could see: the only right way to live is in harmony with the rest of nature. All else is dishonest. He travelled through Asia and Europe, staying with communities to see how people lived in their environment. Wherever the human footprint was large, the rest of nature shrank. In Mongolia, he bought a horse and travelled on horseback across the steppes in search of the last nomads. They were old and alone, their children sucked into the cities. The Mongolian nomads were fading into history with their horses. Then he lived on a boat in the south but the south was too busy. The north pulled at him.

'I bought a van and lived in it. I moved from job to job.'

This is how he came to the Highlands. He got to know people, like the Cougies. They'd go fishing in summer and he'd horse-sit for them. It was bliss – just him up there with twenty horses.

'The Cougie horses are the best kept. Free.'

Nomad was shod at first, but one of the shoes came off and

Dylan didn't want to have it nailed back to his hoof, a barbaric invention. So he had all his shoes removed.

'We work together. I talk to Nomad. He works because I ask him to.'

Sometimes he rides Nomad but saddle-less. You can just hold on to the mane, as Roddy showed me. Nomad is too big for most people to ride but Dylan and Nomad are joined at the hip.

'We're practising a couple of moves at the moment.'

In a couple of weeks, they'll take the road for the first job of the winter season on the west coast. They'll be working in a forest they know, but this time it's a steeper section and Nomad needs to practise turning on a slope.

Another week, Dylan interrupts his repair work on a trailer and takes me on a tour of his riparian wood. Riparian means on a river bank. He manages about seven acres of it. It's a mixed wood, one of the nicest around.

'But none of it is native. It was all cut and planted, harvested and replanted. And not very well.'

The best is the old-growth hazel grove. There used to be lots of hazel in the Highlands. Now there isn't. Britain is the least biodiverse country in Europe. But with intelligence and dedication, things can be turned around, and this is what Dylan's life is about. He started by regenerating the trees around the cabin, and it now looks more vibrant than the rest of the gorge. The forest floor is richer.

'It took a while but the animals have started to appear again. The red squirrels. Pine martens, deer, badgers, there's even a hedgehog.'

He rescued the hedgehog from a logging job – a standard one of the brutal variety, with heavy machinery. The hedgehog was about to be squashed.

'They really don't care in commercial logging, you know.'

I know. He put it in his safety helmet and brought it home. But the hedgehog is out on his evening walk now.

'All of this work, I do it for them. For the animals.'

We look up through the crowns of the trees. They are varying heights.

'It's about floors. These small ones will be mature in fifty years' time, and these tall ones have come to the end of their lives and will fall. You have to not think in human time.'

The slow growers who live to an old age are oak, Scots pine and beech. He has just two beeches in his forest and some oaks. The fast growers, who also have shorter lives, are birch, willow and ash. A birch lives to eighty years at most. Regeneration requires two main things: thinning out where trees are planted too close to thrive, and planting the right saplings in the cleared spaces. A healthy forest needs light and space.

We go down to the river and Nomad follows for company. The ground shakes with his steps. He is like a buffalo. He weighs half a ton. Bunches of felled birches and branches are stacked as mini-habitats for insects, birds and animals. And for firewood for Dylan's own use, though he can also sell them if he wants to.

I am startled to learn that Dylan never uses a chainsaw to fell a tree in his own compound. Too brutal, he says. Only a hand saw. Or an axe. An axe! He smiles.

'It's a gesture of respect for the tree. It's part of the old ways. A time bridge.'

Only once the tree is felled does he use a chainsaw.

On the west coast where he and Nomad sometimes work, there are old Caledonian pines that bear axe-marks from attempts to cut them down a hundred years ago.

'But the lumberjacks gave up. Too big to cut, too hard to transport. They abandoned them.'

And the pines recovered. The same goes for the old oak forests on the west coast: enormous trees, 500 years old. Their remoteness saved them. They are the last ancient oak communities in Scotland.

And the osprey nest?

'They're further down. I've been trying to lure them here. I reshaped the tops of the pine trees. But they've stayed put. They like it where they are. And there's a hawk nesting in that pine.'

In the forest, Dylan is indistinguishable from the trees. That must be the way of all true woodsmen. It's just that I don't know many of them. Because there aren't many – men who are prepared to hand-saw trees and use solar-fed living machines like Nomad. The heavy limp is still there.

I stumble over an iron triangle with a hook.

'A swingle tree,' he picks it up.

An old tool for pulling timber through inaccessible terrain. You attach the swingle tree to the choker chains that carry your bunch of timber. That's how you drag large volumes of timber without damaging the logs or the forest floor. He uses the forwarding trailer or the bogie wagon.

'Injury goes with the territory,' he reassures me.

Of the three most dangerous professions of the Highlands – cattle droving, dam-building and logging – just one is left.

'An old hawthorn.' Dylan touches it. 'See how it's grown that way into the light.'

The thing about September light is, gold begins to seep into everything, even the red of hawthorn berries. It seeps through the clear spaces in Dylan's forest and for a moment haloes his face. I see the Hangman of tarot. He hangs upside down from a tree, his arms crossed and a smile on his face. He has surrendered all personal craving.

The water is full of emerald. A buzzard hangs over the cliffs on the other side, where I stood on Dun Fionn looking down this way. When you have water like this, there is hope.

'When I'm here and working for myself, I sometimes stop and just sit here or lie down. And listen to the birds. I don't have that kind of time when I'm on a job. But here there is time.'

This is a good moment in history to be doing restoration work, Dylan believes. It's finally gathering momentum.

'It's been slow. But in fifty years' time, I hope people will look back at us now and say: that's when the tide turned.'

When the subcontractor came, he showed Dylan where they want to put a pylon 60 metres high: in the clearing with the crescent of rescued trees, and where Dylan is building a barn for the horse and a polytunnel for vegetables, and where he wants to train the next generation of timber craftsmen.

If he doesn't voluntarily leave, they would issue him with a *compulsory purchase order*. That's eviction. The only thing that differs from the Clearances is that they buy you out, instead of shipping you off to Canada. Then the land is grabbed by a speculator and money squeezed out of it quickly, like blood. Eventually, the speculative venture fails. But you will never return, and the land is bloodless.

The company would hand him a cheque and level this place – forest, cabin and all. But they haven't made up their mind yet – they might just erect the pylon on the other side of the gorge, where the neolithic people's Dun Fionn stood and where for ten years I walked among the blaeberries, wood sorrel, chanterelles and deer that flashed through the trees like gods. Of course, that woodland would be felled by the new line.

'These contractors are well paid! And the way he talked

about it was – I'm basically in their way. It gave me a sense of how they operate. They really don't care.'

Like the loggers with the hedgehog. Like the tacksmen of the Clearances with the glen's folk. The job description is *land management officer*.

'I'd hate to lose this place,' Dylan says without anger. 'But I'd equally hate to see the forest on the other side destroyed. Or anywhere else. We need renewable energy, but this is just wrong.'

His winters are busy on jobs, and summers with getting his compound into shape, and in early spring he plants. He does it when the sap starts running in the birches. Used to be March, now it's February.

How do you know when it rises?

'I can hear it. Like this.'

Glug-glug-glug. The birches glug their own sap and get giddy on it. It rises through the roots and makes the leaves green and juicy. There is a birch forest nearby, owned by a rich man. The whole place is rigged with tubes tucked into incisions in the bark. He likes to collect the birch sap. Like a vampire. Dylan would never do that. He only hurts a tree if it must die for the common good, like the birches he girdles, to slowly waste them away over a year or two, and when they fall, that'll bring light for the younger ones.

Once out on a job, the only thing that stops Dylan's work is 70-mile-an-hour gales.

'Nomad doesn't mind the rain and the cold. You get used to it. And in the forest, there's always shelter.'

The remnant of Caledonian rainforest that Dylan and his helpers are regenerating is run by the community. His work is to clear Sitka spruce planted in the 1960s among the native Scots pine. This will make space for a new generation of Scots pine. The forest will never be cut down, everybody agrees. The work of felling and clearing spruce will be done over five years. If it succeeds, horse-powered forestry may be introduced more widely and this may ennoble the way non-commercial forests are managed, and already the project is closely watched by the forestry sector. The place is reached by a barge across a loch. I can see them: Dylan, Nomad, the loggers. Standing room only. I can see them glide through the fog to the forest of the future, powered by hope.

'What time is it?' Dylan shudders in his jacket. 'I must fix the trailer.'

We've been sitting on the porch listening to rain falling on leaves. It makes different sounds on different trees. The forest is an orchestra waiting for the wind, rain and sun to play it. Potted trees rescued from garden centres wait to be planted. Already in the ground are young medlar and quince which I've not seen before. Hazelnuts in a mug.

How to live? Should people colonise other planets? We forgot that we are animals and became the unhappiest of them all.

In an industrial society, home is defined by the degree of separation between your personal indoors and the outdoors. The greater the separation, the grander the home. Living in a forest is different. Instead of watering your house plants, you check up on the trees. I know other people who own woodlands and care for them, like my friend the blue-landscape artist's husband, who planted a million trees on their land. But he inherited that land, worked offshore in the oil industry and made enough money to retire at forty and potter at home. He didn't have to give anything up. Dylan is different.

How do you read at candlelight? Camping lamps, rechargeable. The phone charges up in the truck. There is a large generator but he doesn't like to use it because it's noisy. The insulation of the cabin is very good and there's a log-burner. Water for washing is heated on the gas stove. That's all. His parents died and the family farm is gone. This is his place.

'The place is a part of me and I am a part of it. I don't know how else to say it.'

We looked to the clearing where Nomad stood motionless looking at us, and where they want to put the 60-metre pylon.

'All I need to do is finish the barn,' Dylan said, 'and put up a polytunnel, and it'll be ready to – enjoy.'

Next time I stop by the gate, he'll be gone out west. Nomad, the pick-up truck, the log crane, the horse box, the trailer – gone. Yet he will be everywhere. The willow baskets, old worker's jackets, grouse feathers, shed stacked with logs – all his things will be here.

Everybody likes Dylan even if they don't know him well. His mission is noble and its inherent value is apparent even to those who don't understand it. People get it that he has not run away from human society, it's just that he is in service of nature. It seems that the two have parted ways. And he is building a time bridge across the chasm Anthropos has extracted for itself like a mass grave.

Many in the glen are repairing the damage already. But others are still extracting. It's like a fork in the road. You take the high road, I take the low.

To some, the time bridge looks like something from the future. But it is here, right on time, a kind of Noah's ark.

The last time Dylan lived in a house was during university. It's not that he minds houses, but he could not afford to buy one in a place like this, and he longed to live intimately with a forest. A Scottish phrase: *I belong to*. Meaning I am from. Dylan belongs to the great forest on the receding edge of the world.

October. Gold enters the riverside willows. Their fish-like leaves chime a yellow-green tune that evokes the baskets woven by Dylan. In the estuary, cold wind comes in from the Firth and ruffles the heads of trees, birds and humans.

The geese that flap overhead in geometric formation are those that are staying through the cold months. The black elderberries hang low. Birds will snack on them en route to Africa for strength. I have bottled my elderberry syrup to give to those who are overwintering. Like my neighbour the ex-soldier who is just back from Bosnia. He tells me how he met another ex-soldier there, a Bosnian, whose mother was a shaman. They invited him to stay with them and the mother said: 'You must die and be born again. This land was raped and the only cure is to make love to it again.' She gave him a potion to drink and buried him in a shallow grave. He went journeying into his past, the land's past, and wept bitter tears. When he emerged from his grave, he felt different. He tells me this under the old elms. Evening falls and the ruined monastery looks like the outline of a forest.

In my garden, a hedgehog surprises me. It snuffles in the grass and brings tears to my eyes because I remember the last time I saw one. I was a child.

When I drive past Dun Fionn again, there will be more horses, people, journeys. Smoke puffs from the chimney. Should I stop and become a part of the mission, should I hang upside down from a tree with a smile?

No. Our paths run parallel.

It's not really a person, it's the ghost behind the face I

seek. The country behind the country. I have found it. It is wherever someone is devoted to a place like to a person. The spirit keeper. The one with an eye. The one that reseeds this shrinking world with his very last seed.

Second sight is when you see the totality of the present. First you need to throw away the veil of greed and delusion. The clarity of it, too bright for those with barely first sight or none, the shining harsh truth of it, the forking in the road – it is here.

If Aigas gorge escapes the boot of industry, one day someone will stop by and walk down to the moss-green river, compelled by a presence. They'll pull sorrel from the spongy floor and chew it. The hawks will watch from the top of the pines and the hazel trees will shake their fair heads like horses.

Chì mi

Early morning in the glen one February. Quiet.

I see the roadside fountain of St Ignatius, drinking tin attached to chain but no water. The pipe is blocked. The goodness of a roadside spring is not needed but it will be needed again. The water lurks in the forest floor which looks dead but in May it's a living carpet, green and shouting with victory. I always stop here to greet the fountain and see about unblocking it, one day.

I see inside myself. Though I'll never live inside this glen again, neither will I go too far from it. I don't know if this makes me happy or sad but this is how it feels to belong.

On the road I see the twisted body of a run-over hind, and slow down.

Deer People

The Stalker

On the ground is a stain in the shape of the Affric Hotel and from here the mother glen goes three ways. The middle way is to Glen Affric and that's where I am joining Steve in his pick-up truck which isn't his. Even his clothes come with the job.

'It's more a way of life. You've got to love it or don't do it.'

Steve is head stalker and keeper of a large private estate in Affric, and today is a working day at the end of hind season. Deer stalkers are doubly remote, by nature and by location – difficult to get anywhere near them. Unless you hire them for the day, they are like the banshee. You hear a faint gunshot and that's it. Or you see tracks in the forest. The glens are deep, the hills are many, the stalker's face is out of view. I met Steve through Ali of Silver Falls.

'Ali? Don't believe his stories.'

Friendly competition. They went to school together. They're the two faces of the gillie archetype. Ali is storyteller of the water. Steve is soldier of the hill. The gillie is old, since the time of the clan chiefs whose main pastime was hunting. There was always a *gille* (lad) at their side. The gillie is one of the folk of the glen. He bridges social class, and he bridges dimensions: one part human, one part animal and one part place.

Steve has that grounded manner of the keeper who takes

your measure without judgement and will be polite to the end, but never false.

'You have to bite your tongue sometimes.'

Decades of dealing with the privileged, unseen by them but seeing them, Steve the stalker whose name they forget and his face too because they see so many faces on their worldly travels, Steve who guides them to the hills they can't climb, stalks a deer for them, showing them where to lie in the grass without getting muddy, and delivers the prize to them so they can say they've shot a stag in the Highlands of Scotland. He even takes a photo of their triumph. Afterwards, he carries the dead animal out of sight, leaving the guests to their plush rooms and whisky-doused parties. And drives home mute with fatigue, the dogs asleep in the back of the truck. The indigo silence of Affric comes down like a curtain after the last act.

Steve's parents came to Cannich for his father's forestry job. Forestry was a big local employer. Now there are three men left. Steve trained as a joiner, but shadowing his father in Glen Cannich gave him a taste for the hills. His father was hired as pony boy on stalks and young Steve helped with the lifting. It's the way in this profession: you start as pony boy and end up head stalker. The bodies of stags and the packed lunches of guests were carried on horseback. Then the Argocat arrived in the 1980s and deer hunting became more like a drive-in safari.

'But we still have three horses. We'll feed them first if you don't mind.'

I don't mind. There's a naturalness about Steve. He doesn't use superlatives, and I see it now – when you live in the hills you are more like nature than like human society. Between the two is a chasm.

The horses are overwintering in Tomich because Affric is too high and even the frost bowl is warmer. The three horses come, his two Labradors jump out of the truck, horses and dogs are glad to see each other. He doles out grain and nutritious powder in rubber bowls. In May the horses are taken to Affric and used by estate guests for riding.

We pass Fasnakyle power station which may grow to an industrial hub that takes up the entire end of the glen. We pass Fasnakyle church for sale, and climb the steep road above the first loch.

'When they're generating, you can see the old road along the shore. And the tops of the buildings that were submerged.'

Achagate, once a fertile croft known for its potatoes. A stalker's family lived here once.

'And this is Brewer's Burn.'

The brewer is gone but the burn is so full-bodied, it lives for two. What do you need for whisky? Peaty water. This was the place for it. There were over thirty stills once. A still could make over 1,000 litres and the quality was as good as a single malt today. Evading the Excise men is an oral genre in itself because the state was mean but the glens were cunning. Whisky smugglers often travelled disguised as women. Stills were dauntingly remote – like Pait, whose last whisky maker and smuggler was photographed in 1917, in a stalker's hat with sunken unshaven cheeks. One day, the Excise men were suddenly there. Cornered, the father and son smugglers came up with a ruse: they took the Excise men to their own stills, acting as informers. And they got a reward. In another episode, back when Affric had a community, the Excise men came and searched homes but couldn't find anything despite the smell. An old woman sat at a spinning wheel, wrapped in a long shawl that covered her – and the whisky barrel that was her stool. A brewer was known to carry a whisky barrel on his back and hide under a waterfall until the hated Excise men left. The small victories of a colonised people.

Whisky brewing constituted an entire local economy, bartered with travelling traders for tweed and food, and sold in large quantities to east and west.

The old stalker of Affric met the last of the illicit brewers. The man said: 'Could you do with a drop of the cratur, Dunkie?' and showed him where bottles were concealed inside a dyke wall. The whisky was 'a bit fiery to swallow, but once down its warmth was soon felt'. That was the 1930s but the barter system of the glens continued into the 1950s. People swapped eggs and butter for meat and bread. Money has little use in the hills. That's why the cash economy didn't arrive in the Highlands until the end of the nineteenth century.

And inside the hill to our right is a 3.2-mile-long tunnel that brings the water of Mullardoch into pipes that run sharp downhill to Fasnakyle station. Three lochs' worth of water going into three power stations. Fasnakyle, Aigas and finally our one at Kilmorack. The tunnel tigers worked from two ends: here and Glen Cannich. Two hundred and fifty tons of explosives later, they met in the interior of the hill.

At the official opening of Fasnakyle power station, the Hydro-Electric bosses boasted about two things: how the glens would have cheap electricity, and how the dams would put an end to the seasonal flooding of the rivers because now they were mechanically controlled.

We have improved the flow of the river, said the head engineers of the Hydro-Electric Board.

We will leave an improved biodiversity, said the spokesman of the energy giant seventy years later.

What can we learn from this? That power and truth have parted ways. That once trashed, a place is twice trashed, and thrice. The first flood after the dams, in 1966, was on a scale not seen in the glen. It broke bridges, moved the bed of the river, and altered the strath. And we know how the cheap electricity turned out. Today, those living in the north of Scotland have some of the highest electricity bills in Europe. It's because the electricity generated here is not for us at all, no more than the oil extracted from the Niger delta is for the people whose environment was trashed by British Petroleum.

At the time, the deer stalker of Cannich and his family dug their heels in and stayed, even as the rising water of Mullardoch lapped at their house. The Board was forced to give him another house and a job: warden of Fasnakyle station. No more hills with ponies. His new job was to show visitors around the power station that had replaced the ecosystem of Glen Cannich – and his way of life.

But the old keeper of Affric kept his house and job after the dams. His son took over in 1990, Steve joined him, then took over from him. Just as Steve's son will take over from Steve. Tired stalkers go back to being pony boys.

'You come full circle.'

A game keeper's wage is modest but adds up in perks: a car and fuel, outdoor gear, a supply of venison, and whisky from clients.

Glen Affric is handsome but it is just like other empty glens – organised around visitors. There's no one left to tell you what happened here, except Steve. The road ends at the last of four car parks and two of them are being enlarged. You can walk round the lochs or go on west and squeeze through mountain passes until you reach the kingdom of the Five Sisters of Kintail and the coast. It's the drover's road.

'You should walk it,' says Steve. 'It's beautiful.'

Affric unfolds in the cold sun. The pines on the first loch are a precious remnant of Caledonian forest. This part of the glen is owned by the Forestry Commission and their regeneration has been a success. A few sheep graze in the trees. They shouldn't be here.

'There were more sheep and the Forestry requested them to be removed. But they weren't so they shot them.'

Shot them! In the old days, someone would have rustled the sheep to lower ground but it takes time. Industrial humans have no time, even when they work with trees.

The old stalker of Affric recalled walking at night along the river and seeing the torch-like eyes of wild cats atop the dyke wall. He tripped on stoats and weasels. The river thrashed with salmon and trout. There was a lot of everything. Including time. He worked hard his whole life, but he had time.

And that churned-up ground? Feral pigs. When the weather warms up, they rummage for tasty things. Pigs have gone up in numbers – a policy of regeneration – and keepers don't like them, but Steve is neutral on wild pigs. They like forests, just like deer, but without munching them. Everybody likes a forest in this wet and windy land, surely!

'Well, I like the open moor. And they killed off all the deer. You won't see a single deer in this forest.' He says it without bitterness, only regret. We drive on and up.

Deer management is a never-ending story. How many deer should be allowed, where should the boundary fence be, are those young trees growing or have the deer nibbled them again? It's a matter of life and death – for deer, forests, professional stalkers and ecosystems.

Who killed all the deer in this thriving forest so that it could thrive? Contractors. Hired killers, the stalkers call them, because they don't seem to abide by the traditional rules. These contractors are hired by the Forestry Commission to cull deer. They are rangers, and the culling is done to protect the forests of Scotland, protect people against Lyme disease from deer ticks, protect carbon-capture in the race for net-zero, protect peatland from deer that churn it up, and protect the national economy by supplying venison – in the words of the Forestry Commission. Deer stand guilty of every crime. But the crime is ours. We are the monoculture. We are the nibblers and the disease. I've heard that deer contractors can make a fortune. They are paid per deer killed and it's always open season. A year's quota in a month. In about three years, 3,500 deer were killed in Affric. That's what I was told by local stalkers and gillies. When the deer-killing was at its peak, Cannich witnessed a scene. Cannich is used to scenes but this was different. Fresh out of Glen Affric, two trailer-loads of dead deer stopped outside the shop and the contractors went in. Children were coming out of the school, which is next to the shop. Blood dripped from trucks piled with bodies – pregnant hinds, young stags, the lot.

This is how the Affric Roar ended.

Local stalkers like Steve abide by the rules. They observe the traditional calendar down to the day, following old Highland hunting cycles. Stag season starts on 20 September – the Gaels called it *the day of the roaring* – and it ends on 20 October. Then it's hind season to the end of February. Pregnant hinds and young stags are left alone at all times. No deer stalker worth his hernias would become a mass killer. The last time deer were killed in such large numbers was during the Second World War – for food.

What is it, with our urge to eradicate one species and supplant it with another, more useful one? The post-Culloden lairds had it. The industrialists have it. And the rewilders have it too. The tree project has been successful and it's a shared dream to see the Scots pines come back to their homeland, from where they were eradicated generations ago. But the wiping out of populations in the race to some target – that's the military-industrial approach. The cold expediency, the persecution of long-time dwellers, the messianic zeal of the *improver*.

What is the answer? Once an ecosystem is wrecked by a monocrop (sheep, deer, potato, humans) how do you restore it? Gradually. The way it would restore itself, with a bit of help. But we have run out of time. We have the machines to extract wholesale, and quickly. In the panicked rush to correct the error that got us here, we make the same error in a different place. Industrial time, electrical time, virtual time – they form a grid that uproots us from the Earth and we run faster and faster on that grid like rats in an experiment. Who owns our time on Earth? The grid.

I once saw a long brick wall in rural India. At one end, men were building it. At the other end, men were demolishing it. They seemed in a rush. The net result was not good, but it kept them busy.

It is odd, having these two types of deer stalkers that stalk the glen but don't meet. The boundary is a fence. A deer fence. In the Age of Improvement, they fenced off arable land. They fenced off forests to make it easier for the rich to shoot deer. Finally they fenced off forests to stop the overly populous deer destroying them. The fence tore the living web. Everything was separated from its kin.

The wind whistles the arboreal tune of Affric through the glorious pines. The oldest granny pine in Scotland is 300 years old – there she is, twisted and full of story like a Cailleach.

A tree or a deer? One must die. It's a terrible choice because it's unnatural.

We enter the grounds of the estate. The trees become scarce, then disappear. The gate of the compound soundlessly opens, remote controlled so you don't get out of the car. The compound is a small peninsula. The buildings are new, but the keeper's cottage and the lodge are old. The lodge was built in the 1870s by the owners of Giusachan, who took a long-term lease on this land from the then-clan chief with the castle where Laughing Lachlan fixes broken things.

The white-washed keeper's cottage faces east and sees the sunrise. This is the best place to wake up – built with a feel for the land, and it's where the old keeper lived for fifty years with his family until he retired in 1989. They would be snowed in for weeks. During the Second World War when the glens emptied, the only people that passed through were tramps looking for food and shelter in exchange for odd jobs. Then the estate changed hands, from the local clan chief to a local city provost. Two generations later, it changed hands again, from the provost to an international developer. And he developed it.

When the old keeper moved in, he was young, keen and living out his dream. The place was set up for basic living. It had the old lodge where he first lived with his sister until he married, the lodge for guests, cow byres, deer larder, bothies (stone huts) for seasonal gillies, boat sheds, stables, kennels and a hay barn. They grew vegetables and kept grazing animals for milk. One of the buildings served as a side school for the itinerant teachers who travelled from glen to glen and stayed at remote keepers' houses, becoming part of the children's family. The old stalker's family were the last residents.

I remember when the old buildings burned down to a stain, like Hotel Affric. Then the little peninsula was developed into a bespoke mini-resort.

The new buildings are immaculate. Offices, bar and dining room, round windowless gun room well-stocked with hunting clothes and paraphernalia, even a greenhouse – but nothing edible grows, it's an exotic orangery with carnivorous flowers and a banana tree.

'I don't think we'll get bananas,' Steve says. 'This is Scotland.'

Everything is façade. Where luxury is king, there is no substance. But there is death, and it's the mingling of luxury and death that disturbs. Buildings are overheated, including the lodge where nobody is staying this week. The kennels have underfloor heating. There is a surplus of electricity because the estate built their own Hydro scheme; until then it was generator-run. Every room is festooned with deer antlers. Antlers on the walls, antler candleholders, all crafted by Steve. It's a shrine to a deer cult. The humans come and go but the deer remain. Dark clouds pass through me and the glen like memories. I have said to Steve that I don't want to shoot anything but I'll tag along.

Furniture is upholstered in pretty moss-green tweed. Every estate has its own tweed. But this one is a neo-tradition, another façade. What, you can set up your own tweed?

'Aye. Not the same thing as tartan though!' Steve sees my confusion. Tartan has bigger squares than tweed, that's the main difference. And tartan you can't fake.

The oldest tartan in Scotland was found forty years ago in a peat bog in this glen. The Affric tartan. Who found it? Forestry workers is my guess, like Steve's father. But nobody in the glen remembers. It dates to somewhere between 1500 and 1600. Oh how I want to know the one that wore it! Until a century ago this was clan land, but the wearer could have been anyone from local to visitor, traveller, drover. It's a rough plaid. Travellers didn't go anywhere without a plaid over their shoulder. At night, your plaid became your bed. Where was the wearer of the oldest tartan going? Kintail to Affric or Affric to Kintail.

On pony, bringing glad or sad tidings, a basket of potatoes, a herd of cattle, or a barrel of whisky.

After the battle of Culloden, one woman waited for years. Though the battlefield was only on the other side of the Ness, she held out hope for her man's return. Until one day, a family of Travellers passed through, and among their wares was a long piece of tartan, washed from the blood and mud, and she recognised it because she'd woven it herself. Then she knew he was dead.

After the Hydro-Electric Board left, the glen's neurology changed and it's only one-way for wheels now: east to west because that's the way industry penetrated the glens and the roads follow industry. You drive in and out the same way. But the paths crossed from glen to glen like the threads of a tartan weave. From here I can see the bealach (pass) where two-leggeds and four-leggeds walked together. The glens didn't end with a dam or a parking lot. They ended with the sea. Before the Hydro, a postie walked twice a week from Kintail to Affric with the mail in a leather bag, in snow and gales, alone. Respect! Boozy priests, itinerant teachers, naturalists, scholarly ecstatics like Ronnie Burn the first compleat Munroist, tramps and Travellers – their trails are here. And every few miles, there was a smoke, and a 'wifey' in a white apron or bearded stalker in a tweed jacket would offer you a jug of fresh milk and a bed for the night, and a peaty fire with stories of fairies, fiddlers and smugglers.

All that survives of the people of Affric is a piece of cloth.

A photograph from 1914 shows an earlier stalker wearing a different, large-chequered tweed. His name was Scott and his father came up from the Borders 'with the sheep'. In the photo, he and his Hebridean wife are seated with their seven girls.

Today Steve and his son wear the everyday uniform of the game keeper: olive-green waterproofs and woollens, with gaiters. When a paying guest arrives, they dress up in the territorial tweed. The stalker's hat signals the territory, just as your name once did.

And *what* is your name? People would ask so they could place you. Now your name could be anything, and you can make up your own tweed. Once, everything from pigment to cloth came from the land – its mosses, its sheep's wool, its plant fibres. Now it's more like festooning yourself. Gillies and their guests always wear three-piece tweed suits. Is it out of respect for the animals?

'And maybe for the sport itself,' Steve says.

Soldiers of the hill are literal people. The only poetic deer stalker I've met is inside Neil Gunn's *Second Sight*. That's Alick who has the second sight.

Large identical pots of lavender sit outside the greenhouse, blown by the icy wind.

'It's a fine morning,' Steve says and almost smiles.

Next: change of vehicles and feed the stags. But first Steve slides open a door.

'Are you squeamish?'

This is the larder which sounds like a deli but it's what comes before the deli. It's where the dead deer are brought from the hill. Once a deer crosses this threshold, it transitions from corpse to meat. The first chamber is a butcher's room with hooks and sinks and a drain along the floor. The smell of blood and guts is faint but ever-present. The inner chamber is refrigerated to 3 degrees Celsius. Three carcasses hang on hooks, headless, skin on. They're tagged and ready for the game dealer who will skin them, dismember them, package them and sell them to shops. But first, they hang here for ten days. Any less and the flesh is tough. The flesh relaxes while it hangs.

No, I am not squeamish in the face of death. Better to have an honest, grim gaze on it. There is nothing luxurious about death and the deer bodies look worryingly like human bodies. I've always wondered what's inside these big sheds without windows that stand next to hunting lodges. Death and taxes, the underworld, and Steve moves around, solid and reliable, but there is no hidden darkness about him. The darkness is elsewhere. He is not Pluto, the lord of the underworld, he is more like the ferryman on the border river. He takes you across and brings you back. He has no agenda. He expects little in return. It's just – this is his place.

'Let's head out to the stags.'

Steve gives me a pair of waterproof trousers that rustle when I walk and make me chuckle because once when Ali was working with Steve, they were given two pairs of expensive stalkers' trousers by an appreciative client, but walking in the hills they discovered the trousers had a fatal flaw: a rustling noise that the deer picked up and the joke was on the stalker.

I meet the mellow son. He runs the office. And Steve's younger brother is a handyman. Here he is, black beanie on, his face skinny and humorous. There is a burst pipe. There is always something. The maintenance is constant even when there's nobody home. He lost his partner and is raising kids alone. They had an older brother who joined the Navy and was killed in Northern Ireland. Loss is in the glen, it sticks to you like an old piece of tartan from the bog. The three of them run the whole place. But they stay in Cannich and prefer it that way. Last week two young women arrived to be housekeepers and live on-site. It's an adventure – I can see it on their faces – to hang out somewhere between the centuries, posting selfies with a too-tidy background of a wilderness, and celebrity-spotting when the helicopter touches down. There's an artificial pond for those too timid to venture outside the mini resort. This is what happens when you have too much money. You put a decorative pond in the middle of Loch Affric. I feel trapped. Let's jump the fence and run for the hills!

'It's like being inside *The Monarch of the Glen* here,' I say to Steve, who at once takes me to the lodge to show me – the Landseer room!

I had no idea this was here. It's incredible. Edwin Landseer the Victorian artist painted this room floor to ceiling. Against a pastel green wash are hillside scenes with horses, men, birds and deer. It's the glen inside one room. He used graphite and water. The draftsmanship is so good, every line is alive. And – at the upper door corner, his signature, a little mouse.

Inspired by sojourns in shooting estates like this, Landseer painted a portrait of a stag that became the most reproduced Scottish painting of all time – *The Monarch of the Glen*. This lodge was built after *The Monarch of the Glen* was painted, and the summits in the painting look like the Alps, but the stag, the misty atmosphere – it's very Affric. And there's no escaping the fact that the royal twelve-pointer stag is perfectly centred in the sight of a gun, to be shot, and not by the gillie from the glen whose mother took the sheep to the shieling and whose sister scraped lichens off rocks to get dye for tweeds – no, the stag is on display for the guest who comes to shoot, sample and reminisce.

Landseer was sponsored by the establishment and *The Monarch of the Glen* was commissioned to hang in Westminster. Today, he would be funded by a bank or an energy company. His portraits of animals, gillies and shepherds show how the Highlands were seen by their colonisers: a playground where visitors could view the natives in the flesh. It was during the Highland Potato Famine that Landseer wrote to Queen Victoria, asking if she would like him 'to illustrate the peaceful and sunny side of the Highlander's character in preference to mist and savage treatment.' The queen wrote back: 'Highland Lassie should be all peace and sunshine – on the other hand the Highlander should represent the national sport of the country but perhaps without actual storm.' The result is a brooding portrait of a game keeper holding a dead eagle in a snowy non-storm. Highland Lassie stands by a burn, barefooted and with her skirts submissively hitched, two roe deer by her side. But she turns away – Highland Lassie has no face. She is the invisible servant in castles, shooting lodges and milking pens, soon to be wrapped in the black shawl of the war widow. Behind Highland Lassie are the Great Sheep that replaced people and turned her country into a safari park.

The two new girls sip herbal tea in the overheated kitchen of the lodge. How long will they last? Steve's son glides past us in an Argocat. On his peaceable face I see my own thought: this is a bit unreal. A world in which there is no difference between too much and not enough is like that.

On the walls of the lodge are the mounted heads of famous stags. The White Gate Stag, 1937, and name of hunter. The stag from Gleann nam Fiadh the Deer Glen, and name of hunter. Hunter and prey are briefly joined at the moment of the kill but forever joined in hunt chronicles. I stare at the fairie head of the white stag.

A white deer is an anomaly and, to the Highlanders, a magical augury. In a century, only three white deer have been sighted in Britain. It was in his first week that young Duncan was entrusted with a young woman, a friend of the son of the shooting tenant, one colonel. It's always a colonel. When she heard of the White Gate Stag, she said to Duncan the stalker: It's him or nothing. There was a gillie and a pony man too. They climbed hills. Hours of waiting, the wrong kind of wind, and a herd of 150 unsettled stags. The stags were heading towards the Sanctuary. That's an area where deer can go and not be shot. The White Gate Stag fell just fifty yards of the Sanctuary burn. Beginner's luck.

When famous stags enter the annals of the dead-deer cult, the name of the gillie never appears.

'To be fair,' Steve says . . . Once, the boss got a trophy stag and was kind enough to put down, next to his own name in the funeral directory of Affric stags, the two stalkers who were there with him – Steve and his son.

Deer hunting is fairer than it used to be. Before the Second World War there was no market for venison. Urban people didn't eat it, only communities like these, embedded in the land. Stags were shot for their fine heads, end of story. Then the war came and emptied the land of men and the shops of goods. The old stalker of Affric and one of his brothers were exempt. Someone had to stay behind. They stayed in the glen and shot the deer – this time to feed the nation. Cattle and sheep were re-introduced in large numbers for the same reason. A local meat purveyor took over several stalking estates and struck a deal with the stalker: he was required to shoot a hundred stags and a hundred hinds each season, with the help of a pony boy. The stags were so well-fed and hefty, they had to cut off their heads to lift them onto the ponies. The taste for venison stayed. Now venison is part of the nation's diet and the whole animal is used. But without the skin. Deer skins are out of fashion and get thrown away. Tony and I once picked up a man with a tea-stained beard along the west coast road. What's in your rucksack, we asked, and he showed us deer skins. He went round the shooting estates for the discarded skins and made rugs and cushions from them. Because it was a pity for the deer.

'I'm a deer man,' he said, then we dropped him off in the middle of nowhere and he walked to his next estate.

Steve walks across the tar-sealed compound, with electric lights strung up all around the peninsula. What would the old stalker make of these *improvements*? We both know the answer. He was content with two cows, a vegetable garden and some chickens. And he lived to a hundred. Black Sandy the last drover lived to eighty-nine and walked to the end. With dogs, cows and sheep, his beard stained with tea. They would have sniffed at the Argocat. But the Argo is a great invention. It's an amphibian. It bumps over rocks, climbs soggy flanks and crosses lochs.

First stop in the Argo: feed the stags. The stags are lined up on the nearest ridge and come down when they see Steve. He pours small piles of corn for them.

'Yalayayalaaa!' he calls, just like the highlanders of the Balkans. I've never before heard it in Scotland. Away from the oppressive luxury of the gated compound, here in the muddy churned-up ground with red-coated stags breathing steam through their nostrils, the world is real again. I laugh with relief.

The stags come. Their antlers are cathedral-shaped. They surround Steve. He knows them all: here's the hornless one, Stephen the pet, the others . . .

The hornless one is unlucky. It's genetic.

'If I see him again next season, I'll cull him.'

To stop him breeding. The old stalker of Affric recalled a hunt for 'the hummel stag'. That means hornless. There was once a hummel stag in Affric, minding his own business. The stalker left him alone but made the mistake of mentioning him to the shooting party renting the lodge, and a young guest became obsessed with the hummel. He had already killed several stags but now he wanted the hummel. So they went looking for the hummel and shot him. But his head was discarded – no antlers. It was just for the thrill of killing a freak. Humans are the most savage beasts.

Stephen the pet can't ever be shot. He is lucky. Two of the stags that come to feed have extra big crowns. Hunters call each branch a point, so you have a six-pointer, a ten-pointer and a twelve-pointer.

'I'll keep those ones too.'

The best heads are left to breed because that's what shooting guests want. It's deer pornography.

He picks off the medium ones to cull when he is on his own. The hinds don't have spectacular heads, which is why hind season is quiet. He doesn't mind, he is used to working in all conditions.

'I'm hoping to get something today,' he says. 'I still have a few to get before the end of the month.'

The numbers to cull are agreed in advance in the deer management groups. Each group includes estates that are neighbours. The western neighbour here is the National Trust and during stag season, Steve's estate leases some of their ground – and helps them get rid of stags. There's no getting around it. Many deer die of starvation and wet cold. Then there's the natural cycle of ageing and dying. And there are too many of them.

'But not everywhere,' Steve shouts over the engine. He is half-deaf from all the shooting and the Argo engine doesn't help.

In parts of Scotland, deer are more numerous and the centralised approach that treats the deer population as a unit causes problems. Especially since that approach does not make enough distinction between roe deer, red deer and sika deer, who have different habits and don't mix. Here, it's red deer. Roe deer in the Central belt are more numerous than red deer up here but the recommended culling numbers are the same.

'That corrie up there is the Sanctuary,' Steve shouts over the engine. 'Every deer forest should have one.'

This is one of the golden rules. And in a land without tree cover, corries give refuge from the elements. In the old Fasnakyle deer forest which had plenty of Caledonian wood, the Sanctuary comprised 6,000 acres, which was over a quarter of the entire shooting estate. Here, the Sanctuary is a large corrie that starts at the top of a waterfall called Sputan Ban.

That means the Spring of Bean. There are other springs in the realm of the Great Glen that bear the name of the first missionary of the glen. He came from Iona; maybe he was a cousin of Columba.

We take a turn up the hill and climb a burn to a corrie. It's awesome, a deep shadowy crevasse split like a giant deer hoof, as the old stalker liked to say of these hills where everything looked like a deer to him. The peaks are many, and the higher you go, the more there are. They're all Munros. We've come this high to check up on the private Hydro scheme. But at least this scheme doesn't piggy-back on the national grid, since the estate is off-grid and needs energy to come from somewhere. Before, it was powered by a generator. Steve checks the cistern through its slatted wooden top. It's low. That's because a residue of grass blocks the sluice after the rain. He clears the build-up and the intake surges and the water goes up in the cistern. Hydro-keeping is one of his chores. The old keeper of Affric used to take rainfall readings. He could tell you how much snow fell in, say, November 1942. He did it for pleasure and because that's what this lifeway is about: taking note of everything, from rainfall to wild cats' eyes. If any.

On the hill are small deer called knobbers. That's young stags whose horns are still little knobs. They are trusting and sweet. I'm surprised they're not afraid of the Argo. That's because the stalkers never shoot from the Argo and so lull them into a false comfort. Our small ruses . . . They come down close enough that I can see into their eyes. The Gaelic for deer is *fiadh* (feag), and *fiadhan* (feagan) is to be in a state of deer hunting. But also to be shy and to be wild. It's how it is. Those who are wild are shy of human society. And those who are civilised are afraid of the wild but at the same time want to be more like them. Maybe that's why they kill them.

Shy, wild, deer-like, and deer-hunting like – all faces of the deer god. But to be in touch with the deer god, you must hoof it, the true highland way. You must live it. Not buy it.

Do these youngsters know whether we bring food or death? They're taking a chance. But we bring neither. We are just passing and they are passing us, hello!

I find a chewed-up antler. They cast their antlers from late March onwards, and the antlers get nibbled by other deer. It's nutritious for the hinds, especially in the hungry wet winter. The antler is full of marrow. It gives me thoughts of survivalism. If you were living out here and ran out of supplies, you could boil a broth with this!

Steve pulls a face but wouldn't rule out anything.

It's a lonely profession. In one of his younger jobs, Steve lived in a very remote estate and one of the conditions of the job was: you must be single. No relationships. Just you and the deer at the end of the world.

Yes, the stalker must be content on his own yet good with

animals, people and weather. The stalker has to feed the stags and look after the hinds but not flip out when ghastly guests touch ground from helicopters and demand to shoot the white stag before dinner. The stalker is proud to be unmarried but longs for a warm hearth after a day on the hills. The stalker is a drinker but has the most sobering job of all. This life isn't for everyone. Even with an Argocat.

The old stalker walked everywhere. When he was made head stalker of all three beats of Affric estate and moved into the damp old lodge with his sister, they brought little with them from their parents' humble house in Fasnakyle — a gramophone, a paraffin lamp and a kettle. Apart from killing and dragging back 200 deer per season, he was given another war task: to keep an eye on the trail to Kintail. The Home Guard gave him a rifle. All bridges in the glen were ready to be blown up if the Germans landed on the west coast and entered from that direction like bad weather. But it never happened.

What happened was that the shooting lodges were occupied by military personnel. And the glens were bled dry. Men didn't return from the war or returned maimed and broken and died before their time.

'That's a cairn to a shepherd,' Steve points at a pile of stones uphill. 'He died here with his flock.'

Heart attack. Pals built this cairn for him. It's a long way up, but last year his grandson came to visit and Steve was glad to bring him up. We drive on. Steve stops and spies the hills through binoculars. Back when it was a long retractable round binocular it was called the glass.

'They're out of view because they're sheltering.'

He knows which side of a corrie a herd of hinds could be. The wind carries smell, and when the wind is in our backs, they can smell us. If you don't want to be sniffed, have the wind in your face.

There was once in the glen a poor shepherd. A banshee came to him. I'll grant you a wish, said she. I wish to sail the seas and gather a fortune, he said. Done! The banshee gave him a boat and wind in his sails, and flew off with a screaming laugh like this: *hí, hí, hí*. He sailed with the wind in his back and gathered a fortune. Years passed, he missed his glen. All he wished was to pass his days on the river and the hill and stalk the deer. He came home but – no luck. He couldn't get a single deer. Because the wind was in his back.

'This life is all about the weather,' Steve shouts. 'The best days are when I come down the hill after a day's stalking and I'm not soaking wet.'

Bang, splash. I get his meaning. I am soaking wet and that's without walking. We are crossing a surging crazy burn that flashes like liquid mercury down the hills. It has dug out the path and Steve, brother and son must fix it before the spring. Because this is also the hikers' path. The icy wind batters my left side and I know I'll get a chill but don't roll down the plastic flap because I want to be close to everything, even when it hurts. It's the harsh and vitalising fronts rushing in from the west like sprinters down a fast lane. The snow cloud moves in from the west. Trouble and thrill come from the west, it's always been that way. The fertile east coast was pastoral and peaceful in the Middle Ages, but the west had less arable land and clans made incursions into their neighbours' glens. Reivers, drovers, rivals, they came from Kintail, and the people of Affric were waiting for them – always a watchman on a dunn, trying not to fall asleep. It's hard to fall asleep when a weather front blows in from the west like this.

'Not always,' Steve shouts. 'Sometimes another wind comes in from the east. And the haar comes with it.'

We're too far inland for the sea haar that rises like a thousand clammy spectres and wraps you in its damp sheets. But if you are a game keeper of Affric for twenty years, you see everything. The world will pass through this glen, east to west and west to east, and you will witness it without complaint and no one to tell about it. Because you are alone. Your guests are passing through, it's hellos and goodbyes. Only the deer are permanent.

Once, when Ronnie Burn the first compleat Munroist stayed with a keeper's family, they sang him a sad Gaelic song at the evening ceilidh by the fire. It was the time of the Great War. The song was for bagpipe and voice, written by a stalker who missed his mate killed at the front. Ronnie jotted it down straight into rough English translation:

> As I was going up Druim Garaidh, my heart was very sore.
> I saw deer, but I had no pleasure in them that year.
> Going to the hilltop I had little pleasure
> Since the man I liked so well is gone.

The chorus picks up a refrain often found in Highland folk songs sung by lonesome gals and guys out in the hills:

> I am tired and I am sore
> By myself on the hill
> Going to see the deer.
> I had no pleasure in sport that year.

Sung from ceilidh to ceilidh, this melody exited the glens with the last of the stalkers, leaving cold ashes behind.

I don't know whether it's because we're not talking, but a sombre mood takes over the Argo ride. Affric opens up ahead. The brown hills, the cascading burns in their steep funnels, lead into a churning, cold afterworld. We have crooks tucked up behind us. We won't need them but you always take one. Like a shepherd. I suddenly find myself inside *Second Sight* but without a role. The novel is set in a glen like this.

Three local stalkers endure the company of rich, bright, well-meaning guests from the south, come for the summer to shoot stags with good heads, sample whiskies in an empty land and reminisce by the fire. India is mentioned. Why, the Highlands are a bit like India. The colonels and company men that run the empire are everywhere, shooting, sampling and reminiscing, dressed in tweeds and served by the few remaining locals who are a bit wild and shy, like deer. Just the way the visitor likes them.

The story opens with the stalker Alick's frightening vision of a dead man in a shroud carried by four others. He sees the faces of the four but not of the dead man. The most arrogant among the guests never stops mocking Alick and his second sight. That man becomes obsessed with bagging the head of King Brude, the emperor stag with the crown of horns. And the under-gillie who lets him do it in the end, out of duty and against his instinct, will forever be haunted by his part in this, the evisceration of his hills by the colonists – because it's clear to both native and colonist that King Brude is 'the spirit of his [the gillie's] forest, its incarnation, its reality, its legend, its living truth. For this man – this man – to shoot.' And he does. For the gillie to finish off and eviscerate, and carry over the hills on pony back in a foreseen funeral procession that stands for the murder of the Highlands. Its head will be displayed as a trophy in a plush drawing room somewhere down south.

That is the true story behind *The Monarch of the Glen*.

And here are the deer, still on the hills. After the Highlanders are all but gone. Hunted by everyone. By the rich, the bored and the mercenary. The deer can't be left alone. The deer is trophy or vermin.

When in the last pages of the novel the premonition of Alick the stalker comes true, he knows that he must leave his glen. His clients will forever hold him responsible for the death of one of theirs, even if it was self-inflicted, even if he was a bastard, even if all the stalker did was deliver the truth, just as the other stalker delivered King Brude to the bastard.

'We must go – and take the things with us. That has always been our small tragedy,' Alick tells Mairie the maid. 'Pity, for I like this country well enough. It's good enough for me – perhaps because it is my own country.'

And the only bright note is that Mairie will go with him to the south, to the lowlands where dispossessed Highlanders go. And take *the things* with them – language, story, second sight, first sight, knowledge of river and hill, fiddle, bagpipe, memory and love. The things.

The dead hind is heavy even without her viscera. A single person can't lift her.

Once shot, a deer must be gralloched there and then. Steve makes a quick cut under the throat. That's called bleeding. Then a long slash down the belly and the balloon of the stomach rolls out. It makes a wet squelch. I can't stop seeing a human being. We have the same guts. The stomach is large, then the small intestine, the large intestine, the matter at various stages of digestion from grass to excrement. All the processes of life are slow and complex, and how suddenly it ends.

Steve ties a nylon rope around her neck. I don't know if she died on the spot or dragged herself to drink from the burn. The other hinds are standing on the ridge, looking at us. We are the evil ones but there is no blame. They are just looking, with that understanding animals have.

He drags her down the slope. I walk behind. It's bleak. My jaw aches from tension. Rolling next to me is the stomach. It won't be left behind. It follows us. It's a lesson in anatomy. It's a lesson in everything. When it stops, it quivers in the wind. Steve clocks me and the stomach.

'The ravens and buzzards will get it.'

Oh good. Some kind of natural chain is at work. This is not just senseless murder. We reach the Argo and heave the hind in the back with effort – Steve normally does this on his own. That's why he had his third hernia operation last autumn. And back on his feet and on the job a week later. There was no one to replace him. He shouldn't be lifting large animals after three hernias.

'I'm all mesh now, it's fine.'

It's his sacrifice: his guts in exchange for the guts of the deer.

We drive on west just to enjoy the hills. Like a funeral cortege with our cadaver. Our stalkers' sticks lie on top of the eviscerated hind. The wind helps with the numbing. A line of poetry comes like rescue remedy.

> I can't give to the deer
> all that's their due.

'Praise of Ben Dorain'. The Gaelic ode to the deer mountain by Duncan Ban MacIntyre. He was poet-hunter-soldier. It's the story of the deer people seen the indigenous way – from the roots up.

DEER PEOPLE

> The deer in us
> drinks to its fill.

The deer people inhabit the Highlands. The stalker roams the mountains. He must shoot the deer, it is his destiny. In doing so he shoots the deer in himself and he knows it. But the shapeshifting mountain spurs him on. He runs like a deer. One dies but the rest carry on. Next thing they swap places. It's not personal. It's kinship. Steve is in that lineage. A black snow front comes in from the west like a column of furious banshees. We are small and transient in our Argo and we know it. The smell of petrol fumes is mixed with blood and guts. At least it was instant.

It all happened very quickly with the hind. Steve spied the hinds from the Argo. This was the moment. He got out with intent and picked up the gun with the silencer from behind the seat. It is precise and military, with a tripod, like a camera.

'Walk behind me,' he said.

There are the hinds, naturally shy and friendly.

They are natural people. I can see their stance, the cocked heads curious like children, coming down the slope to check us out. We creep up the wretched sodden earth and Steve takes up position on a small knoll. He is soundless, almost weightless, focused on a single point. I could be next to him, the gun in my hands, looking through the crosshair, choosing which hind to shoot. He could be delivering the baby of death for me, a midwife with a firm hand. The true gillie loves to deliver the stag to the client – I almost said the patient, though Steve calls them guests. It's always been like this and it's his favourite part of the job: getting someone their first stag.

I see the hinds and want to shout – Run!

But I am with Steve, not with them. If I was with them it

would be different. Maybe that's what it's about – who you share the journey with. The journey has a beginning, middle and end for us today. This is the middle.

And here it is, the moment of consummation between hunter and prey. Steve is at one with the boggy land. The twitch of a hind's ear makes his own ear twitch. He is deaf and blind to all else. I look down at the steely loch. A fog rises. We should be wrestling this herd of hinds with our bare hands if we were honest animals. Steve *would* wrestle the hind with his bare hands. He takes aim. I crouch a few metres behind him. This is what stalking is – tracking, spying, zeroing in. Then a single shot. Quiet because of the silencer. So quiet it almost couldn't be deadly. Steve folds up the tripod and gets up. He's missed!

'No, I think I got her.'

He never misses. You aim for the shoulder when it's a far shot of 200 yards like this, and that gets the lung. If it's a closer shot, you aim for the neck. We climb to the fold in the burn. I hear a pitiful cry, like a child. It sears me. Is it some bird I've never heard before? Steve is too deaf. The cry again. The hinds are gathered above us. One of them starts down the hill again. Maybe it's her crying.

Life can end so suddenly. From a stalking viewpoint, that is the objective.

'There she is.'

A single shot through the shoulder. Later I realise this is good marksmanship but right now all I realise is the fact of death. She lies with her face by the stream, her neck twisted, a bit of blood seeping from her mouth. The hill holds her in its brown arms like a Pietà.

The water continues to mould the land. It's not over. It can't be over when so much water is coming down. New waterfalls unfurl like ribbons, then furl back in. Some have names but are not here. Others are nameless but gush down the slope.

You chase something that moves across the land. Your reptilian brain is alert. You chase it, you strike, overpower it, you are bloodied, then it's over. What have I done? Or it's you that bites the dust.

The hills are the colour of the oldest tartan. Perhaps that cloth really was dyed in this glen and worn by its people. Woad was used for indigo-like pigment, though you wouldn't guess it from its yellow flowers because it's the leaves they ground to a powder for the dye. It's a lot of work. Those painted people the Picts might well have used woad to paint their bodies blue but by the time you saw them in that awesome state, you were at war with them. And for that orange-red of Affric? Lichens and mosses of course, scraped off the stones by the sister of the eternal stalker of Affric.

To wear these hills like tartan through an eternity of sleet, for all our sins to be washed in the burns that suddenly surge and sweep us off our feet and life ends without warning – it's what Steve does every day.

Just one preference he has – he doesn't like stalking stags alone. Stags are an occasion to be shared and it feels wrong to go kill a stag on your own. They're also very heavy.

The stalker is lonelier than the river gillie. It's the remoteness. On the river you're never far from friendly things. But the hills are different. Steve nearly died a few times. He was after a stag one October, in a corrie up that way, and he got the stag but the burn suddenly surged and couldn't be crossed. But to not cross the burn meant overnighting in the corrie, which was sure death from hypothermia. Crawl into the freshly gralloched belly of the stag? He and Ali did that another time. This time, he went to cross the burn and was swept down. Somehow he pulled himself out of the raging torrent and walked back to the lodge, six miles with icicles on him. And didn't even catch a cold.

'Last summer – it's not nice to say it, but this guy turned up. Still young. With a tent.'

He'd spent childhood holidays in Affric, it was his special place. Three years before, he was diagnosed with cancer. Steve befriended him over the week, took his phone to charge it up at the lodge. Then one evening, on the way home Steve stopped to drop off the phone. But it was not needed anymore. The guy had died in his tent.

'It was pretty upsetting. I'd got to know him a bit.'

If you can't live here, at least you can die here.

There was the taxi driver who came to the loch and quietly asphyxiated himself in the car. You want a last glimpse of beauty. In the same way, people come to Tony's gallery for last rites. One woman died hugging a small painting.

In the larder where guests are too squeamish to go, Steve hangs the carcass on a hook. It takes time. The head is cut off, the forelegs are cut off and the organs are taken out. Heart and lungs are thrown in a bin. Every estate has a pit where animal remains are buried. Then the inside of the body is hosed. The smell of blood and guts is like nothing else. Once it enters your nostrils it never leaves. In a few days, I will sit down with a venison steak that Steve has given me. A sad and grateful cannibal. To eat another conscious being is to eat yourself. Every bite is choice. I don't have to eat this hind. But I'm part of the food chain and I know what it takes to get to this point.

Steve puts aside the liver for a friend, but there is a spot on it – liver fluke – and he discards it. Fluke gets in when the animal is exposed to boggy ground. It's a parasite that rots the liver. He shows me the teeth – just two are left! The hind was old. She may have died at the next frost. This too reassures me. Steve shot an old hind to reassure me. How can you tell her age from such a distance?

It's the ribs showing through the skin, no fat. The flesh is lean, and a bit tough. When I eat the venison steak, I will be swallowing something more than flesh. People who butcher animals know something that others don't. When you've handled a carcass that was a living being with light in its eyes, you know that you too must give something up. Even if you don't think so. It just happens.

Like a surgeon, up to your elbows in the patient's innards, solemn and not speaking, you cannot make a mistake. The sternum is held open with a small instrument. Finally, the carcass is wheeled into the fridge room to join the others. Steve has done it without gloves or apron. Not a drop of blood on his clothes. It's also a statement: I am not a butcher or a surgeon. I am a game keeper.

'I use gloves with the stags though, I learned my lesson.'

A few years ago he nearly died of blood poisoning. This happens to stalkers.

During the rut, stags' blood is near toxic from all the adrenaline and everything else that gets into it on the hills. If you have a cut and his blood gets into yours, it can be fatal. He was rushed to hospital. The doctors started opening thick books to read up on it, so he briefed them before going into septic shock.

It's the revenge of the stag – your blood for his.

Last, he feeds the dogs. We exit the glen. We sit in the truck and I think: we humans always travel in our machines feet first. Feet first – like corpses. It's only when we walk across the land that we are alive and aligned with other beings.

Today has been like a whole season. I can't imagine doing

it every day. Steve has a few more hinds to cull. He spends the long winter evenings making things from deer antlers. His girlfriend is a local archaeologist. She chips away at buried secrets, mining the Old Statistical Account for the detail that will reveal all about the illicit whisky stills in the forest, or the lime kiln or the lead mine. Steve would still be living this life if he had no salary. He would still be there on the hill. His girlfriend too, map in frozen hand, scanning the body of the land for signs of life.

What is the difference between the pastoral approach to the land and the industrial approach? It's the difference between custodianship and extermination.

The Ranger

Kintail and Affric are the two faces of this epic glen. Each looks a different way.

It's late summer. The wettest in Kintail's memory – but that's what they say every year! Water falls down vertical hills like a prophecy. Then the sun comes out. The ranger and I stand at the watershed. It's where the backs of the Janus twins meet.

'On this side the rivers flow west to the Atlantic. And on that side they flow east.'

Bella chews a deer leg. The ranger is tall, friendly and impersonal. His passion is the path. We climb for ten hours and his stride doesn't change. Weather passes through him but doesn't move him.

Once upon a time, Affric and Kintail bickered over their boundary. To resolve it, each clan sent a powerful old woman.

They met here at the watershed and fought until one surrendered. But each clan insisted that their Cailleach had won and still couldn't agree on the boundary. The people of both clans are gone from the glens but new people came, like me and the ranger. The ranger came as a volunteer and stayed until he was offered a job. He studied Zoology and this is all he ever wanted: to roam these glens tracking short-eared bats – there's one right there! – and eagles, there's two types here, golden and white-tailed. He is a soldier of the hills like Steve, but without a gun and on foot all the way. He is also the next generation. The ranger tried his hand at deer stalking but it wasn't for him. Someone else is employed to shoot the excess deer. The hills of Kintail are vertical so stalking is done the hard way – on foot and pony back. The ranger and Steve know each other from a respectful distance. Like guard dogs, they keep to their territory. And they prefer silence.

The story of how the National Trust for Scotland came to own 14,000 acres of Kintail is incredible and true. For centuries this land was in the hands of the clan to which belonged Coinneach Odhar, the Brahan Seer. Their lands stretched over 125,000 acres. Then, through illness and decline, the chief's line came to an end. Just as predicted by the Seer.

In the 1930s, these mountains came up for sale for the price of £12,000. The man who bought them was a philanthropist and mountaineer called Percy Unna. He bought them on behalf of the Scottish Mountaineering Club, then gifted them to the National Trust. Already he could see the way the wind was blowing, that the hills would come under more pressure from industry and touristry. He bought several other mountains and gifted them anonymously to the Trust, and in time a fund was set up to make the transferral of land easier. He died while climbing in 1950, a smile on his face even in death. No monument because that would desecrate the land.

Everyone who walks the Kintail-Affric way is here because of this man. He was Danish and devoted enough to the Scottish hills to buy them and give them back to the Scottish people. But under rules. The Unna Rules he set up are stark because they serve nature. Here are some of the rules:

> That 'primitive' means not less primitive than the existing state. That Sheep Farming and Cattle-Grazing may continue, but that Deer Stalking must cease, and no sport of any kind be carried on, or sporting rights sold or let. That the hills should not be made easier or safer to climb. That no facilities should be introduced for mechanical transport; that paths should not be extended or improved; and that new paths should not be made.

The final rule ends with this:

> That this may create a precedent . . . in other mountainous districts not only in Scotland, but also in England and Wales.

And sure enough, others followed the precedent of 'the man who bought mountains'. The Trust was inspired to continue acquiring land, abiding by the Unna Rules as far as possible.

'This is why we try not to use gravel on the paths.'

The ranger is using our ten-hour hike to track the state of the trail after the rainy summer. Gravel would be an easy fix, but gravel is interference with the land, and using it supports extraction. So the ranger's team try to find natural solutions – like moving stones to stabilise paths and shoring up the disturbed peat.

Walking behind the ranger this endless day, I learn the code of the mountain path. Even when the trail is flooded, you stick to it. If you go off-trail to avoid getting wet boots, you disturb the peaty moor.

'Peat hags are on the increase. It's not good,' says the ranger. 'But there's not much we can do. Environmental change. It's a cycle.'

Peat hagging is when the peatland rises like tables from the ground and becomes exposed. We see a lot of it. They're like giant mushrooms. It's caused by flooding and erosion, and herds of deer trampling the ground.

But the upside is: the rising peat has thrown up the roots of ancient trees. We see them – white roots in the peat, four to five thousand years old! Climate change caused the great forests to die back.

'The Highlands might have been at their most forested four-and-a-half to five thousand years ago.'

This is a shock to me. So long ago! Natural processes of die back and return, and die back. The ranger accepts this without struggle. Faced with the monumental Five Sisters of Kintail and the bealach lochs of the mountain pass, which seen from below look like a dark quartz palace we must impossibly climb – well, when you walk these harsh drovers' paths, you learn how little control you have.

I learn from the ranger that we should appreciate the midge and just wear a face net. Because a healthy midge population feeds pipistrelle bats, swallows and fish. If the midge disappears, others will pack up too. Thank you, midge, but you are vicious.

We began in Kintail in a sea of bog myrtle useful against midges, past the ruins of settlements backed by these vertical hills and destroyed first by avalanche then the Clearances. Past the dyke painstakingly repaired by rangers and volunteers. The dyke was built during the Highland Potato Famine. Men from starving families were brought in by the lairds to build walls like these for sheep enclosures. They were given food as payment, and the glen remembers that these men had to walk both ways, for miles along the merciless drovers' road to Skye, skinny as convicts. Projects like these became known as Destitution Roads. Is there anything more vicious than the midge? Yes, the nineteenth-century landlord and his factor.

Some of the Kintail crofters, traditionally growing oats and raising black cattle, were kicked out by landlords and became pauperised cottars. Once evicted from their fertile glen, they were forced to eke out a living on comfortless cliffs where only bird eggs and seaweed could be harvested. And some landlords were so pathologically mean, they charged folks a fee for the rocks on which bird eggs were collected. One of the large estates here was bought by a man who made his fortune in the opium trade in the Far East.

Past the canyon with the two old bothies, now fixed by the National Trust, where you can stay almost gratis, if you want absolute silence and darkness. The last stalker and the last shepherd used to play the fiddle to each other across the river.

We leave the Five Sisters behind but their protean shapes remain etched in my mind like a dream. They are goddesses. The ranger names them: Sgurr na Moraich, Sgurr nan Saighead, Sgurr Fhuaran, Sgurr na Carnach, Sgurr na Ciste Duibhe.

'And that's Spaniards' Peak up there.'

Because Spanish soldiers spent the night up there after the 1719 battle of Glen Shiel. Jacobite clans against the British Army. Three hundred Spanish troops arrived to support the Highland rebels. They were defeated after the British Army fired mortars at their fortified positions higher up, setting the heather on fire — this was the first time mortars were used against the Highlanders, who could not respond in kind. The clan chief lost his lands and fled to France (but was later pardoned by the Crown), and the Spaniards were taken prisoner by the British and housed in Edinburgh Castle where they enjoyed the treatment given to professional soldiers, and it seems that many of them stayed on. Not so for the captured Highlanders who were executed as traitors.

Through the chasm of the Ugly Pass in perpetual shade and surging waterfalls, so named by cattle drovers because to squeeze through here in a storm with a herd of animals is ugly. You try not to fall off the path that didn't exist then; it was built in the nineteenth century for stalkers, and the ranger and his team maintain it now. Even in winter, when waterfalls wash out the path they restored last season, the team will squeeze through the Ugly Pass, spades strapped to their backs, and fix it.

But at least they don't have to survive by bleeding cattle and drinking the blood the way desperate drovers did. Blood, whisky and thin oatmeal gruel was their fate. It took them many days to move the cattle through the glen to reach the Monks' Place. I see what it took — the land is rough, the weather dreich, reivers on horseback want to slash your throat and steal your cattle, and your only warmth comes from the dogs you sleep with. After Culloden, the carrying of arms was banned and the only people exempt were the drovers. They wouldn't survive otherwise. But the pasture, the pasture of Kintail! So juicy, it makes you want to be a grazing animal. Easier than being a drover.

An obituary for a drover in the early nineteenth century reads:

Died on Thursday the 16th curt, Mr Angus MacEdward, tacksman of Kerrowmeanach [the Middle Quarter] in Badenoch, in the 44th year of his age, after a short illness brought about by fatigue in the execution of his business as a drover. He was an honest, industrious and useful member of society . . .

The language of the Age of Improvement. In another drover's account from the late nineteenth century, I learned that along the forty miles of this toughest of trails, there wasn't a place for a drover to sleep, eat or drink. Not one. There were empty houses and lodges but the estate owners didn't want the drovers trampling through their deer forests cleared of people – and trees.

Past the bothy that was once a home to a stalker's family and then stood empty, and was restored by volunteers. Two stark stony rooms with bunks without mattresses, and an empty hearth. The ranger frowns at the small pile of kindling left behind by the last overnighter. You're not to break off branches from the precious planted trees. You are to bring your own logs, on your back like everything else! It's the Unna Rules.

The ranger is the only person I know who has read the book about Ronnie Burn, the first compleat Munroist. The ranger and I don't have to speak. We're turning the pages of the hills like a book. Like Steve the stalker, the ranger is content to take on the personality of the hills. He needs no other personality.

We turn the page and fall back a century.

At Alltbeithe, the Burn of Birches, the chimney puffs.

Two girls carry baskets of peat indoors. The Scott family! Eight girls. How did Mrs Scott give birth to eight children here, fifteen miles from the next house? She was lucky and tough. She came from an island without trees.

The postie comes from the west, the teacher and the priest come from the east. It's not as lonely as it will be half a century later, because over the hills in Mullardoch is the family of shepherd-keepers with their ten children. There was Black Sandy the drover with his family, and the whisky smuggler with his sister.

The ranger shows me a crevasse in the rock with running water. That's where the illicit whisky still used to be.

The ranger spies a band of breakaway sheep that have gone feral.

'They'll roam the tops and never come down.'

We can almost see their grins.

I've lost the ranger from view and someone is behind me. Quite far, but I make out the woman walking with a pony. She has straight long skirts and piled-up hair. What a long way she has come, from the Monks' Place where my future street is still an orchard. She has just enough clothes, a second pair of shoes and a pot of cold cream in baskets tied to the saddle. This is the teacher, coming to stay with the stalker's family. The eight girls will be waiting for her. Soon they'll be scratching words on boards with chalk. A hundred years later, their school room will be a youth hostel. And hikers will put on the fire the boards with the girls' names, not knowing they were burning history.

Oh and here's the smoky cottage of the glen's last bard with the cows. One winter his cows were lost in a snowstorm. He composed a song for them that he recited to anyone that stopped by and one day, the bard left. Maybe he became a tramp. He was nothing without his cows. You may see him walking the loopy old road of the west coast, his hair dreadlocked, his face peaty, hitching a ride, dropping in on estates to get deer skins off them, or antlers, to turn them into something beautiful.

It's 1913. Black Sandy is returning from the cattle mart with eighteen black Highland cows. He has walked from the Firth to here, dressed in a three-piece suit of fine wool. The cattle are for his boss, the Colonel, who is the shooting tenant of Affric. Black Sandy and his wife used to live one glen up, at the west end of Loch Lungard. One day, the burn next to their house rose so high, it ran through the house and they escaped through the windows.

And who's that coming down the Gael's Corrie? Hundreds of woolly sheep! Three men whistle to the collie dogs. The aim is to keep the flock together and reach the lower part of Affric as a group. The sheep are heavy with wool; it's shearing time. Must be 1966, the last big drove of sheep between Cannich and Affric. The drover's skills are dying out. It's not easy, in 1966, to find someone who can take sheep from one glen to another.

Before the Hydro-Electric Board arrived, Lungard and Mullardoch had grazing flocks. They'd move between the lochs in search of pasture. Then the two lochs became one. They had to be brought all the way over the pass into Affric to be shorn, before being taken back the same way. A day's droving, each way. The men shout and whistle. And vanish in the mist.

The ranger's back comes into view. Are we nearly there?

A small, odd-looking man is coming from Kintail. His canvas rucksack gives him a hunchback. He walks fast and has a shepherd's stick but is not a shepherd. As he comes closer, I see his humorous face, and the sole of one boot is unstitched. It's Ronnie Burn, the first compleat Munroist! He doesn't see me but I know where he is rushing to get before nightfall, this lonely lovely man, this *very strange priest*, this poet among clergy, accidental champion among vain mountaineers, optimist among gloomy Gaels, who wanted to climb all the peaks of Scotland but not for glory and oneupmanship. He climbed all 555 of them several times. As if lured by singing banshees. He was looking for home, that's why – a home for his sky-high spirit and his pure heart. And the stalker's family at the Burn of Birches became one of his favourite homes. With them he would get not just 'a bed and some place names' but a family for a day or two.

'Would I could be buried there in sight of my own ben and in my clan country,' he wrote in his diary of an evening. He did not want to go back south.

Ronnie was as much story hunter as hill bagger. In his diaries are recorded forgotten hills and corries, songs and stories. Already in his day they were being forgotten because the people of the glens were leaving. He was passing through his homeland at the end of an era. To go higher and lower and get dangerously lost when the wind rips the map from your hand and the mist comes down is to know the Highlands with your whole being.

We've been walking so long it feels like another day. If the ranger's back wasn't there to keep me on track, I'd go off-piste and trample the peat like a herd of deer. I'd go in a direction opposite to that of Ronnie so that I'm going where he's coming from. For instance, to the Fannichs – which are a family of hills, though they sound like people. Peaks *are* people, a stalker in a remote glen told Ronnie. That's why no less than five hills are called Peak of the Cailleach. The women and girls of the glens are gone, but the Cailleach can't die. Something is there, even when you think the glen is empty forever.

Ronnie Burn stayed with a keeper and his sister. They had five other brothers who were shy like deer. You would stumble in from the mist, starving and frozen, and the deer-shy, deer-friendly brothers sniffed you out from their hiding places and if they liked you, they approached and maybe took your shoes and coat and offered you a jug of milk. They never said a word.

You creep along the corridor of Affric and you're like a scuttling crab on the bottom of a sea loch. Yep, I smell the sea, acrid and iodine. The Five Sisters of Kintail do not move their priestess heads but they see you.

The last time Ronnie walked this way was in 1920. The war had ended. He didn't know that his favourite family had left their Burn of the Birch. Imagine Ronnie's shock, arriving on a blizzardy evening, full of aches and hunger, to find that his friends were gone and the hearth was cold.

'The glen is not the same to me now,' he wrote in his diary, typically self-restrained.

Affric, Cannich and Farrar became places where no friendly smoke was seen. You would not be given a jug of milk, an oatcake or a bed. The last Ronnie heard from the keeper with the sister and the five deer-brothers was in a letter after the war. They were still there but Ronnie would never visit them again. To the end, the family of keepers kept a door open for their friend the very strange priest.

'Trusting that you may yet step in some evening,' they signed off.

On our descent to Kintail, we pass two lush oases in the barren hills. It's where the National Trust has planted trees. They call them exclosures. The air is fresher inside, the burns run though a woodland and not a wasteland. It's incredible. This is how the Highlands were. Back when deer, sheep, cattle, goats, wolves, horses, birds, fish and humans were in scale with the land.

Is this the difference between having grazing animals and not having grazing animals?

'Yes.'

And the ranger inspects a tear in the fence where deer have come through. The team will come and fix it.

'It's okay. Deer are part of this country. And the trees are getting older so it's fine.'

The Ranger crouches by a small waterfall and drinks like a deer. He has not brought a flask or a cup. The sun sets in a blaze. The Five Sisters of Kintail fall into shadow, one after the other: the One that Looks to the Sea, the One of the Arrows, the One with Many Springs, the Rocky One and the Black Kist.

I once had a dream. There is a waterfall and I start climbing it. It's crazy to climb a waterfall, but I know there's something at the top. I emerge on a forest clearing. It's full of deer big like myth. Thunderdeer. Their heads are gilded with sun and lichens. The world rests in their crowns. It's incredible, incredible. I look up at them in awe and a couple of them let me in. I take my place among them. I've arrived just in time. Oh, it's been worth the climb! I found the deer people in their deer forest, my ben, my clan country.

The Glen

By the Kilmorack dam is a new bench dedicated to Willie the gillie. At the bridge of the Crossing Place, subcontractors are *core drilling*. They're prospecting for —

'No idea,' they say grimly, and it's true. Bridges, roads and fields are being drilled, measured, marked with orange and fortified by the energy company ahead of their preliminary operations, that's what it is. To take the weight of the industrial gear needed to build the substation in Talorgan's Place, the bridge would need to be replaced by something much larger. But the riverbanks can't support it.

Despite these problems with access, not one but two new power stations are planned in the glen. One in Talorgan's Place and another one near Silver Falls. That takes a moment to sink in. Because I know that the only access there is a beautiful rural road narrow as a birth canal. They want to dilate the birth canal to force through a substation platform, two Super Grid Transformers, three large future bays, four smaller future bays, a new double busbar and ancillary equipment, a new control building and new access roads.

The Cougies' horse-riding business would be destroyed. The new transmission line would rip through Giusachan forest and Aria's woodland. The additional large battery storage system that is planned on the river is a toxic hazard if it goes on fire. All the water in the river wouldn't put it out, and the lithium would leak into the river and poison everything that lives.

In Talorgan's Place, twelve households fall within the marked-up industrial zone. Tenants are already being forced to leave, others may be stuck on a construction site for years, and those who put up their houses for sale can't sell them. The industry traffic will consist of a large vehicle passing either through Talorgan's Place or the Monks' Place every minute of every day for several years, like a perpetual music festival, but the music will be the smashing up of the glen.

Mo ghleann.

The *upgrades* to the three dam substations in our glen are approved. We discover that they are not upgrades at all, but brand-new large industrial hubs – and quite far from the dams themselves. Until now, the substations were integrated in the dams, but they stopped maintaining them: there's no money in maintenance. The new Kilmorack substation will be on a hill with a Druidic grove above Tony's gallery, and next to the cattle farm. The company will hack a new road through the last grazing field, lined by old oaks. Human and environmental health, land and agriculture, electromagnetic radiation, and major accidents and disasters – once again, ignored.

The government buckles under lobbying pressure from the power and construction industry and, citing *energy security*, decides not to go with zonal pricing. This is a blow for everything that lives on the land, and good news for large energy developers, investors and the extractive industries that prop up the renewables industry: steel production, quarrying, mining, industrial transportation and the fossil-fuel industry which works overtime (but *not in our backyards*) to produce, transport and install all the components. The energy giant can now get on undisturbed with their plans to trash land and sea under the banner of clean energy. Both transmission and generation can continue with their mega-expansion of the grid, and export energy from the north of Scotland to the south of England. This model is not smart. It is the most expensive, least resilient and most destructive to human and environmental health. It also means that other new hungry industries will creep up north, to hook onto the grid: hydrogen plants and data centres.

Around the same time, citing *national security*, the government bans a non-violent protest movement in support of the Palestinians in Gaza. The protest group's crime is to spray-paint a British fighter jet. The government proscribes the group as 'terrorists' and continues to support the genocidal Israeli state.

Up at Loch nam Bonnach the Cake-shaped One, the energy giant has started prospective core-drilling for the bases of pylons for the new transmission line that would hook into the new station that hasn't yet been approved. Which makes their drilling illicit but apparently not illegal. The blue artist walks up to the loch and paints it – in case it is obliterated. I used to walk up there, and now I don't.

Near her croft, in Farley, the hills are being prospected by a German wind-farm developer. This is because the absentee inheritors of the castle in-glen own these hills and invited the developer to build thirty-six turbines 230 metres high. Plus battery storage units, access roads, fences, gates. Thousands of tons of concrete will be dumped into the peatland of Farley. Prospective drilling is taking place there too. For convenience, men in large vehicles are driving over the ruins of the Five Forts of Farley. Over our bones.

People have started walking places marked up for destruction. It is grief pilgrimage. Walk, paint, write, film, make love to the land now, shout, scream, before it is extracted by appointment to fulfil a target. If you resist the destruction of the place you love, the extractors and their political allies call you a *nimby*, perhaps even a *terrorist*. If you collaborate with the extractors you become a *stakeholder*. And the land? A *marketplace* apparently waiting to be pounded with *global investment*.

'Since you have preferred sheep to men, let sheep defend you,' went the heartbroken farewell of Highlanders to their chiefs. And they boarded the ships.

Since you prefer *global investment* to places and people, the day will come to eat investment, drink investment, and breathe investment.

'We have to reseed the world!' Tony is saying, and doing it. He is planting trees like one possessed. We are all becoming possessed. People's mental health is suffering. Twice Tony has collapsed with vasovagal syncope when bad news reaches us about more core drilling and more extraction by the energy giant. I worry that reseeding the world takes time but destruction is quick. That the damage is irreversible. And me? I have recovered some of my health but things will never be the same. Grief is lodged in my chest and I go into a state of fight or flight at the sight of the energy company vehicles. They are everywhere. Just the sight of their logo makes me see red. They have become the biggest employer of young people. It reminds me of how during war, the biggest employer is the army. War *opens up a marketplace*.

Thousands of jobs, community benefits to the war widows and orphans, a renewable extermination. Wipe out the population and replace it with something more useful. Because — where is the profit in mere people and mere places?

Inside Strathfarrar, the energy giant is trying to buy more

land from the Middle estate – to open a new quarry. Thirty thousand tons of gravel from the flanks of the Farrar for the new roads needed for the 'upgrade' – which hints at the size of it. Dougal is bottle-feeding his lambs and worries that the lambing sheep will be stressed by the noise.

'I'll take them across, there's still good ground on the other side of the river. I don't want them to pine.'

The postie died before I could go on the postal round with him. His wake turned into a feast. It was held in a village hall once purpose-built by the Hydro as a cinema for workers. Drinks and memories, hugs and hearsay. Roddy the Cougie held his latest grandchild – at least someone is working to repeople the inner glen! Ali sold him his metal detector. The new gate keepers of Strathfarrar are here, bohemian types. Steve the stalker of Affric tells that the two new girls have left the estate. They lasted one season.

The new Corrimony wind farm is approved. Fourteen needless turbines 149.9 metres high will go up on a hill above it – unless subsidies dry up or the company goes bankrupt. Once chipped by industry, the bowl of Corrimony may end up smashed. If Ciara leaves, the walled garden will fall into weeds. But the robot will continue to harvest the field of pumpkins. It doesn't mind one way or another.

This summer there are wildfires in the Highlands. But woodlands continue to be felled to make way for yet more overhead lines and underground lines. More, more.

Climate change is a symptom of an Earth in turmoil, fighting for her survival. You cannot treat the symptom without addressing the root cause: the genocidal, ecocidal greed of the global industrial-military complex whose appetites are incompatible with the survival of a human Earth.

★

In the glen, word has it that an 'X-ray' has been taken of Monar dam and it showed cracks 17 metres long and wide enough to 'slot a credit card in'. It showed that the dam had been in-filled with industrial junk – tools, engines, wheels. The builders had wanted to get rid of detritus with this last dam. This last dam that was not needed.

Monar dam is tired, that's why the reservoir is not used to its full capacity. This gives two prospects. Loch and river will be reunited when the dam fails. Or repair, which would cost a lot and come out of our pockets, as everything does. I don't want Monar dam to retire. There's no other curved dam like it. I've been in the glen too long!

In their preliminary maintenance work, the energy company partially drains Mullardoch dam – *de-water* is their term – and it reveals the two original lochs with the river running between them, the way it was before the Hydro. It's where the path was – you crossed the river between the two lochs and you were on the other side. That's the trail dwellers, hikers, shepherds and stalkers took until the dam merged the two lochs. It's incredible to see, even if the only person who actually sees it close up is the man with the boat. No access from the shore, too treacherous with all the mud that's revealed – 40 metres of dead mud.

The stadium by the bridge over the Firth is in trouble, and to generate easy money it decides to build a battery energy storage plant on its own site. The handful of Travellers and their horses will be chased from this garbaged land, and once again pack up their caravans and horse boxes. But is there anywhere for them to go? Or for any of us to go.

This summer, seventy-seven whales were stranded in Orkney and died. Entire families. Last year – fifty-five in the Isle of Lewis. This is not normal. They were driven away by sonar noise in the sea, having picked it up with their collective true north. Core drilling, prospecting, transmission cables, floating turbine platforms and emissions of every kind. The noises of a militarised, industrialised sea chases them the way the felling of a forest chases the birds, then everything else.

A few months later, and the Travellers must be relieved that the battery energy storage plant will not go ahead after all because it has been recognised by the local authority as a fire hazard. The spot is too prominent. The bridge over the Firth going up in flames would not look good.

These days I am haunted by the ghost of Calgacus. The writer Tacitus was nothing less than son-in-law to the general Agricola who aimed to enslave *the last of the free*, and Tacitus may well have invented the famed Calgacus speech, playful in his victor's smugness, rolling the imagined words of the *Picti* in his mouth like a cat with a mouse. But there's no smoke without fire and it must be that the gist of what Calgacus said to rouse the motley tribes of Caledonia travelled from mouth to mouth until an imperial writer put it down in his own tongue with sympathy, so it may reach us across twenty centuries and two extinct languages – Pictish and Latin – and ring with truth. His real name was Calgaich the Swordsman.

> 'These plunderers of the world, after exhausting the land by their devastations, are rifling the ocean: stimulated by avarice if their enemy be rich, by ambition if poor. Unsatiated by the East and by the West, the only people who behold wealth and indigence with equal avidity. To ravage, to slaughter, to usurp under false titles, they call empire. And where they make a wasteland, they call it peace.'

Two millennia later, the plunderers of the world are large energy and tech corporations that grab land and squeeze the life out of it. They are here today, gone tomorrow.

But we are staying.

The hermit of Kilmorack died in the spring. There is poetic justice in the fact that she lived in this parish where women were persecuted by the church for being like her – a green hermit. I'm guessing a green hermit is what the original Morag was. I'm pretty sure that Kilmorack was named after her – a local cult of a healer called Morag. The keeper of the spring, the merciful mother of the glen, the green lady that haunts ruins, the banshee that screamed in warning and may yet have the last laugh.

Her daughter comes to the house to pack away her mother's things. She invites me in and I enter for the first time. A painting of a green waterfall presides in the living room; the water moves like a perpetual dream. Who was the artist? The scene is familiar. Do you want it? Yes! We try to lift the painting but the frame is nailed to the wall. The wall would have to come with it. Maybe it was the Spanish guy who left his colours and hands to my friend. The hermit of Kilmorack had been custodian of the outsiders and the ones in pain. The workmen she hired for small jobs were Laughing Lachlans – gypsies of labour, tenants of rooms that leak. She is cremated in a humanist ceremony in the hills above Inverness where fiddlers and fairies once gathered.

Fasnakyle church sold to a couple from the south.

Struy church sold cheaply to an investor. No plans, he fancied owning a church in the Highlands. Margaret was diagnosed with polymyalgia, which means pain in many places. Sounds familiar.

'However!' she says brightly, popping a pain killer, the good news is —

Rose is returning to the river after her maternity leave. Ali and Rose will continue to track the salmon, even if this year the salmon are struggling because the water levels are all over the place.

Dun Fionn is a hub. Good luck to the bulldozers and those who want to drill in a steel tower to reach a target.

Passing Stas the dam-builder's son, I see that the shack no longer leans and has been painted.

In the Monks' Place, my neighbour the ex-soldier has started cleaning up the riverbank. He dismantled an old fridge in the reeds and carried it on his back to the dump. It was leaking poison into the river and the river is full of birds and otters, and some salmon, still. Then he continued with the bottles the tide has washed up. I started doing the same. My God, so much glass and plastic, tin and silicone and rubber, tubs of petrol – and so much of it half-full. After a few weeks the reedbeds started to breathe again.

I found the forgotten clach (gravestone) of Talorgan! Turns out that Talorgan is a Pictish name which makes it, like the Farrar, one of the oldest names in the land. Several Pictish kings and subkings bore it, and their Druidic priests too. This could even be the burial place of Talorgan the brother of Brudei, King of the Picts, who welcomed Columba. Or a Druid who cursed the land that the Lovat clan claimed for themselves a thousand years later. We are at the heart of Caledonia here, a powerhouse of spirit. These glens are a web of energy meridians that run over the body of the land. The power grid wants to seize the land's arteries and suck their life force, like a vampire.

But when you dig up Talorgan, you don't know what else will rise from the ground. A few of us are in fact rising from the ground. A circle of women has started gathering in Talorgan's Place, which is marked up for the new power station. It's the lynchpin in the proposed new mega grid. It would be the largest in Europe. All the wind farm prospectors are hanging on that.

This is where something haunts the field. Or maybe protects it. We meditate. We invoke Brigid the Celtic goddess of light. Just to let the place know that somebody is still here – and to console ourselves. Everyone has lost something precious – a dream, a relationship, a forest, peace. Industrial capital has damaged the fabric of life. But crisis has brought people together and renewed old connections, from the ground up. I am meeting new people all the time, as anger and sorrow grow and the slow-to-be-roused Highlanders eventually rise to their countryself, the way they did when they fought for the Crofters Act. Nature abhors injustice. Under assault, a community pulls together to fight for its survival and discover who they really are. You find that you can take a leap – and you are not alone.

Tony takes a leap and buys the hermit's place from her daughter.

The bungalow is rundown, the garden is a tip, it needs work. It's all on a shoestring budget and all will be upcycled. Tony envisions it as part of the gallery and a salvaging mission – to reunite this sacred ground above the waterfalls of Kilmorack. He takes out plastic fittings, rips out old fences, digs channels for the spring to flow better, plants native trees, repaints walls and rewires cables. We've been each other's person for fifteen years but I still don't comprehend this quality he has – this crazy electrical force that erupts from the peaceable nature and manifests the impossible, Prospero-like. From the midden come decades of rubbish. Old chairs, sinks, mattresses and television sets. Tony extracts them from the ground with glee. I buy stuff for the house from charity shops. Going to the recycling dump is a special occasion and one of the many things we still do together. The dump is a happy place because it's the end of the road. A certain peace comes with that. It's like living next to a cemetery.

'I want to live at the end of a road one day. Not in a Crossing Place,' Tony says.

Tons of breezeblocks emerge from the garden – but they can be crushed and reused as gravel. We'll never buy gravel again. The garden begins to breathe, the spring flows, the trees burst into blossom, and – what about some bee hives!

'Am I gonna be the keeper of Kilmorack?'

'Yes,' I say.

'Do you regret coming north? You were elegant, once.'

'And now I wear my jumper back to front like you.'

We sit under the horse chestnut. When you sit under it, your foot touches the feet of those who walked this ground.

And you see this countryself the way it was when it was entire. Waterfall, springs, gorge, woodland. You see the green hermits who understood people and plants. The silent Druids by their oaks, and the chatty priests who boarded the exile ships with their countryfolk and preached in Gaelic until they died on foreign soil. The painters, potters, growers, collectors of stories. Under the chestnut, you see that hope is not yet gone.

You see a timeline where we move slowly across a quiet

Earth, barefoot like penitents, seeking to salvage something. Anything. One of us stops and calls out banshee-like —

Oh I see, I see the painted waterfall! It's the one I climbed with the deer people. I wish we could have seen it earlier. That without the living land we are nothing. That we are cursed, cursed! Until we learn to love again.

Acknowledgements and Sources

I acknowledge the people of the glen whose lives I have witnessed and shared over the years. Most living people appear with pseudonyms. The important clans mentioned are: the Frasers of Lovat, the Chisholms, the MacKenzies, and the Macraes who were affiliated with the MacKenzies.

The Monks' Place is Beauly. It emerged as a Benedictine monastic community, the Monasterium de Bello Loco. Over time the name divided into its constituents and both are used today – Beauly in English (from the French *beau lieu*) and A'Mhanachainn in Gaelic (the Monks' Place). I call it the Monks' Place because the ruined priory remains its symbol. Similarly, the Monks' River is the Beauly River. I use this earlier name as a reminder of this kinship. Lest we forget that rivers are lifegivers. Talorgan's Place is my name for Fanellan. Talorgan's Village is Kiltarlity. The church of Talorgan is the old Kiltarlity Church. Kiltarlity derives from Cill-Tarlan (or Talorgan). *Cill* (kee) means variably hermit's cell, chapel, church and graveyard.

The two energy companies which used to be one are Scottish and Southern Energy (SSE) and Scottish and Southern Electricity Networks (SSEN). They are the inheritors of the North of Scotland Hydro-Electric Board. At the time of writing, SSE owns 75 per cent of SSEN. The other 25 per cent is owned by the Ontario Teachers' Pension Plan. SSE also owns multiple wind-farm companies operating and prospecting in the Scottish Highlands and Islands.

SSE is owned by a portfolio of global investors including BlackRock.

The wind-farm developers who were stopped by local activism were ABO Energy and Druim Ba Sustainable Energy, a subsidiary of the Louis Dreyfus Group. Among the larger companies invited to our area by landowners and the government to build wind farms are EnergieKontor and Statkraft.

The company that extracted our woods is Breedon Group. The Pictish burial cairns and large hut circles were marked on maps, yet industrial enlargement was favoured over natural and cultural wealth by the local authority. The cairns were dug up in phases, during the expansions of Breedon Group and SSEN. An archaeologist from the North of Scotland Archaeological Society (NOSAS) wrote an essay I cite below.

'We don't inherit the land from our ancestors, we borrow it from our children' is an adage associated with Native American wisdom and has become a common phrase in the American environmental movement. While it cannot be attributed with certainty to one particular source, it encapsulates an understanding shared by all indigenous peoples around the world.

These works and sources have been helpful in my research and may be of further interest:

A History of the Parish of Kiltarlity and *The Glens and Straths: Parish of Kilmorack*, a monograph in several volumes by H. W. Harrison

ACKNOWLEDGEMENTS AND SOURCES

An Element of Regret, a documentary by Edwin Mickleburgh, 1984
Burn on the Hill: The Story of the First 'Compleat Munroist' by Elizabeth Allan
Carmina Gadelica by Alexander Carmichael
Children of the Dead End by Patrick MacGill
Confessions of a Highland Art Dealer by Tony Davidson
Crofting Years by Francis Thompson
Culloden, docudrama by Peter Watkins, 1964
From Loch Ness to The Aird by Edward Meldrum
Glen Shiel, Kintail by Glenys Macmillan
In Search of the Picts by Elizabeth Sutherland
Isolation Shepherd by Iain R. Thompson
'Lament for a Once Magical Place – or the Agony of a severely traumatised pair of Archaeological Sites' by Meryl Marshall, North of Scotland Archaeological Society, https://nosasblog.wordpress.com/tag/balblair-wood/
More Than a Legend by Constance Whyte
My Yester Years in Glen Affaric by Duncan MacLennan
Pintupi Country, Pintupi Self by Fred R. Myers
Place-names of the Aird and Strathglass, Inverness-shire by Simon Taylor, Ronald Maclean and Jacob King
Ravens and Black Rain: The Story of Highland Second Sight by Elizabeth Sutherland
Scottish Gaelic Place-names by Charles M. Robertson, editor Dr Jacob King
Second Sight by Neil M. Gunn
Strathglass Heritage Association www.strathglass-heritage.co.uk
The Dam Builders: Power from the Glens by James Miller
The Dark Mile and other True Highland Tales by Iain MacKay
The Drove Roads of Scotland by A. R. B. Haldane

The Gaelic Otherworld by John Gregorson Campbell, editor Ronald Black
The Highland Clearances by John Prebble
The Hydro Boys by Emma Wood
The Last Highland Clearance by Iain MacKay
The Long Horizon by Iain R. Thompson
The Man Who Bought Mountains by Rennie McOwan
The Poor Had No Lawyers by Andy Wightman
The Prophecies of the Brahan Seer by Alexander Mackenzie, with a foreword, commentary and conclusion by Elizabeth Sutherland
Tunnel Tigers by Patrick Campbell
When I Was Young: Voices from Lost Communities in Scotland, in four volumes by Timothy Neat